RATTLESNAKE DADDY

A Son's Search for His Father

For Karen —
with best wishes!
— Brent

Brent Spencer

BRENT SPENCER

The Backwaters Press

Also by Brent Spencer

The Lost Son, Arcade/Little Brown, 1995
Are We Not Men?, Arcade/Little Brown, 1996

Rattlesnake Daddy: A Son's Search for His Father © 2010 Brent Spencer.
Book design by Susan Ramundo.
Proofreading by Aaron Anstett.
Author photo by Miriam Berkley.
Cover design by Andrea Shahan.

First Printing: March 2011

2009 Winner of the Little Bluestem Award in Non-Fiction

Rattlesnake Daddy: A Son's Search for His Father is printed as a cooperative effort between the Nebraska Arts Council and The Backwaters Press in order to honor the winners of the Nebraska Arts Council's Distinguished Artist Awards. Brent Spencer won the Distinguished Artist Award for 2009, which included a cash award of $5,000 and the publication of this book.

Published by: The Backwaters Press
                  3502 N 52nd Street
                  Omaha, NE 68104-3506
                  Greg Kosmicki & Rich Wyatt, Editors

                  http://www.thebackwaterspress.org
                  thebackwaterspress@gmail.com

ISBN: 978-1-935218-18-0

For Sheree, Mark, & Mom

Grateful acknowledgment is made to the editors of the following journals in which sections from this book first appeared: "Red-Eyed Dog" was first published in *Witness*, XIX, 2005, and "Mystery Ways" in *River Teeth*, 11.1, Fall 2009. I'm also grateful to Creighton University, Yaddo, and the Nebraska Arts Council for grants of time, space, and money that contributed to the writing of this book. My thanks to the many people who shared their memories of my father, some of whose names have been changed to protect their privacy. Any mistakes are my own. And thanks also to the fellow writers with whom I've shared these pages, especially to Jonis Agee, whose keen eye and true heart keep me going.

I'm a rattlesnake daddy.
You better get down on your knee.
I'm a rattlesnake daddy
. . . from Tennessee.
I'm a rattlesnake daddy.
You better let me be.

—*Bill Carlisle*

CONTENTS

1

WHY I WENT

It was the fourth time the phone had rung in the last ten minutes, so I broke my unbreakable rule and answered it. The unbreakable rule: never answer the phone. Not under any circumstances. Let it ring. Let it bleat. Let it call down fire from the heavens, for all I cared. The phone always brought bad news: bill collectors, angry former girlfriends, telemarketers. And besides, I had thirty freshmen composition essays to grade. I could tell it was bad news. A certain glee in the ring, a certain smugness, a certain I-told-you-so quality to the reverberation of the hollow after-note that hung in the air.

"No," I said aloud to the second set of rings.

And to the third.

But finally, at the fourth, unable to resist, I raised the phone to my ear with all the eager dread of a man raising a gun to his head.

"Yeah?"

"Brent?"

"Yeah?"

"Brent, it's Sheree."

"Yeah?"

"He's dead."

"Yeah?"

I knew she meant our father, the man we never talked about, the man who'd been out of our lives for thirty years, but I didn't quite know what to make of the news. Neither did she. I could tell from the sound of her voice. Sadness, yes, but more a sense of wonder, as if some eternal monument had suddenly disappeared. My father's death was the emotional equivalent of the Berlin Wall coming down. I don't quite mean that. There was no dancing in the streets. The sky wasn't filled with rocketing champagne corks. But even absent for so many years, my father still stood as a shadow, a force forever at my back. Without him in the world—the stories of his naval exploits, the memory of his madness—I wasn't sure I'd know how to live.

Toward the end of his life, after several years of living in a camper, my father moved onboard a sailboat in the Florida Keys, a 46-foot, 14-ton cutter-rigged sailboat designed by Philip Rhodes and built by Kreutzer Boats in 1938. He'd sailed for years, even taught a sailing class to women, but until now he'd never owned his own boat. Its hull was made of mahogany planking over oak frames, with teak decks, white oak timbers, and bronze fastenings. Its mast, booms, and spinnaker were of Sitka spruce. The Sea Dragon. The boat had been meant to be the start of my father's new life, but in the end it killed him.

His dream was to sail from place to place, meeting new people, having new experiences. But after only a few months he had that most exotic of all experiences, his own death. He drowned in a sailing accident off Key West. A lifelong sailor who had joined the Navy at sixteen, lying about his age, he'd never learned to swim. Since his death, I've found that this is true for many career Navy men. Was it faith in technology and in his talents that made him think he'd never need to know? Or was he just a fool who died a fool's death?

Bad swimmer. Bad sailor, too, I guess. He hung his boat up as he entered the Northwest Channel on his way to shore, hung it on the east jetty, the submerged wall of granite marking the passage into and out of deep water. The Coast Guard report describes the event as a "collision w/fixed object." A beginner's mistake. Dumb.

The sea was calm that night and not especially cold, but the Coast Guard had trouble responding in a timely fashion, and before they could get there, the sea took him. Hypothermia. Pulmonary Edema. Dead at 60. Some say the death is suspicious. But I guess we always say that when someone dies too soon.

Our troubled history makes it impossible for me to claim his body. When I say "troubled," I mean he was the kind of father who did his talking with his hands, belts, straps, a razor strop, and with his diver's knife. The kind of father who beats you for an untucked shirt, a sign that you are unworthy in the eyes of the Lord. But all that was so long ago. I've moved on. I'm an English professor in a Nebraska college. I've done fine without a father. To claim the man now, to look him in his dead face and say, "Yes, he's my father"—it's just too much. How can I claim the man who never really claimed me? The thing is, I don't want to do anything that might be interpreted as honoring him— identifying his body, shipping him back home. My sister Sheree did it. Jumped onto a plane and flew down there to identify the body and make arrangements for its return to Indiana, the ground of his making.

It's not that I'm afraid of death. That's not why I wouldn't go down there and identify the body. I'm afraid of my father. Afraid that if I stood next to his dead body the energy of my anger would somehow reanimate him. His dead eyelids would flutter. His stony head would turn. His gray gaze would fix on me. And once again, the hammer of his hand and the hiss of his blade would rise against me. No, I didn't want to be the one to go down there. Besides, how could I identify him? I barely know what he looks like, and, anyway, he was never a father to me. To identify him now would be to participate in a charade of family life.

But without warning, and without fully understanding why, I drive from my home in Nebraska to hers in New Orleans to meet her when she comes back from the Keys. I show up late at night, shamefaced, a little drunk, filled with explanations about why I couldn't go to Key West but can be here now. As it turns out, no explanations are necessary. I knock. She pulls open the door and hauls me into the house in one motion, as if I'm expected, saying, "Brent, that place is beautiful!" For twenty minutes she goes on about the wonders of Key West.

My sister is a big woman with a big heart. Her face shines as if lit from below by an armful of imaginary flowers. She's the hugger in our family, the one who reaches out to the rest of us. She was a runaround as a teenager, smoking with boys in back alleys, doing other things, I guess. Maybe because she knows every trick, she keeps a firm grip on her own kids. Firm but fair, like a good boxing referee. Now in her forties, she's become a person who delights in simple pleasures. Her kids are a constant turn-on for her. The whole idea of family gives her a big kick. She is not, I mean to say, a person who takes the death of a father lightly.

When she finally takes a breath, I say, "So you identified the body?"

"Yeah," she says, searching distractedly through her Polaroids for the one that catches the exact blue of the sea, the water that killed our father. "Oh yeah," she says, showing me the picture, a blue so rich you could fill a fountain pen with it. "Yeah, I did. But really, Brent, believe me, you have got to see that place!"

I guess you can say my father occupied an ambiguous place in our family.

We—Sheree, my brother Mark, and me—are my father's first family, the one he'd pretty much erased from his mind until Sheree reached out to him twenty-some years after the divorce. She tracked him down, wrote to him, called him, lured him out of the shadows. All of it on her own, without a word to my brother or me. Slowly, over many months, she recultivated the relationship.

After a while, he even made regular visits to her. Think Frankenstein in the woodcutter's cottage.

Tonight, after she runs out of things to say about the splendors of Key West, she says, as if in apology for the absence of grief, "We didn't really know him very well." This doesn't say as much about her as it does about him, about the essential mystery of the man, about the distance he kept between himself and the world. And now here he is, dead, the undiscovered country of my father.

"There's something else," Sheree says, putting down her pictures and leading me out to the empty carport, where she's stacked a half-dozen bulging green garbage bags. "Most of this was still on the boat, but the salvage company had to fish a lot of it right out of the water."

"Most of what? His garbage?"

"His papers."

"What papers?"

"All of them." And when I still don't get it, "Everything."

I kneel down to the nearest bag, spread open its mouth, take in the rank scent of seawater, and peel up the top sheet of paper, a letter from my father to his doctor dated more than two decades ago, a copy he made by hand in his careful, squared-off printing:

Dear Dr. Sorenson,
You treated me recently for a skin condition which I have had for 29 years. It has been called nomular eczema and you called it winter itch . . .

I remember the handwriting vividly from my childhood, the dead even lines, the words not inscribed so much as erected. I look up startled, expecting to see him standing there in the carport, about to whale on me for going through his stuff. But it's just Sheree and me and the sea-smelling bags of swollen paper, hundreds and hundreds of sheets, bales of it, pounds and pounds of pages fished up from the sea—checkbook ledgers, diary pages, letters, recipes, shopping lists, reminders, class notes, lecture notes, every piece of paper that had ever passed through his hands.

"Have you gone through all this?"

"I had a look. It's mostly old receipts. Stuff like that."

I show her the letter I've been reading, the blue ink fuzzy with dampness. Not words at all but the ghosts of words, the bones of thought.

"Yeah?" she says, handing it back.

"Winter itch," I say, tugging at my pant leg. "He's describing the exact same rash I have on my leg."

"Yeah? So?"

She isn't getting it, and I'm not sure I can explain it. My heart is pounding but I keep myself calm. "Well, I just think it's interesting is all."

But it's more than that. That rash is a connection as real as a fingerprint, as revealing as DNA. My father and I suffered from the same skin condition. At last I've found something that ties me to the man. The realization fills me with an exhilarating mixture of pleasure and disgust. Maybe I'm my father's son after all.

For the rest of the night, I sit on the floor of the carport, carefully lifting wet slabs of paper out of the bags, peeling back the layers like some kind of archaeologist.

Along about dawn I come across a thick wet sheaf of pages stapled along one side, a journal in the same careful printing, *The Mexico Log of Commander R. C. Spencer.* Along with his impressions, private thoughts, price comparisons, and lists of necessities, the log includes detailed maps of his routes, the places he stayed, the people he met. I knew that, for the last ten years or so of his life, ever since his second marriage ended, he lived in a camper. Now I know that he spent a good deal of that time lurking along the U.S./Mexico border, a place I've always thought of as mine.

Was he somewhere nearby that last time I went to Nuevo Laredo? Or was he walking in the street below that balcony bar in Tijuana? Or was he following me? He might have been. According to his log, he was in both of these places when I was there, and many more besides. The thought that we might have passed each other in a Mexican street makes the connection between us seem more real than a rash. Like twins separated at birth, we suffered the same ailments, felt drawn to the same landscapes. We were closer, I now realize, than I ever thought possible.

The new day is gearing up. I can hear noises from the neighbor's house—heavy, clomping footsteps on the stairs, the chatter of a radio. By the time Sheree puts on the first pot of coffee, I know what I have to do. I have to go back to the border. To the places he went. Have to look for signs of him, clues to his mystery.

When Sheree brings me a cup of coffee, she shakes her head at the blizzard of paper. Every square inch of the carport is covered with old receipts, letters, photographs, calendar pages, and more. I tell her my plan.

"It's all here." I can't keep the excitement out of my voice. I hold the damp journal in front of her face as if it's a treasure map. "The places he went, the people he talked to. Not just in the journal but in lots of these pages." I spread my hands over my night's work. Damp, translucent sheets of paper are spread out all over the floor of the carport.

From the look on her face, you'd think I've turned into a maniac. And maybe I have.

She looks doubtfully at the carport full of papers. "The body is already on its way back to Indiana," she says. "If you make this trip, you'll miss the funeral."

I haven't thought about that. "Then I'll have to miss the funeral," I say.

"But why?" she says. "Why now? Why go now? Why not wait until after the funeral? You're his son, the oldest."

Because, like identifying the body, going to the funeral is one more thing I can't bring myself to do. You drive your kid away with boards, belts, blades, and the hard, calloused flat of your hand, and now you want that same kid to claim you, to grieve over you, to stand at the graveside and cry hot tears into the open hole? No.

Or maybe going to the border is my own way of honoring his memory, or at least of trying to recapture the man, restore him to us, the story of his life, the story of my life, at least a part of it, his days on the line between worlds. Yes, that's the pretty spin to give it.

"I can't do it, Sheree," I say. "I can't be there. I can't do the grieving family thing. I can't sit there and listen to all the relatives say what a great guy he was when I know he was—"

"Let it go."

"I can't."

Sheree looks at me a little sideways, on the verge of speech, but she knows better than to try to talk me out of it. She has her own history with my father.

Going to the funeral would show respect for a man who doesn't deserve it. Guess I'll show him. My message is actually meant for the family, who worshipped him his whole life. I want them to know that someone else in the family has a different view. I want my absence and my silence to drown out their false praise, their meaningless sorrow. Guess I'll show them.

What a child I am. I could avoid lots of mental anguish by just claiming the body—yes, that's him—and dragging it back to the farmlands of his making. I think I'm depriving him of honor, but maybe all I'm doing is depriving myself of something vastly more important. But what that is I don't really know yet.

So, instead of going to the funeral, I load up the trunk of my Taurus with the heavy green garbage bags filled with his past—thick moldy sea-smelling bales of it. They're so heavy and smell so bad that as I lift them into the car, the green plastic bags going drum-tight, tighter, it's all I can do to keep from thinking I'm hoisting hunks of his actual body into the trunk. In a way, I guess, I am. I don't know what more I'll find among his papers, or if I'll find anything at all. I just know I have to move, have to retrace his steps, have to find a clear space to rethink everything I think I know about my father. And about myself.

⤜⤛⤚

The purpose of my odyssey along the border of old Mexico is threefold. First, I wish to escape the coldest part of the winter to a place which is warm enough to sun, sail, and see old friends and business associates, many of whom have retired or are currently active along the border. Second, I want to enjoy the sights, the people, and the environment of this older, less developed nation. And third, I want to find an area, quickly accessible from the U.S. in the event of an emergency, sudden change in circumstances, or political exigency.

Truth to tell, a couple of marriages have gone bust on me, and so I've outfitted my F-150 with a camper back, re-designing the interior until it suits my every need. I have a television that works off two spare batteries (one is always recharging while the other is being utilized). I have a working sink, a camp toilet/shower combination, a table leaf that folds up into the wall, even a modest bookshelf rigged with a rail to keep the books from tumbling out during sudden turns. My survival supplies are completed with a SIG-Sauer semi-automatic handgun with a polymer frame and a stainless-steel slide.

The loft area over the cab gives me ample sleeping room as long as I don't try to stretch out and as long as I don't take a notion to sit up in bed, the ceiling being a scant twenty-two inches above the tip of my nose. I fit into the space the way a hand fits into a glove. The only problem is the heat, air conditioning being one luxury I have had to do without. The only other improvement on my mode of conveyance that I can imagine is that it be made seaworthy.

There's nothing like a long stretch of open road for sorting out the whys and wherefores of your life. I have made mistakes, it's true. I'm not one to deny that. But my greatest mistake may have been my tendency to have too much faith in people. Your human being is, by and large, little more than an out-of-tune engine. I have had to face the fact that I have neither the time, talent, nor tools to make the much-needed repairs.

Better, I have decided, to take to the open road, where I have only myself to account for. I will take whatever adventure the road brings to my door.

But why the border, this place neither here nor there? To be quite frank, and to say more than I'd ever tell a living soul, I find myself at this stage of my life a little at loose ends. I'm no longer sure what world I belong to. I'm not referring to the great nations of Mexico or the United States. I mean, what is a man's true country? Son? Husband? Father? Sailor? Scientist? For the time being, I'll drive the line between worlds and stick it out inside the four walls of this camper, a world unto myself.

On the subject of marriage, I have but little to say. No marriage fails without the cooperation of both parties, or so I have heard repeatedly. There may be truth in this; however, my own research has shown that sometimes one party "cooperates" more than the other. And besides, I choose not to use the word "fail." What others call a failure, I call an unexpected outcome.

And so I have come to believe, after my share of clinical trials, that the human male is not well adapted to the condition of marriage. The presence of the female alters a man, changes him, makes him a stranger unto himself, unto his powers, unto his very divinity.

❧❧

2

LEGEND OF PARTS

M y father lived with us continuously, under the same roof, for only one year of my childhood, the 1960–61 school year, the year that would split us up for good. He was a sailor who rarely stayed on dry land for long, but now, after having driven us apart so many times, the Navy had finally brought us together. While serving as a gunnery inspecting officer over the amphibious forces stationed at Little Creek, Virginia, he redesigned the Mark XIV sight used on the 20-millimeter anti-aircraft gun. I pictured him on a destroyer, at the turret of some death-dealing cannon, laying waste to every ship on the sea, every city by the sea, every everything.

As a reward the Navy was sending him to Purdue to study electrical engineering. Because Indiana was the home place, the place where both my parents had been born and raised, it all seemed like destiny, a coming together brought about by desire, talent, and fate.

The train ride took three-and-a-half days from Wilkes-Barre, Pennsylvania, where my mother, brother, sister, and I had been living while our father was overseas. The best commuting distance, he said, from where he was stationed at the time—the Brooklyn Naval Yards. We left that gritty mining town behind, the train crawling between slag heaps, past breakers, past the tumbled-down shanties of the mine workers and finally out onto the pristine plains of the Midwest.

We'd been on the train for two-and-a-half days. Tomorrow we'd be in Indiana, the place where we belonged, to live with our father. He had been such an infrequent visitor that we kids—my brother, sister, and I—barely knew what he looked like. So, on the third day, a few hours before our arrival, my mother took us to the dining car with great solemnity. My father had sent us enough money for the tickets and one meal. The rest of our meals my mother pulled from a satchel—peanut butter and jelly sandwiches mostly, which was fine with us. But the dining car, that was special. She parked my sister and me on one side of the table, Mark, my little brother, on the other side, with her, where he could eat from her plate the way he liked. Sheree and I split the Salisbury steak my mother ordered us, but we insisted that she cut the meat, peas, and scalloped potatoes into exactly equal portions and divide them down the middle of the plate. We spent the rest of the meal arguing over whose food was touching whose.

After the plates were cleared, while my mother had a cup of coffee and a cigarette, she showed us a photograph of a man in a naval uniform.

"This is your father," she said slowly, handing the picture first to me, making me hold it and look at it until she counted to ten. "Memorize it. I don't want any slip-ups."

He had a square jaw and dark eyes and a mouth as set and stony as the seam between two rows of bricks. He didn't look like a father. He was dressed in a white seaman's uniform with a dark neckerchief and a stiff white cap. He was looking way into the distance, past all of us, from a world and to a world none of us knew anything about.

When my ten-count was up, I passed the picture to my sister, slowly, as if I were handling plutonium. She stared at it as though she were peering through a drinking straw. We must have been a strange sight, passing the picture from one to the next while my mother counted slowly to ten, but we needed the tutoring. None of us kids would have recognized him if he walked right up and sat down beside us.

When Mark, whose head barely cleared the tabletop, got the picture, a man came into the dining car looking for a seat. Mark clutched the picture and closed his eyes before he'd even looked at it, chanting, "Oh, Daddy, Daddy, Daddy!" By the time my mother had counted to three, he'd slipped under the table and out into the aisle, running to the other end of the car, to the man, yelling, "Daddy, Daddy, Daddy!" He ran up to him and threw his arms around one of the man's legs. "Oh my daddy!" he cried, looking up into the stranger's startled face.

The man, whose face seemed older than his rich, black hair, looked down in helpless alarm, then around at the other people in the dining car. Except for being tall, he looked nothing like the man in the picture. He was just a man, an adult. But in my brother's eyes, that was close enough. By the time my mother peeled him off the stranger, apologizing, and dragged him back to the table, his eyes were red with tears. It was as though he'd lost his father all over again. I wonder now whether this explains my brother's interest in history, in his passionate interest in getting the facts right. When I think of telling him the truth about our father, I remember that day. I won't put him through that again.

For once Sheree and I didn't make fun of Mark. We knew we could have made the same mistake. How would we recognize our father in real clothes? We were just as capable of calling out to the wrong man, to the milk man or the man at the door who only wanted to ask us were we ready for the rapture. It didn't occur to us that we'd know instinctively, that blood might call to blood, skin to skin.

That was the kind of father he was—not merely absent much of the time but out of touch all the time, beyond our understanding and even beyond our sight. But Indiana was a fresh start for our father, for all of us. That's what we thought. That's what we hoped.

At the end of three-and-a-half days, it seemed that the train pulled right up the curving lane to the cracker box that my father had rented, our new home. When we arrived at the houses, he was out, so we waited for him in the bare living room, sitting on our suitcases as if this was only another stop on our way somewhere else. Eventually, a lanky, smiling man came into the house, a man so tall he had to duck through the doorway. That moment should have warned us. The house wasn't large enough for him. No house would be. No family either. He strode across the room and knelt to us. It's then I realized that only his mouth was smiling. His face was like the faces in my little brother's flip-book: the bottom half didn't match the top. The bottom half smiled while the top half looked at us the way strangers watched in supermarkets as my mother counted out food stamps.

After his mistake in the dining car, my brother wasn't taking any chances. He hid warily behind our mother, chewing the heel of his hand, peering out from behind the flowered dress our mother had sewn for the occasion. Our father lunged for him, hauled him up over his head, and held him there at the end of his outstretched arms.

"Look at you!" he shouted happily. "Look at you!"

Mark, breathless, looked down on us from up near the ceiling, his eyes wild with joy. Our father had won his heart forever.

It was probably my father's finest moment. From there, things went downhill in a hurry.

And yet the house and neighborhood were the best we'd ever lived in. Sure the ranch-style house looked like most of the others on the block. The same simple plan, five rooms and bath. An identical young pear tree was leashed to each lawn. And yes, maybe the walls had all the tensile strength of balsa wood. But there wasn't a broken window—not even a crack—in the place. Not like our old apartments, where rats and roaches scrambled across the floor at night. And the street had so much class it wasn't even called "Street." It was a "Court." Emerald Court. Like Emerald City in *The Wizard of Oz*. We were coming up in the world all right.

A train track ran behind the houses on our side of the street. The only drama in the neighborhood was the hourly shaking of the ground as the next freight train came shuddering by. Otherwise, life moved at an almost southern pace. The sun bore down on the tarred roads, the cicadas whined, and we all moved with the well-ordered precision of a drill team. It was a made-to-order place for a made-to-order life. It all looked so clean, green, and hopeful that we had no idea we were falling apart, that this would prove to be the ground of our unmaking.

In many ways, life there was idyllic for an eight-year-old like me. We'd been living in a series of crummy apartments back East, the only kind my father could afford on a sailor's salary, home to every kind of vermin imaginable. Once a week or so I'd find a mouse in my shoe. To this day, every morning I still turn my shoes over and knock the heels together, just in case. And there were so many cockroaches my sister and I liked to trap them under overturned drinking glasses. The floors were always studded with these small monuments, but somehow the roaches disappeared by the time we came back to check on them.

That first day in Lafayette, I found a praying mantis in the yard, what we called an Indian Walking Stick. It came stilting toward me through the long grass, a green stick that had come to life, one twig-like leg carefully feeling its way forward, and then the other. I was completely undone by its prehistoric charm. In Indiana, even the vermin were cool.

Our new neighborhood had lots of kids to play with, but I was the new kid, too shy to join in. My father solved the problem our second day there. He blew up some balloons and tied them to the back fence. Then from a cardboard box he pulled a fiberglass bow and arrows with target tips. "Time for target practice," he said. "Inside of thirty minutes, you'll have all the friends you can handle."

The bright green bow was taller than I was and, unstrung, looked more like a large version of the Walking Stick's strangely shaped leg. He stepped into the bow and strung it expertly, fit an arrow, and let fly. *Pop!* One less balloon on the fence. The arrow itself had passed through and was sticking in the side of the railroad embankment just ten feet beyond the fence.

"What if they still don't want to be my friend?"

"Then," he said, handing the bow to me, "shoot one of them. The rest will come to their senses right quick."

I just stood there looking blankly back at him.

He let a long moment pass, then said, solemnly, "That was a joke." Another moment. "You knew that, right?"

"Uh-huh," I said weakly.

He left me in the yard trying to hit the balloons. The best any of my arrows did was to nudge one aside a little. But he was right. In less than thirty minutes, the yard was filled with new friends, all of them wanting a turn with the bow and arrows.

Plenty of kids lived on Emerald Court, kids with bicycles, wagons, go-carts, basketballs, footballs, and even one odd kid who went around bouncing a white patch-work ball off an upraised knee.

When we weren't in school or playing with my bow and arrows, my new friends and I played marbles for keepsies, dragged wagonloads of comic books to each others' houses to trade, and built go-carts out of baby carriage wheels and flimsy fruit crates that sagged when you climbed in and fell completely apart halfway down the first hill. One kid smelled strange, another wore his hair in a Mohawk, and another was fat and mean. We were as brave and fearless outside as we were quiet and obedient at home. We ordered younger brothers and sisters not to follow us as we went to the empty field, where we played war and hatched noble plots against imaginary enemies in a deep pit we'd dug and camouflaged with a pile of brush. We passed our small hands through the flames shooting out of trash barrels. We dared each other to hop slow-moving freights, telling stories none of us ever questioned about the boy who'd lost his legs under the turning wheels, about the severed hand found in the tall weeds by the tracks.

The school was so progressive it frowned on homework. For me, though, the best thing of all was that I had at last come to my true home. Both sides of my family were here, people I didn't even know. Like the Walking Stick, I had come, fragile step by fragile step, back to the land where I would find myself, where I would learn my place in the clan.

The parents were all young, like mine. The men worked and wore suits; the women stayed home and wore aprons. Everything happened almost at once on Emerald Court. Kitchen lights came on at first light. The fathers all left within twenty minutes of each other, driving their big, angular American cars. The kids trudged off to school at the same time. The mothers all stood watching from the front step, drying their hands on dish towels. Their biggest worry seemed to be whether they'd have time to clean the house while everyone was away. Like a lot of people, we mistook all this regularity for happiness.

At the end of the day, the kids would come home first. Then, an hour later, the fathers, looking a little roughed-up by their day. Kitchen lights came on at dusk. If you were to walk down Emerald Court at that hour, you could smell cooking meat, hear the sound of slotted spoons banged against the edges of pots.

And later the clatter of supper dishes being collected and washed. After a while, the picture windows were jumpy with gray TV light until, house-by-house, other lights came on, trailing the occupants from living room to bathroom to bedroom and so on into the dark. It was an orderly life, a meaningful life, a life meant to prevent surprises. None of us knew what was to come.

My parents grew up on farms in southern Indiana, though my father's people were closer to the big city of Columbus. My mother's parents' place would make the crossroads in *North by Northwest* look like a busy intersection. The difference showed in their personalities. He was the talker, she the listener, the watcher.

She was raised to be a good homemaker and not to make a fuss. She's never talked much, as if she believes others are smarter and more important, and that her job is to keep their coffee cups and highball glasses filled. She's still, past 70, a woman surprised by her own insights and endurance. "Who said that? *I* said that? I guess I did!"

My father's talk took the form of aphorisms, rules for living, and tales about the strangeness of the human race. I don't think any of the other fathers on Emerald Court were college students. They came home with sample cases, briefcases, and lunchboxes. My father came home with a leather book bag. At twenty-eight he was old to be in college, but I didn't realize this until much later. At the time, I thought of him as a kind of scientist who left home each day to go to a lab where he wore a pristine lab coat and watched over beakers filled with boiling blue liquid. He was what my grandmother called a "deep thinker," a man, she said, "with his eye on the back-forty." It was not until years later that I came to think she might have meant that as a criticism—a thinker rather than a doer, a man whose gaze was focused on the far away instead of the here and now, as in,

"That faucet of yours still broke?"

"Bob's studying on how to fix it."

"Oh yes, my, that man of yours is a deep thinker, he is."

Of course, my grandmother would never say such a thing. Not outright. She'd have rather eaten a gravy boat of buckshot than talk like that about anyone. Even more than my mother, she was a woman who said little, required little. During her visits to our house toward the end of her life, I only ever remember her smiling contentedly in the corner, hands folded in her lap. "I'm jist fine," she'd say. "Now don't go bothering 'bout me."

These were not the days when you were encouraged to talk about your problems, to share your pain. You were, instead, encouraged to shut up and get on with it. Therapists were for celebrities and psychopaths, fleas from the same dog, if you asked my father.

So the decorated sailor was now a man of science. His math and science books all over the house proved it, passages underlined so carefully and notes written in the margins so neatly that I thought books came from the publisher that way, with all the important parts marked and noted. His most exotic tool was his slide rule, a Post Versalog, which he wore in a hard leather scabbard that hung from a belt loop.

Sometimes I'd find the rule lying on the end table with its scales extended, as if my father had just found some kind of ultimate answer and had rushed off to tell some bigshot like Wernher von Braun. I liked the weight of the slide rule's heavy mahogany in my hands, the shine of the cursor's glass face. I liked the delicate articulation of its parts, the way the hairline indicator slid over the tiny numbers. When I played with it, I was always careful to slide the scales back to the settings at which I found them, though there were many rows of microscopic numbers and it was hard to be sure.

That year together in Indiana was the longest time we ever spent under the same roof. And for a while, it felt as though it might work, this experiment, this idea of a family. My parents were impossible to know, but that's what all parents were like, I thought, strange monoliths like the ones on Easter Island we'd read about in school, only these had moving parts.

Eventually, I came to learn that when my father was out in the world—at large—the forces inside him had a way of venting. But put him under a roof and within four walls, and the charged particles of his rage had no way to disperse, except in barely controlled bursts of ritualistic violence.

And yet, before long, I began to admire my father—the keen mind he was said to have. After a while I began to imitate his distant gaze, the corners of my eyes crinkling, the lines of my face sharpening (as if, at eight, I had any lines to sharpen).

The high-point of my regard for my father came the day The Whizzer arrived.

Late one Friday afternoon, just a few weeks after we'd moved in, a panel truck backed into our driveway. I watched as a small square wooden crate was offloaded along with a couple of dozen heavy cardboard boxes of all shapes and sizes. The driver left them in the gravel driveway at the side of our house. My mother had me sit with them, keeping guard, until my father came home.

An hour or so later our two-tone green Ford Crestline pulled slowly into the driveway, and, more slowly still, our father climbed out, a look I'd never seen before on his face—wonder. He walked slowly to the crate, set his book bag down, and slowly circled it. The crate was about two feet square. On each side was stenciled a single winged word—"Whizzer."

I was bursting to say something, do something, but I had no idea what was in the crate and boxes. I said, "I was watching." When it seemed that my father hadn't heard me, I said, "Guarding mostly." I spread my arm to take in the whole array of boxes, then dropped it. "All of it." As if I had chased away the curious and fought off thieves. As if I had kept the weather at bay. As if I had kept the boxes themselves from sprouting legs and wandering into the weeds beyond the railroad tracks.

He shifted his gaze to the boxes scattered around the driveway. He turned back to the crate and tapped it with the toe of his shoe and then, at last, looked at me.

"'Walking's too expensive, Joe, when you can ride a Whizzer!'"

I was stunned but knew better than to say anything, to show it. Joe? Didn't he know my name? Had he forgotten? Years passed before I found those words in an old magazine and knew that he was only quoting an advertising slogan. But at the time it only added to my father's mystery. Like most mad geniuses, he was too preoccupied to focus on incidentals like his children's names. And besides, some of his excitement was rubbing off on me. I didn't know what was in the boxes, but I wanted to be part of it, whether or not my father remembered who I was. I wanted to be useful. More than that. Indispensable.

"Sir," I'd say after my father spent hours of frustration over the Whizzer, "I think we can demogrify the transversal if we realign the stervick nodes."

"By George!" he'd say, standing up, his white shirt grimy with failure. "You're a goldang genius, son!"

But this wasn't likely. For one thing, I never saw my father sweat, never saw him wear a wrinkled shirt. He was on the go so much that the backs of his knees were never creased. And for another thing, my father never needed help from anyone. There was nothing he couldn't do.

He rubbed his hands together. "Time to put this doohickey together."

"I can help," I said, stepping forward.

He stepped toward me, put his hands on my shoulders and walked me backwards until I was standing on the twelve-inch strip of gravel that ran alongside the house, saying, "I'm going to need you to stand down, sailor."

I knew better than to push. I watched as he went to the garage for the big blue metal toolbox and came back with the sleeves of his white shirt rolled up, ready for work. I watched from the sidelines as he knelt down and pried open the crate with a claw hammer and fished out a squat metal thing with fins, chambers, and a light coating of oil. It looked like a robot's heart.

"The engine," he said.

From the broad flat box he pulled out a bicycle frame red as blood. From another, smaller box he pulled the gas tank, so red it looked like a lung ripped fresh from a lion's chest, except "Whizzer" was embossed on the sides in gold. From other boxes he pulled chrome tubing, a headlight, a writhing coil of belts, and what seemed like hundreds of mysterious parts, some as shiny as mirrors, some with sharp, dangerous-looking edges, some thick with grease. There were bags of screws and clamps and belts. There was a rat trap for the back fender, where he could clamp his book bag.

"Normally," he said, not looking up, "the Whizzer comes fully assembled, but I know a fellow who knows a fellow." He lifted a pair of black saddlebags from a box. "Look," he said. "Not leather." He held the saddlebags towards me. "Leather-*like*." I was to understand that this represented a vast improvement over mere leather.

It took him a long time just to unpack the boxes, lifting the pieces carefully, as if they were fine china, and searching each box thoroughly to make sure he wasn't missing a sack of bolts. He cut down the corners of the big boxes with a single-sided razor blade and all the precision of a medical examiner, folding the walls down like the petals of a big ugly flower to expose the contents.

"This creates a cardboard pallet under the part," he said. "Less chance of losing things."

When he was finished, the entire driveway was littered with glittering chrome, black hoses, flanges, rods, bolts and nuts of every kind and size, not to mention the packing material—wads of paper, rolls and folds of cardboard, clouds of golden Excelsior. There was no way, I thought, that he could keep track of all the parts. But then he unfolded what looked like a roadmap of some vast empire.

At the top of the open sheet was the heading "Legend of Parts," below it a diagram of what must have been the Whizzer. It looked like someone had drawn the thing just as it was being dynamited, all its parts zooming away from the still center. He stepped slowly among his field of parts, consulting the legend, murmuring the name of each part as he found it: engine assembly, carburetor, air cleaner, CDI module, rear sheave, belt sheave brackets, slotted chrome belt guard, long rear belt, short front belt, clutch pulley, clutch arm, pulley bearing, right-hand control, left-hand control, compression release cable, and an endless list of brackets, bars, clamps, hoses, tubes, and belts.

At last, when he was convinced that he had everything he needed, he sat cross-legged in the middle of it all and began to read the thick manual.

I was the kind of kid who read a lot of comic books—Batman, Superman, Green Hornet—but I knew they were just stories. The real superhero was my father. More than most kids, and probably because we'd spent so little time with him, I believed he had unlimited abilities. He could build anything, solve any problem. What's that? You say they need someone to replace the hinges between the earth and sky? The Martian canals need draining? Heaven's floor needs refinishing? My dad's your man. Isn't he the one who redesigned the Navy's anti-aircraft gunsights? Sure. The Whizzer wouldn't be a problem.

And it wasn't.

When he was finished reading the manual, he flipped it back to the first page and pinned it open with the heavy kickstand. He reached between the open wings of the blue metal toolbox and lifted out the rolled-up canvas pouch that held his wrenches, rolling it open like a surgeon readying his instruments.

Slowly he began to assemble the Whizzer. Time stopped as he worked, fitting things together, screwing pieces in place, applying exactly the right amount of torque to each bolt.

The Whizzer, it soon became clear, was some kind of bicycle. This much was obvious when he pulled out the blood-red frame, the spoked wheels clad in Goodyear double eagle whitewalls. For a wild moment, I imagined the bicycle was for me. But there was something about the intensely private way my father went about building the thing that made it clear The Whizzer had nothing to do with me.

Supper time came and went. He kept working. My mother showed up at the side window once in a while, but she knew better than to interrupt him. I did, too. I had to pee but I stood on the gravel strip as straight and silent as I could, watching. I thought of it as a kind of training exercise.

Once he had the wheels on the frame, he picked up the bloody muscle of the gas tank, the word "Whizzer" lettered in gold on its bulging side. He perched it on the top bar of the bicycle, then began the laborious process of affixing the engine below it, with its intricately related parts, cables, belts, and chrome cowling. The exhaust was a curved chrome horn. This thing was more than a machine. My father's hands were so sure, the process of assembly so smooth, that he seemed not to be just putting it together, but to be inventing the thing. Nothing stopped him, not even the gathering darkness.

As he worked, he talked, more to himself than to me: "The original Whizzer was manufactured in 1939 by August Breene-Taylor Engineering, a Los Angeles maker of airplane parts. This is the '300,' designed in '49. Bigger exhaust ports than previous designs. Cylinder block is heavier, too. It's a three-horsepower engine with a trigger for compression release and a twist grip for the throttle. I could have got one with a kick-start, but what if I feel like peddling?"

The last pieces he installed were the headlight and the brown leather seat. Finally, he filled the crankcase with oil and the tank with gas he siphoned from the car. When he was finished, he stepped back, wiping his hands on a shop rag. It wasn't the motor bike itself he was taking the measure of, but himself, his workmanship. Then, without a word, he lifted a leg over the Whizzer, settled into the seat, and pushed off, pedaling for an awkward ten feet or so, his long legs as ungainly as a grasshopper's, until the motor caught and jerked him forward, past our car and out into the street. He made a wide, sweeping right turn and then was gone. Nothing left of him but the tinny buzz of the engine fading up the dark street. Once again my father had disappeared.

Was he gone for good? I stepped off the gravel strip and stood among the peeled-down boxes, tools, and leftover parts, feeling as though I had witnessed some final transformation. It was as if the boxes were cocoons that had split open, my father evolving into another life-form, like Superman, strange visitor from another planet.

His labor over the Whizzer had somehow kept back the night, but now I could hear the cicadas again and the jittering hum of the streetlights and, from somewhere, the slam of a screen door, the rattle of a garbage can. I walked to the front of the house, but the street was empty as far as I could see. It was Friday night. My mother, brother, and sister were in the living room watching Red Skelton. None of them knew what had just happened to us, that our father was gone, probably forever. The prospect frightened and thrilled me.

I waited at the end of the driveway for what felt like a long time, waited while the night deepened around me, just to make sure. A sudden breeze flattened the grass for a moment and then was gone. The hard stars burn above. The longer I waited, the truer it seemed: my father was finally gone for good. He hadn't just stopped off at one of his haunts—the Dari-King, the Dog 'n Suds, Bulldog Lanes, or the Happy House Shop. He'd gone much farther than any of those places. He'd gone all the way back to his home planet.

Our picture window was greasy with TV light. I heard laughter. I heard applause break out like the sound of popping corn. After Red Skelton, I knew, was *Highway Patrol*. I headed toward the back door, back to my innocent family, who knew nothing of what had just taken place. As I climbed the steps and pulled open the storm door, I thought that now, with my father gone, I'd be allowed at last to stay up late and watch Friday Fright Night on Channel 8. There'd be time enough, after the second feature, to tell them the terrible news.

☙ ❧

The internal combustion engine has to be the most primitive invention ever to come from the mind of man. So primitive, in fact, that they should have called it the "infernal confusion" engine. With no more than two hundred miles of my trip under my belt, I've already had to patch two hoses, replace a fan belt, and plug the radiator. And now the dang thing has done quit on me altogether, and it's beyond my poor powers how to make it right. Inauspicious beginnings.

I think of Hannibal crossing the Alps by elephant. I think of the Norsemen crossing the ocean in a primitive sailboat. Surely I should be able to drive a few miles in a pickup truck with a camper back. Sometimes I think the Machine Age was a big boo-boo.

Here in Mexico they use burros, small mules, and a very few small horses for individual transportation. As I stand beside my disabled machine, I begin to understand the wisdom of such a life.

While I wait there for inspiration, a man comes by riding a burro, his wife walking behind.

I ask him why he's riding while his lady walks.

He answers, "She doesn't have a burro."

Earlier that day, my electric water pot stopped working due to a dance on the highway with my suitcase. When I see one lashed by its handle to their saddle pack, I offer six dollars for it.

They ask for seven.

I give them eight.

The Mexican people don't appreciate it unless you bargain.

Once I make it to town, inspiration having deserted me for the time being, I leave my camper in the capable hands of a Mexican mechanic whose garage is no bigger than a phone booth.

I decide to make an opportunity of my misfortune and purchase a quantity of traveler's checks and a bus ticket for parts unknown.

I find that, as I travel deeper into Mexico, the people along my paths are different than the Mexican-Americans and Border Mexicans. They tend to be more Indian. They are gentle and kind. In all my time in Mexico, I have never seen a fight or heard an argument or a voice raised in anger.

They are honest. I have never seen or heard about any theft, burglary, or even any attempt to shortchange a customer. There are no bums or hustlers or questionable charity collections.

They are sober. I have never seen a drunk on the street.

Family activities center about the children. Parents are more permissive than Americans but less so than Japanese. However, children do not take advantage of their freedoms, nor do young adults behave badly.

Most adults seem to work ten- to twelve-hour days, six days per week. Children work after school.

Most of the villages have a place for worship, often a small Catholic Church. However, I have seen only one Priest. Services are generally conducted by laymen. I'm told that the Catholic Church is having trouble recruiting Priests for Mexico. The church buildings are kept clean and left open. Worship appears to be a mixture of Catholic and Indian, with more Indian features as I go deeper into the country. A common aid to worship is a cross outlined on the floor with pebbles or sand, and burning candles set at each corner.

There is no police harassment. Other than border and roadblock guards, I have seen only three police officers in the past six weeks. I talked with one roadblock guard who humorously teased me and took my teasing in return.

Mexicans keep themselves clean. Even though they might live in a degree of filth and even though odorless water is at a premium, they and their clothing are clean and neat. Even the young children are nicely dressed. The water is not drinkable or usable for anything except closed-mouth showers.

It is considered fortunate to have a lizard in your bedroom to reduce the insect population.

⤛⤜

3

LA BOCA

'm standing at the mouth of the Río Grande, where it sprawls into the Gulf, having driven my car right down onto the nearly deserted beach at Boca Chica. I'm gazing out at the green, then gray, chop of the waves, trying to imagine my father's death, my father's life. I might as well be trying to stare across the Atlantic, to see the face of God.

On this side of the river, a few solitary fisherman whip out their lines for spotted sea trout. Near me, an old couple walks grimly past, the man saying, "Maybe this shouldn't be the way it is, but this is the way it is." On the other side of the river, in Mexico, it's party time. Several families and couples have fired up barbecues, and a couple of teenaged boys have a good-sized bonfire going. Mostly the beach around me is studded with flattened plastic jugs, soda bottles, beer bottles—Negro Modelo and Bud Light.

People swim and wade in the river from both sides, some of them walking completely across, wading through thigh-high water to talk with those on the other side. Three-hundred years ago, the river was said to be as wide as a musket shot and thirty-six feet deep. Now it's a wading pool. In another few months, the river will give up completely and, for only the second time in recorded history, will no longer reach the Gulf, falling short by five-hundred feet. From Río Turbio to Río Tardo.

I settle down in the sand near the rusted carcass of a Volkswagen to think. My plan is ridiculous. I am ridiculous. What am I thinking? What can I possibly get out of this trip? The death of my father has thrown me into some kind of tailspin. I need to turn back right now, put the silk noose around my neck and drag my sorry ass to the funeral. So what if the family gets all weepy over their fallen hero? Be a man, I tell myself. But I can't. I'm not ready for that. I don't want the story of the man, and I don't want the grim perfection of the face in the open box. I want the man himself. And the only way I'll find him is to search him out the way a cop would—in his last known whereabouts, among his last-known associates. The places and the people he describes in his *Mexico Log*.

Here at La Boca the party goes on. There's no sign of La Migra. Everything is very civilized, except for the guy in the Waverunner who keeps racing up and down the river every few minutes. Could he be border patrol? Somehow I doubt it. He's enjoying himself too much. On the other side, mimicking the Waverunner, a carload of teens from the bonfire race up and down the beach in an old Impala, arms draped over the sides, cruising, radio loud with the bouncing polka rhythms of *conjunto* music, and the echoing cries of announcers: "The most powerful Tejano hits in the Valley!!!" and "Coke—*siempre tu pasion!*"

On this side of the river the fishermen work with poles, on the other seins. Besides sea trout, they catch blue crabs, redfish, shrimp, and more. A seagull splits the air with a self-pitying shriek. Lying next to me are the brilliant blue remains of a jellyfish looking like some alien's used condom. The river here is pale brown and translucent. The gulf is blue and green, except for the cloud of brown river water seeping slowly into it, already being choked off by silt, sand, hydrilla, hyacinth, and overuse. Soon the riverbed will be so dry that they'll mark the border by driving a wooden stake into the sandbar at what once was mid-river.

I'm leaning back against the rusting hulk of the Volkswagen, staring out at the Gulf when a man who has been standing in the river chatting with other men walks across the river and up the sand to me. His wet iron-gray hair is swept back. His chest is a wiry gray thicket. His rust-colored Speedos are so tight I can see all the fruit in his basket. He looks at me, then out at the Gulf.

"You look for the dead zone?" he asks.

I'm sitting up now. "*Cómo?*" How does this man know about my father?

"The dead zone," he says again. "Gringos say we pollute the river, but your Mississippi is the one." He gives me a sidelong look and points out to sea with his chin. "Farm runoff poisons the Gulf. The dead zone." This is years before the BP spill threatened to make the Gulf an even deader zone.

"What state are you from?"

"Nebraska."

He says the word quietly, then, "Which one is that?"

"The big square one."

He shakes his head. "*Ese,*" he says thoughtfully, looking out over the water, "they're *all* big square ones. Anyway, the dead zone is the size of Nebraska."

The sun is warm. The sky is blue with a scribble of white clouds. The dead zone is the size of Nebraska. It's the width of the line between worlds, the envelope of air I move through, the sack of skin in which I stretch my bones. The man wades back across the river. The Waverunner makes another pass. The Gulf comes throbbing softly up the sand, the water where my father died.

⁂

The Color of the Ocean

The color of the ocean varies from place to place. Near the equator, the color is a beautiful deep blue. As one travels northward the blue begins to fade. North of the Caribbean the water becomes a blue-green. Approaching the thirtieth parallel, one discovers the blue is almost entirely gone, and the only color left in the sea is a beautiful, deep green.

The green water of the North Atlantic is a thing to fear and to respect. The green sea shows no mercy to the uninitiated seaman. It may cast its body into many forms so as to cause the seaman's ship to weather badly. It may glaze its surface and still the wind and leave the sailor lying-to. It may bunch its mighty muscles and smash the tiny thing that dents its surface like a pin.

The strength of this green water is beyond man's conception. It sucks the blue water of the Gulf Stream north along the coast of the United States, and merges it with the Arctic Stream at the Grand Banks. Here it gathers up its strength and hurls these waters eastward. Even when all this water has traversed the entire Atlantic, it still has enough momentum to wash high upon the shores beyond. Herding this water into a pool once more (a pool three hundred miles across), the green water races with it southward, gaining speed as it goes. Nearing the blue waters once again, the green releases its captive, sending it racing, rolling, jumping thousands of miles before the green once again sucks the blue into its possession.

The Destroyer USS Danning rolled and pitched in the heavy seas. I stood on the bridge. I had the con. A shipmate stood the watch with me, just a pup who hadn't even crossed the equator yet. Too new, even, for me to know his name. He was an extra pair of eyes, keeping his binoculars trained on the spray.

Wind screamed in the rigging and drove pellets of rain into our faces. The waves crashed over the bow and ran foaming across the deck. The bridge was awash with slippery spray. We held tight to a stanchion. Our feet were dead frozen things. The binoculars hung heavily from my neck. I took them off and put them aside. What was the point? I leaned peering into the wind, trying to see if there was another ship out there, but the weather was a solid wall. Impossible to see through. I had slowed the ship to ten knots, just to be safe, trying to hold her head into the sea. With every plunge, the bow tore the waves into phosphorescent foam.

The seaman's voice sounded thin and distant, even though he stood right next to me. "Light ho!"

I cupped my hands around my mouth and yelled, "Where away?"

He pointed. "Starboard bow close aboard!"

I turned to the watch in the pilot house. "Full left rudder. Engines back emergency. Sound collision. Call the Captain to the bridge." It was only after the words left me that I realized I'd been screaming. In seconds the ship began to heel to starboard, vibrating as the screws and rudders fought against the motion of the ship.

Ahead, off starboard, a shaky line of lights began to take shape in the howling spray, at first faint, then brighter. I stood there helplessly as the line of running lights came snaking closer. They were almost abeam now, the lights and the tall wall of steel they were attached to. I was afraid that the big freighter wouldn't answer her rudder in time and that her bow would cut us in half. Oddly, as I waited for the ship to be torn in two, it was the words of the poet that came to mind: "For fog and fate no charm is found to lighten or amend."

Our crew had begun to stream on deck, running to their collision stations, half of them still in their skivvies. They cut the huge hemp fenders from the lashings and threw them over the gunwale to hang from their suspension lines against the hull. The ship was beginning to answer her screw, so I ordered the rudder shifted, knowing this was the last act I could perform to save her. I heard the boatswain on the forecastle yelling orders to his men over the piercing shriek of the ship's whistle.

The Captain, in bathrobe and slippers, appeared beside us. "I'll take the con, gunner. You two go see to the bilge pumps."

"Aye-aye, Captain. The rudder's right full. The screw's back emergency." We lunged down the nearest ladder.

I heard the Captain advising his talker. "Tell the black gang I want all the steam they can give me."

But it was too late. As the new man and I landed on the main deck, there was a scream of tearing metal, and the deck was swept from under our feet. I landed in the water-way and clung to the lifelines as a wave broke over the side. As the wall of water slapped and pawed at the deck, I realized I couldn't see the new man. I scrambled to my feet, but he was nowhere to be seen. I didn't even know what name to call. "You!" I yelled. "You!"

Now the huge freighter was sliding past, slowly crashing up and down against us, a darker wall in the dark wall of weather. High up, I could see the hazy line of running lights rising and falling with the waves. The freighter moved with terrible slowness. Every time the two hulls touched, bright sparks sprayed into the driving sea wind. The shrill aching groan of metal on metal turned in my gut. I gained my feet and fought my way forward to the bow, where a crewman was already playing a flash down our injured flank.

Much of the starboard plating had been sheered off. Twenty feet aft of where the eyes had been appeared the innards of the boatswain-locker. The starboard side was so battered, crumpled, and torn that we looked more like a broken toy than a warship. It must have been terrible noisy, but all I heard was the ugly sound of the ship taking on water like a big tin ladle dipping water out of a bucket.

We closed off all the bulkheads we could but had no idea if they would hold. All we could do was hope.

Somehow we made it, limping back to port, listing to starboard the whole way, bilge pumps running day and night along with a 24-hour bucket brigade. We lost only the one man. Plucked right out of his shoes by the storm and the force of the collision. There one minute and gone the next. Nothing left of him but his shoes. That could have been me, I thought. And sometimes I think it was me.

Since that night I've stood many watches on many ships through many storms and swells, most without incident.

The quartermaster calls out, "How's she riding?"

And I answer, "Like a dream, Wheels. Like a dream."

But I'll never forget two things: the way that man disappeared right in front of my eyes and the voice of God screaming in the sea wind.

Robert C. Spencer
Theme for Freshman English
Purdue University, 1960

4

RARA AVIS

N ancy and Frank Wharton are the self-styled pioneers, the advance guard for the Great Texas Coastal Birding Trail, an experiment in ecotourism that, when complete, will take birders to 308 birding sites along its 700-mile length. Two major migration flyways intersect with the Trail. It's a birder's paradise, with a species count of almost 600. Even in winter, it's worth a visit. A drive through the back country will turn up eagles hunting the harvested rice fields. The Trail stretches from the Louisiana line to Brownsville and along the Río Grande to Laredo. The Whartons and I are having breakfast on the terrace of our hotel outside Matamoros, the sister city of Brownsville, Texas.

Frank Wharton was one of my father's shipmates. I found his name and address on a torn-out address book page, a San Diego address. I thought I'd line up a visit, but when their daughter, Donna, told me they were vacationing in Matamoros, just a short hop over the line, I thought my luck was changing for the good. When she told me her father was recovering from a stroke, I wasn't so sure.

The hotel itself is a grand hacienda, but our rooms are in the pink stucco box on the back end of the parking lot. Very large, very clean rooms and not very much furniture. There's a TV as big as a refrigerator, but the only channel it gets repeats the same fuzzy footage of a line of Mexican soldiers being decorated with medals. Meals are served out here on the patio behind the hacienda, a nice change from the echoing box of my room. Here there are hanging plants, cool breezes, brisk waiters, and the good food of Mexico.

The Whartons have ruddy faces, maybe from putting in lots of time outside, maybe from blood pressure, maybe from tightly stoppered anger. They have a conversational style that would be hard to distinguish from pro wrestling.

She attacks with treacly kindness, he tosses words at her like blades and blunt objects. Both have eyes that fix on you for a second and then look away, anxious not to miss a more interesting species.

Nancy wears her white-gold hair in big brassy ringlets. The nervous flutter of her eyes is exaggerated by the thick lenses of her black plastic teardrop glasses. She's wearing a peach-colored pantsuit. the jacket open to show a gray sweatshirt that reads "Permanent Vacation." She talks nonstop. Nervous talk, as if she's determined to fill in the silences left by her husband, who for the most part sits stoically next to her. I decide not to tell them right away why I'm here, why I want to talk with them. Maybe it's the time I've spent in Mexico, but it seems rude to ask outright for information and then leave, too much like robbery.

"I've been looking for you," I say.

"Here we are," Nancy says, pointing at her sweatshirt, "on a perm vac. At least Frank. For me it's work. I'm his nurse. I'm his wife and his nurse. He's the victim, the patient, and I'm the nurse. Stroke, right, honey?" She pats his knee. "But you're doing fine, aren't you, sweet potato? You're, as they say,"—and here she speaks with terrific slowness, dancing her pinched forefinger and thumb tips together in the air as if each syllable is a damp piece of doll clothing she's hanging out on a line to dry—"in . . . re . . . cov . . . er . . . y."

"Can't complain," Frank says, swinging his gaze lazily to me. "Try to. Nobody lets me."

Nancy, ignoring him, says, "Travel while you can—that's my motto. This place is nice. Good views, good food, good tufted titmouse, nice ladder-backed woodpecker. You can see them feeding, roosting, and nesting to your heart's content."

Frank turns his milky blue eyes on me. His lower lids are baggy and dark. "That's what she does mostly—feeding, roosting, and nesting."

But Nancy busies herself with her birding log: "You got your *helmitheros vermivorus*—"

"—Worm-eating warbler," Frank adds quietly.

"Your groove-billed *ani-*"

"—*Crotophaga sulcirostris*."

"Your *sayornis nigricans*—"

"—Black phoebe. Say, I once had a black phoebe."

"Don't you say a naughty word, Frank. Not another naughty word."

Frank has the distant, unperturbed gaze of Buster Keaton as he slowly raises his hand to his mouth and turns an imaginary key.

Nancy ignores him, busying herself with her bird log. Frank takes a sip of coffee. Nancy can't help it, can't resist talking. "How's the coffee, honey?" she asks as if talking to a simpleton. "To your taste?"

Without a pause, Frank says, "Yeah. Maybe you'll like it anyway."

She turns back to me. "The point is, this is a hot spot for serious birders. And we're serious birders. Since Frank's stroke—he had the kind of stroke most people don't walk away from—"

"Hmmm, just like my marriage," Frank says gazing at the pale blue sky,

"Like I say, since then, we go birding, and this is bird country with a capital B!" She draws the letter in the air between us. "The Valley here is about the most important region for birds in the country. It's at the confluence of two main migratory flyways, and on the edge of four major climatic zones."

"Translation: birds up the wazoo," Frank says.

Nancy, ignoring him: "We respond to all the Audobon Alerts. We do the pelagic birding trips out of Freeport. We're big benefactors for the Río Grande Valley Bird Observatory. We never miss the Río Grande Valley Birding Festival. We even plan our trips using NEXRAD radar images downloaded from the internet."

In the most deadpan voice imaginable, Frank says, "We're advanced as all get-out. We come down here all the time. She comes back riddled with worms, and I come back with nothing. There's a reason for that." He pats a folded copy of *La Prensa* that's lying next to his empty plate. When I give him a questioning look, he unfolds it to show a pint of John Power hidden in the fold. "Alcohol," he says with holy awe. "Kills everything." He unscrews the cap and adds a little more to his coffee. He doesn't offer me any, returning the pint to its hiding place.

Nancy gives a shudder and makes a face. "I don't touch the stuff."

"More for me," Frank says, sipping. "She also doesn't eat jalapeños or peppers of any kind, either. That's what kills the microbes." He leans toward me, whispering loud enough for Nancy to hear. "Between you, me, and the Worthen's Sparrow, she's sicker than she knows, sicker than I'll ever be."

Nancy straightens the sweatshirt under her peach jacket and pats the barrel of a curl as unyielding as rolled steel. She says, "You can't beat Mexico for birds! We like any place with a view, but this is our favorite. The Mexicans know how to treat you right." Then she adds, "When they feel like it. After all, Frank can't do much. We travel to see birds. We like to go away for a few days in mid-week. Of course, we need special things. The room has to be on the ground floor. This hotel is nice. Queen-sized beds! Feather mattresses! And so high! Since the stroke, Frank has to go through all kinds of maneuvers just to roll over. I'd rather he jab me with his elbow than risk rolling off the bed. I didn't sleep at all last night. Not at all. This is our favorite place. We spend a lot of time down here. Truth to tell, it's his queen-sized bed. I get the room with twin beds. At our age we don't go in for the smoochy-smoochy. And when we have visitors we make them take the double. They raised the rates, but they used to charge for visitors. Now they're included free. So it's OK. If you're a TV fan, though, watch out. Around here, they got two channels—on and off. And even when it's on, all you get is the Seurat show—all little dots. But the carrot muffins are to die for. Now they have a VCR. We like to watch tapes of long series. We just finished 'World at War,' and now we're starting over from the beginning. We're terrible! We can't get enough of war!"

"Hitler's rise to power," Frank says. "Look out, she's taking notes."

"I don't like to stay away from home too long. Now that we put the maid on full-time, I like to be around to see that she's really working. Of course, when we're away in the middle of the week we aren't around to dirty up the place, so what's she got to clean? Besides, I don't like to leave Oedipus for too long. That's our cat. When we came home last time, he ran under the bed and said, 'I don't! I don't love you anymore.' Cecilia and I had to get on both sides of the bed and coax her out with jumbo prawns." She begins to gather up her maps and guidebooks from the tabletop and pack them in a plaid mesh shopping bag.

"Southern Arizona's great for birds, too. This trip Frank has spotted one hundred species. And I've spotted one-hundred-and-one." Turning to him: "That's only because you missed that famous kite, whatever it's called. I forget. But it's famous. It's beautiful country down here. But it's hard to count your birds."

Frank, whose lower lids are bruise-blue and crosshatched like a lizard's back, says, "You can't count that kite. It was on the Mexican side, and we were on the Texas side."

"But then it went and flew over to the Texas side. Now what am I supposed to do with it?"

"Better start your Mexican log."

When she sees me reading Frank's T-shirt, Nancy says, "You like that? That's his stroke shirt. I had it made special." Tweetie-bird yellow with a red arrow pointing in both directions. Underneath, it reads, "I'm with . . . I forget."

I lean forward. Before realizing it, I find myself gripping the edge of the table. The suddenness, maybe the crazed look in my eye, I don't know, but Nancy stiffens in her chair. "I know you've been sick, Frank," I say. "I know you have trouble remembering. The stroke and all. But the reason I came looking for you—I'm wondering if you remember serving with my father on the U.S.S. Luce back in 1961."

While my question registers in Frank's mind, Nancy's smile fades. "You're not the Prize Patrol?"

After an awkward silence, I say, "No, no, I'm not."

"Shoot. Sorry, but shoot." She slumps a little in her chair, fingers twitching idly at her sweatshirt. "I thought for sure when Donna called—" Then, her voice rising, "Oh shoot, you mean this is just about one of his old Navy buddies?"

"I guess so," I say. "I'm sorry."

Her mouth tightens and she shakes her head. She stands. "Time for this little girl to fix her face."

Frank says, "You do that, honey. You fix that face. If you need help, I've got a hydraulic jack in the back of the SUV."

She shoulders her white pocketbook and says, "Sometimes, Frank, you can be so funny. Of course, this is *not* one of those times." She heads off in search of the women's room.

"Haze gray and underway," Frank murmurs, watching her go. Then to me, he says, "No chopper."

"Excuse me?"

"No chopper. No van. No check the size of a surfboard—I knew you weren't the Prize Patrol."

"I'm sorry," I say again. I feel criminal, as if I've stolen from them, stolen the prize money that's rightfully theirs.

"Not your fault," he says. "If there's one thing I've learned in this life, it's this: you are who you are and you ain't who you ain't. If people realized that, they'd be a lot better off in this world. Your father. Yeah, I knew him. We served together on the Luce Goose, the Brasso Queen. Fact, we were in the same compartment, up next to the Sonar Room. Tall fellow."

"How well did you know him?"

"As well as most, which is not well. Silent-type. Not much conversation in him. Don't get me wrong. He was pleasant enough. Just kept to himself is all."

"But what was he like?"

"Quiet. Like I said." Sensing my disappointment, he says, "I remember one thing. Sometimes he served as the O.O.D. That's Officer of the Deck. So he rigged all the ship's intercoms to play over a bunch of speakers he had hanging over his bunk. That way, even when he was asleep, which was almost never, he could hear what was going on all over that tub. Had the rest of us screaming bloody murder—turn that racket off!—but it made a certain kind of sense when you thought about it."

"He was clever."

"Yeah, I guess. In a crazy sort of way." He gazes off across the empty tables, remembering, or trying to. "I don't think I ever saw him drunk or whoring around. He ran a very tight ship, personality-wise." His gaze shoots back to me. "That's really all I remember."

We sit for a while without saying anything. I'm surprised to find that I miss Nancy's empty talk.

More to himself than to me, he says, "I remember the fellow who hung himself when he got a Dear John letter. I remember another fellow who got his fingers tore up pretty bad. And I remember what a roller the Luce was when the tanks got low. It may be a straight line on the chart but, by God, it's like climbing up and down mountains when you're actually out there in the soup."

Just then Nancy comes back, saying, "Did he remember anything about your daddy? I'll bet he did. He remembers. He remembers plenty when it suits him. He remembers what he wants to remember."

Frank aims the blue-black sacks of his eyes at me and, with mock wistfulness, says, "What's that word I keep forgetting? Oh yeah, I remember—'Happiness.' Tell me again what that is?"

"Well, thanks," I say, standing. "That's a lot." But my disappointment must be clear.

"Considering my age and what all I've been through"—he pats the side of his head with his fingertips—"you should be grateful."

"I am," I say. "Thank you." I reach out to shake his hand.

He brushes at the air between us. "Don't mention it." After a stretch of silence, he says, "So your father is . . ."

"Dead."

"I figured. How?"

"He holed his boat and drowned before the Coast Guard could get to him."

Frank shakes his head and lets his gaze fall on the potted palms. "Sailor's death. Lucky bastard."

• • •

Later that night, when I open the door to my room, the breeze that follows me in lifts the wet wings of my walls. I've covered the bed and floors with wet sheets of paper, pinned hundreds of damp pages to the walls, partly so they can dry but mostly so I can see them, study them, decipher them. I stare at them so long they take on the mystical properties of Egyptian runes. The scribbled restaurant receipt that reads "2 eggs ov, wht, cof." The entries in a small datebook: "Ret JB Fr." The family tree drawn meticulously on a piece of typing paper, generations flowing neatly from one branch to the next, stopping at his name. Everything below that, the bottom inch of the page, has been carefully torn off, as if he were trying to deny he'd ever been married or ever had children.

All the dampness makes the room smell like a wet hole in the ground, and it looks as if it's been decorated by a serial killer. Papers of all shapes, sizes, and textures are pinned to the walls. Hundreds of sheets of bright white typing paper, some of it gone to yellow, Pink while-you-were-out sheets that have faded to dusty rose. Fringed blue notebook pages scored with darker blue lines as fine as drawn wire. Navy records by the hundreds, boxes neatly filled with numbers and abbreviations. Yellow second-sheets, carbons of every letter he ever wrote, with brown bits of wood pulp floating among the faded words. An old paper lunch bag rumpled as the surface of the moon and covered edge-to-edge, front, back, and sides with an endless equation. A torn corner of vellum, mottled ivory, blank as a bone. Some of the sheets have curled up, dry as dead leaves. Others have stuck to the wall. A few still drip steadily. There's no getting away from the dank smell of the papers. And all of it covered with his ruler-straight printing or murky typing or the hazy vagueness of old carbons. It's as if I've laid out his moldering body.

The Whartons are in the next room. I can hear the sounds of "*World at War*" through the cinderblock wall—goose-stepping soldiers, Adolf's grinding bark. I've brought back a few bottles of beer from the restaurant to help me go through more of my father's papers.

He was a career Navy man who told me he enlisted at sixteen, under-aged but eager. But if this is true, how is it that he appears in his 1947 yearbook as a sophomore? Did he go back to school after the war? Another mystery. It was the height of World War II, he said. He trained as a frogman and learned to clear underwater obstructions for landing craft. Some of the obstructions were jungles of kelp. Some were mines. In the Navy, he said, he found a way of life that made more sense than any other he'd experienced. He loved the hierarchy. He loved obeying—and later giving—orders. To him, obedience was a sign of your status as a human being. The simple willingness to obey an order—any order—made a person stand out in the crowd, made a person special. By the time of his retirement, he claimed he'd taken part in three wars—World War II, Korea, and Vietnam.

Along the way, he claimed to have been involved in any number of top-secret projects and missions that took him from the Black Sea to White Sands, from the Lawrence Livermore Lab to the jungles of Latin America, where he claimed to have lived with cannibals while working on a CIA satellite ground station hidden deep in the jungle. Call up "CIA," "satellite," and "cannibal" on a web search engine, and what you get are news accounts of Russell Eugene Weston, Jr., the guy who charged into the U.S. Capitol in 1998, killing two police officers in an effort to capture what he called "the ruby satellite," which would help him put a stop to cannibalism. I want to believe my father, but at every turn I find another wall, another frightening possibility.

He was a man who spent more time away from his family than with them. Home for him was a stopping-off place, a place to kill time while you waited for another mission. At one point he'd been away from home for so long—from the home he'd made with his second wife—that when he called, his six-year-old son, my half-brother, said, "Do you remember when you used to be alive?" My father told me that story as a joke on himself. It gave me the chills.

I've never met my half-brother. So when I call him, I'm not quite sure what it is I want to say, to hear. After some oddly enthusiastic pleasantries, he says, "Look, I plan to attend Bible college in Los Angeles, and I can really use the money. Whatever there is, you know, in the will. Oh, and can you send me the ship plaques?"

I can't think what to say. Does he even realize our father is dead? "Sure," I say, "sure thing."

At the end of a sailor's tour, he's offered a wooden plaque embossed with the profile of the ship and an account of his service onboard. For a reason I was never told, my half-brother had in effect disowned my father some years before. Why he wants such a remembrance is beyond me. Weeks later, when I finally find the plaques and mail them, there are so many the package will weigh nearly a hundred pounds. It's the last I will ever hear from my half-brother.

In Key West, a few months before the end, my father put his camper in storage and began life on a sailboat. As well as the Coast Guard can tell, he was taking the boat out the channel into deep water when, for some reason, he tried to cross the jetty, one of the walls of stone that mark the channel to deep water. The tide was in, so the jetty was underwater. Still, he was an experienced seaman and should have known better.

Sometime during the middle of the night, he hung the boat on the rocks and was thrown overboard, along with the woman he was about to marry. The water was warm. The sea was calm. They were both in lifejackets. And yet they both died of hypothermia. By the time they found him, his body had drifted three miles away from the scene of the accident. Very strange. Even the newspaper accounts pointed out how unlikely an accident it was. Piecing together what had happened was made more difficult by the fact that a salvager began work on the boat before the Coast Guard showed up, in strict violation of maritime law.

It's strange enough that my father kept every piece of paper that ever came into his hands, not just kept it but kept it with him, even on the boat. I mean everything: thirty-year-old canceled checks, bank statements for long-dead accounts, receipts for items he no longer owned, essay assignments and transcripts from his days at Purdue, and almost the strangest thing of all—pages and pages of his signature written out in slightly different ways each time. The handwriting goes from florid to cramped, the name from Cornelius Spencer to Robert C. Spencer to C. Robert Spencer to C.R. Spencer and every possible variation, hundreds of signatures, written every style imaginable—this one with boxy, squared-off letters; the next with loopy curlicues; the next lazy and sprawling; this one tightly circled, like a knot. The name and style that dominates, repeating for pages and pages, is Robert C. Spencer, the skinny loop of the "R" thrown out like a lariat to the end of the name, a kid's idea of a signature.

And the oddest find so far—his birth certificate with his name clearly indicated as "Cornelius Robert Spencer." We always knew him as "Robert Cornelius."

Who was this guy?

Just then the phone rings. I stare at the green Princess phone on the stand between the beds. No one but the Whartons knows I'm here. I consider invoking my unbreakable rule: don't answer it. But I do.

"Hello?"

The only answer is a cluster of fainting clicks. I hang up slowly, as if the phone is a bomb that might go off in my hand.

I haul my backpack onto the bed and pull out the sealed envelope my sister gave me as I left her house. A Polaroid the Coast Guard took of my dead father, proof that he's dead. He survived three wars with barely a scratch. I have to know for sure that he's dead. I stare at the white envelope, the only clean, dry, blank piece of paper in the entire room. I know he's dead. Of course he's dead. Still, I don't have the courage to open the envelope, to stare into that dead face. I push the envelope deep inside my backpack and push it off the bed.

My father, who claimed he never drank, was like this. Everything meticulously arranged. Nothing out of place. For thirty years, from the age of eight to thirty-eight, I never heard from my father. Then one day his camper pulled up in front of my apartment.

We didn't really know what to say to each other. I complimented him on the way he had crafted the camper's interior to get the most use out of the space—the sleeping pad in an alcove over the cab, the combination shower and toilet. His book rack had a hinged railing to keep the books from falling out while the camper was in motion. The rack was completely full. Every time he bought a new book, he got rid of an old one of equal thickness. But the thing that stopped me dead was the roll of toilet paper in his bathroom. It was marked off every twelve inches. He had calculated the amount needed for one swipe, then unrolled the entire thing to inscribe an inky caret at every twelve inches, and then carefully re-rolled the paper. That frightens me more than anything else I know about my father. How could all this order be anything but a disguise for mental disorder? Or is that no more than my anger speaking? Or worse, my effort to explain the man's malevolence, something that finally—like the truest evil—has no explanation.

Maybe all his care and craft were efforts to cling to a world he knew. And writing out his name hundreds of times might have been his way of staying anchored in that world. But what about all those variations of his name? I have no knowledge about the mental health of my father, except that he often seemed to be two people. One was self-effacing, smiling, courteous, a shy country boy who took an interest in everything and everyone but himself. The other one made you wish you were dead.

One Saturday in Indiana, when I was a kid, he told me to rake the driveway gravel smooth. He'd inspect my work when he got back from a study session at school. Maybe it was because I had planned to play football that day, or maybe it was because the day was hot and the job was bigger than it seemed, or maybe it was because I was eight-years-old, but I guess I didn't do a very good job. When my father got home, he dragged me out of the house by my hair and hauled me up and down the driveway to show me all the uneven areas.

"I give you a simple job, sailor, and you muck it up. Look here! And here! You've made things worse than they were. That's quite an accomplishment. You should be very proud of yourself. I'm going to give you some inspiration for sorting out your sorry excuse for a life."

He dragged me back inside and had me strip off my clothes and hand-wash them in the toilet. He looked in on me every ten minutes or so to make sure I was still scrubbing, still up to my elbows in toilet water. After a couple of hours, he let me wash up and go to bed, tucking the sheet tightly under the edges of my body with the hard blades of his hands. "I'm giving you another chance to redeem yourself. Tomorrow you'll want to get it right."

I was awake all night trying to figure out how to do the job. The next day I failed again, and the next night I did more hand-washing in the toilet.

On the third day, I stood next to the driveway, the rake in my blistered hands, my eyes ripe with tears I would not let fall.

As my father left for school, he said, "This is your last chance, sailor. You hear me?"

"Yes, sir," I said quietly, knowing that this time it would be the belt.

Once he was gone, I studied the driveway. Somehow I'd raked gravel into the grass along the edge of the driveway, and there were bare spots, lumps, and furrows in the driveway itself. My father was right: I was a failure.

I was about to begin when my mother came charging out of the house and grabbed the rake.

"Get inside. If you say so much as word one about this, I will kick your ass from here to kingdom come." And she began raking the driveway with short, sharp, vicious strokes.

That evening I sat cross-legged on my bedroom floor waiting for my father. I played with my toy soldiers, small green plastic infantrymen molded into various postures of battle. I had just lanced one of my blisters with the tip of a soldier's bayonet when my father came into the room. This time he was smiling, but that only frightened me more.

"I see that second night of toilet-time did the trick." He smiled more broadly. "I thought it might. There's hope for you yet, sailor. Not much, I admit, but some."

Now, every fall, I'm very serious about raking leaves. I rake them onto tarps that I haul away, I grind them into mulch, I remove every last one from the yard. I tell myself all this attention is good for the lawn, but I know the truth.

It's very late when I decide the pages are dry enough and start taking them down to organize them into piles—personal letters, business letters, bank statements, naval records, receipts, and the rest. He's even got a copy of my birth certificate and his marriage license, though he's been divorced from my mother for thirty years. The divorce papers are here, too, and his marriage license for his second marriage, which also ended in divorce, though after a twenty-five-year run.

Later that night, surrounded by the damp archive of my father's life, the sounds of Hitler's march on Paris coming faintly from the Wharton's room next door, I reread the letters he sent me over the last few years, after we'd reconnected. I have my copies somewhere at home. But so does he, here among his papers, old-fashioned carbons of them all, the letters fuzzy and blue, the paper gray with mold. Absolutely amazing. In several he tells about picking up hitchhikers, my father the Samaritan.

I spread a new generation of damp pages across the floor and around the room, pinning more of them up until the walls are covered wetly from floor to ceiling, papering the walls with what's left of him. I stay awake most of the night reading and organizing more fragments of my father's life. Eventually, I fall asleep surrounded by my father's words, penned in by his dead-even lines. On all the handwritten pages, the ink has run a little from sitting in seawater, each word fading behind a pale blue cloud, disappearing like the man himself.

∽✧✧∽

In Vietnam, I spent some time as a river rat on the Swifties, the Swift Boats, PCFs, which stood for Patrol Craft Fast, and the like. I grew to love Vietnam. The people impressed me with their quiet gentleness—the ones who weren't shooting at me. The countryside struck me as tranquil, not far from someone's notion of heaven itself. But that's not the story I mean to tell.

It was well before dawn and dark as pitch on the South China Sea. The Boat Captain was a Lieutenant JG who made us all wear the uniform of the day, no matter what the weather. Other guys on other boats got by with green T-shirts and even cut-offs, but not us. He was a small, compact man who'd done a little of the Golden Gloves in his youth. His face was a some bit mashed from the experience. Lieutenant Brookstone. Even his name sounded by-the-book. And to tell the truth, the book was all right by me.

It was dark when we nosed up against YRBM-27, a supply barge anchored offshore, actually a flotilla of barges tethered together, a floating city.

"Welcome to the Mekong Marriott, PCF," a voice called out to us from the darkness. "Shut her down for refuel and re-arm."

We shut down the diesels and started to tie up. Just then, somewhere off the barge's bow, a grenade went off, causing some of us to nearly soil our linen.

"Don't fret, gentlemen," the crewman said, handing us up on deck. "It's just the bow watch playing catch with Charlie." He explained that sometimes a VC sapper would float downriver and stick a mine on the barge's hull. An occasional concussion grenade was the crew's method for telling him that such behavior was not appreciated.

"Chieu hoi!" one of forward crewmen yelled through a loudspeaker, trying to convince any VC within hearing to give up.

On the other side of the barge, men were offloading an ammo supply ship, carrying rockets and boxes of ammunition, with belts of machine gun bullets draped over their shoulders and outstretched arms. Everywhere you looked there were gallons of gasoline and oil, crates of grenades, and ammo of every description. If I threw a match, I could have probably blown us all into the arms of Our Eternal Lord and Savior.

We heard rotor blades and looked up to see a Navy helo in short orbit coming in for a hot turnaround on the pad above us. But some wire in the weapons system must have shorted because just as the skids hit the deck, a rocket launched from one of the pods, bouncing off the deck. The men and I grabbed our vitals and dove for cover. The rocket screamed off the steel decking and shot out over the water, where it exploded, lighting up the jungle-choked shore.

When we regained our feet, I said, "That was interesting."

The Captain said, "Let's cut a chogie, boys. Too much drama on this tub."

We resupplied the boat fast, with the help of our friendly host, leaving before our tanks were full and before we'd entirely finished re-arming. But we were back on the blue line in good time and still under cover of darkness.

In general our missions were mostly to go upriver looking for contraband, give fire support, and in general adversely influence the hearts and minds of the enemy. Tonight we were doing a little recon. We'd heard about an ammo dump upriver in one of the VC secret zones and needed to know more about it before the higher-ups could decide what to do. The last thing any of us wanted was to call down a zippo raid on an ammo dump that turned out to be no more than a village of women and children.

Jasmo drew the short straw, which is how we ran operations. He was a tough guy from Wichita with a face like a sweaty fist. His claim to fame was being able to fire an M-60 freehand. Since he was on-deck for the op, we let him relax and enjoy the ride.

It was difficult to move upriver without detection, our boat churning and racketing like an old wringer washer. Usually when we passed villages, the bank would be lined with kids—even in the middle of the night—with their hands out. It was always "Lai dai! Lai dai!" Come here! Come here! But along this part of the river the banks were deserted. Not one of us said anything, but I'm sure we all noticed.

Hours passed. The river was a silent, oily swirl, the only sound the stumbling chug of our boat. I'm not ashamed to say that I couldn't wait to get back to blue water.

Eventually the Captain ordered us to put in, and when we did, Jasmo jumped out and disappeared into the jungle. The dump was not far from there. It shouldn't have taken very long. Brookstone kept us beached so we could pick up Jasmo faster. The jungle wall was less than twenty feet away, which definitely ratcheted up the tight-cheek factor.

We stayed at our stations, each man with a weapon. I had the thumper, the grenade launcher, which would be useless in close quarters, but it's what was available. We waited and listened. I could hear the river hiss. I could hear the soggy clatter of the sea return washing up against the hull. Every minute we waited was an agony, and soon the crew began to get the heebie-jeebies. Nobody spoke but the silence and the light rattle of jungle waste and the oily smell of our own mosquito repellant were starting to get to me, to all of us.

The Captain's voice cut through the quiet: "Stay sharp on that green-eye, sailor. If you see anything but our man, localize on his ass."

"Aye-aye," said the spotter on the starlight. "Nothing yet."

We waited. We waited some more. We watched the jungle and were watched in return, no doubt. After the longest time, the radioman broke silence.

"He's gone, sir," he said. I knew his name was Marty, but nobody seemed to know if that was his first or last name. He had a very busy mouth. Not that he talked all that much, just that his mouth was always working. His lips were always worming around, his teeth darting out to take hold of a lip. "He's gone. I can feel it."

We waited for the Captain to reply, but he just let the silence hang there. Then he said, "Keep it wired tight, gentlemen."

Somebody muttered, "Aye, Cap. Laugh-a-minute."

That held us for a little while, but the waiting was too much for us. The gunner said, "Cap, it's taking too long. We'll lose the tide." He was right about that. No matter how hard you stared into the jungle, you couldn't see more than a few inches into the shadowy green mass. For all we knew, a whole VC regiment might be watching us. And even if they weren't, the chances of that increased the longer we waited there. And still we waited.

That was the night I learned that colors have smells. We couldn't see much of the jungle's green, but we could smell it, the stinging blade of it. We smelled the brown of the earth, too, which seemed to be breathing. And we smelled the musky gray scent of jungle animals, or maybe humans, moving past us in the dark.

The radioman slapped at a mosquito as big as a bat. "This is the absolute pits," he said. "We don't get out of here, and I mean now, it'll be caca-dau time." *I-kill-you time.*

By now the Captain was getting nervous, too. "Give him a click," he said.

The radioman keyed the talk button for a second without saying anything, then let it go. We listened to the static, waiting for an answering click, but it never came.

"He's gone," the radioman said. "Like I said. We got to haul ass. We got to put our shit in motion."

"We wait," the Captain said.

A shudder ran along the hull, as if the river had given us a shove. We were scared spitless and too much in shock to know what it was. We might not have ended up in the fix we found ourselves in if we'd been a little more on the ball. What it was was the tide turning. The real tide and the tide of our luck.

After a while longer, even the Captain'd had enough and gave the order to push off. Jasmo wasn't coming. But when we backed out into the channel, there wasn't any channel. We backed right out onto a big gob of mud. We'd waited too long. The Captain gave the order to gun the diesels, but that just seemed to lodge us even deeper in the mud. The boat was hung up at an angle to the current, its stern higher than its bow.

The radioman was hissing and spitting. "I told you," he said as if he were talking to the jungle, but it was the Captain his remarks were aimed at. "Now we're in it but good."

Normally our captain didn't take any guff, but the entire situation must have gotten to him because he did the strangest thing. He didn't say a word. He just went below. We thought he was going for something, that he'd be right back. We waited. He didn't come back. When I went below, I found him lying in his rack, just staring into space.

"Cap," I said. "you OK?"

At first he didn't answer, didn't even look at me. Then he turned his pale eyes to me and said, "I can feel my heart beating in my eyes."

It was a puzzle all right, but something told me not to bother him, so I went back up on deck, where the men were as close to mutiny as I have ever seen.

"You guys stay here if you want," the radioman said, "but when the light comes, you'll be up to your armpits in Uncle Charles. I'm leaving." And before any of us could stop him, he went over the side.

I leaned over the side and said, "Where do you think you're going, boy? The jungle's crawling with VC, and the river's crawling with snakes. You want to end up like Jasmo?"

His voice came from the dark water. "I'm staying right here." I couldn't see him but I could hear his arms moving in the water. It didn't seem fair. We were hung up in the mud, but there seemed to be plenty of water for him to tread.

"Don't be crazy."

"I don't care. I'll take my chances."

And that he did, staying there for a good long time, at least until we joined him, which confused the radioman something terrible.

I'd got it into my head that we could maybe pull the boat off the mud bar by hand, if we were lucky enough and strong enough. I had the men strip down to their skivvies and bare feet, and we went over the side with a towline I had tied to the bow. It might work, I thought. The boat drew less than five feet. The radioman proved there was at least that much water just a few inches away. It might not take much to put us right.

We took our positions off the bow, up to our waists in dark water, found a purchase on the towline, and, on my signal, pulled for all we were worth.

I right away saw what a dumb idea it was. The boat had a hoisting weight of some 43,000 pounds, was thoroughly dug into the mud, and with Jasmo gone, the Captain out of commission, and the radioman in the drink, there were only three of us on the towline. Ridiculous. But when the radioman figured out what we were up to, he splashed over to take a spot on the line. So that was something. And pretty soon there was the Captain himself on deck stripping down to his birthday suit and slipping over the side to join us. Still, even five men hauling with every muscle God gave us couldn't budge her. But what else was there to do? I could already feel the dawn coming on. At first light we'd be an easy target. We had to try.

So we pulled. And at every pull our bare legs sank deeper into the muddy river bottom. The boat just wouldn't move.

Dawn was coming for sure now. The black tops of the palms stood out against the blue night behind them.

"Come on, boys," I said. "She's nothing but an ornery old mule who needs a little friendly persuasion."

We pulled again, grunting and puffing and straining, all the while hoping the river bottom wouldn't suck us under, hoping the stuff floating past was lumps of grass, not lumps of snake.

Maybe it was a change in the current or a loosening of the mud or the boat shifting its weight, but we seemed to move it, just an inch or so, enough to give us hope.

We pulled again. And this time we—or something—moved it several inches.

And again. A few inches more.

When it seemed like we'd pulled the boat to the point where the engines just might do us some good, we climbed back aboard, even the radioman, all of us looking like mud-caked savages.

"Ahoy!" came a whispered call across the dark water. "Permission to come aboard?"

The next thing we saw were two hands coming up over the side holding an AK-47, and then Jasmo pulled himself onboard, wet to the bone, bruised, and cut up some.

"You utter and complete dog," Marty said, smiling. "You put us in some big-time shit."

Jasmo held out the AK. "Took me a while to find just the right souvenir."

He was back safe and sound. Turned out it was an ammo dump all right, and a heavily guarded one. The VC'd caught him and made him dig a ten-foot pit, then thrown him in, posting an armed guard above. When he saw his chance, he made his move. "The dirt was so soft," he said, "I could climb the wall of the pit like a ladder." He'd opened his man's gullet and inflicted a few more sore throats on a couple of others. That boy was tough.

Having Jasmo back was enough to give us all hope. We fired up the diesels just about the time we heard the hollow scream of the first mortar round. It hit the river ahead of us, sending up a big geyser of water.

We called on the big Allisons for all they had. The boat lunged forward, then stalled, sliding sideways in the current. Another mortar round hit, this one close enough to loosen our back teeth. The next one, I figured, would end all our earthly problems.

Then we smartened some. We gunned just the starboard engine, hoping it might kick us out of the last of the mud. It worked. We were free again, in open water. But just as we were about to make our run for the sea, the third mortar round came arcing our way, landing right in front of us. We didn't need to wait until the smoke cleared to know that the shell had blown the bow right off. The hull was nothing more than a thin skin of aluminum, but it was still a shock to see nothing in front of the pilot house but a ragged, smoking hole. It was a wonder none of us was killed.

The bow dipped. Now there seemed to be plenty of river to go around. We were taking water fast. It was a race to see whether we would die from drowning or from the next mortar round. Either way we were in it. Caca-dau time.

I'd like to say it was quick-thinking, an innate sense of strategy, or some other respectable thing that saved us, but it was nothing more than fear and dumb luck.

I gave her full throttle. The boat bolted forward so suddenly that the torn bow lifted above the water line. And that's how we went down the river—all out with our broken nose in the air. Somehow we made it back to blue water like that, finessing the port and starboard engines until we ran her right up against an LST. I held her close aboard while the men went up the scramble net. The deck dipped out from under me as I stepped off. The captain had stopped halfway up the side of the T to watch our boat sink.

"She's gone," he said when the last of her went under the waves. He stared at the water as if he could see through it to something far beyond.

I'll never understand why he did what he did, stranding us like that. He just disappeared. The brass would call it "dereliction of duty" and give him the boot. Only it never came to that. Nobody ever told what happened that day on the river. We were just glad to be alive and back to blue water.

From the papers of Commander Robert Cornelius Spencer

❦

5

———

LA POSADA

I find, in the big green bags, an exchange of letters between my father and the captain he served under on the USS Danning, a ship that collided with a freighter in the North Atlantic. Leland Fanshawe, a name that precludes any other profession except sea captain. According to the letters, he has retired to San Benito, just outside Harlingen. I've found addresses for other former shipmates now living along the border, which explains another of the reasons my father spent so much time down here. What oddly firing neuron would send so many sailors to the desert? Maybe they needed to get as far away from the sea as possible, like Melville going to Egypt to forget the sea, only to be reminded of it by the wave-like dunes.

I want to meet this man, want to talk to someone who knew my father in the life that meant most to him, his life as a sailor.

Their letters mostly trade memories of that night, the night of the collision. "You remember," my father wrote, "how no one slept? There was no telling how long the forward bulkheads would hold. But somehow they did, and we managed to limp into New York three days later. Thanks to our captain."

"Thanks to luck, you mean," Fanshawe wrote in his reply. "Anytime you put big water and big ships together—especially in the North Atlantic—you're going to have big drama. No two ways about it. We were lucky that night, swabbie, all of us except for that kid blown out of his boots. What was his name? Sometimes it seems to me I used up every last ounce of my luck that night."

I cruise the streets of San Benito, up one and down the next, looking for Fanshawe's house. All the squat stucco houses are beginning to look alike. Overhead, the sky fills edge-to-edge with dark clouds. At last I find it and pull into the driveway behind an old station wagon. A woman stands at the open tailgate looping the handles of several plastic grocery bags over the fingers of both hands. The cargo space is filled with the plump white bags. She grunts a little as she tries to lift a cluster. As I walk up to her, one of the handles breaks.

"Sugar," she hisses quietly, then rearranges her grip on them.

"Mrs. Fanshawe?" I ask.

She looks at me for a long moment and then says slowly, "No . . . no. . . ." Then she looks down at the bags. "It's the handles," she says.

The handles of the plastic bags are stretching to thin filaments under the weight of the groceries. I gather up as many as I can and follow her into the house, through the living room, past five or six Latino men who jump up from the sofas to help when they see us. They're an odd assortment—nervous-looking men of varying ages in T-shirts and jeans, the T-shirts often wrong for them—a Metallica T-shirt on a man of sixty. I don't get it.

We carry the bags to the kitchen, to a pair of battered yellow side-by-side refrigerators. By the time we unload the bags, the men have brought the rest inside.

Once all the bags have been brought in, she holds out her hand and says, "I'm Sister Caroline. Who is it you're looking for?"

To hide my embarrassment, I check my note. She doesn't look like any nun I've ever seen, with her worn jeans and red plaid work shirt. "I'm looking for Captain Leland Fanshawe, a retired naval officer. He's supposed to live here."

"Not for the last seven years he hasn't. My order bought the house from his widow. This is La Posada, a temporary shelter for refugees."

I'm starting to think nothing about this trip will be easy.

As we put away the perishables, Sister Caroline explains that La Posada is under the auspices of the Sisters of Divine Providence, its purpose to provide shelter for refugees, mostly men, seeking political asylum or legal residency. Here they find food, shelter, transportation, communication resources, and prayer. To a high degree, the shelter is run by the residents, who handle much of the upkeep themselves. But it's clear that Sister Caroline, a tall woman with a sure step and a steady hand, is the boss, the kind of nun who can get you to toe the line with nothing more than a direct look.

"These people," she says, gesturing toward the living room, "they come here hoping for a better life. What they find is a jail."

She sits me down in the kitchen and sets an empty coffee mug in front of me. I really only want to talk with Fanshawe, but she won't let me go.

"The Lord works in mysterious ways," she says, pouring me a cupful. We're sitting at a Formica table with a pattern of gray swirls. I find myself staring at it, wishing I were anywhere else. The last thing I want to hear is a bit of evangelizing. "I'll bet you've heard that one before—'God's mysterious ways.' Am I right?"

When I don't answer, she says, "Are you a religious man, Mr. Spencer?"

I smile, trying not to let my words sound like a criticism. "Not especially, no."

She presses her lips together and shakes her head slightly. "It hurts my heart to hear that." She slaps her knees lightly. "Well, God's never shied away from a little hard work. Are you hard work, Mr. Spencer?"

"I don't know. I—"

She brushes my explanation away. "Oh don't pay any attention. This is just me talking. You'll come around to God in your own good time and in your own way. And if you don't, well maybe God will come around to you. Heaven knows he's got enough to keep him busy down here on the border."

I have no idea what to say to this woman. "Look," I say, "I see the good work you're doing here, but I only came to find a man who knew my father."

"I know, I know. But sometimes the people you *want* to meet and the people you *should* meet are two different people." She rises to her feet and leaves the room. I'm afraid I've offended her.

A moment later, a man in his fifties steps into the doorway of the kitchen and looks around the room suspiciously. He has a grizzled moustache and big red plastic glasses that magnify his eyes. Cartoon eyes. Stringy black hair trails into a sparse line of gray beard along his jaw line. He wears a loose-fitting, sweaty tank top that's stretched taut over his big belly. "Michigan" is stenciled across the chest. Later he will tell me he's from Nicaragua, but I know that wearing Michigan T-shirts and sweatshirts is an in-joke for Mexicans from Michoacan, so from the start I have trouble believing him. A ballpoint pen is clipped to the slack collar of his shirt. The large lenses of his glasses make him look more open, I think, than he is. But the eyes behind the lenses dart left and right, like an owl looking for prey.

As he crosses to the table and sits down, I introduce myself and shake his hand. He smiles but says nothing, eyes darting.

"And your name?" I ask.

His gaze drifts to the ceiling, then back, looking not at me but through me.

"Atahuallpa," he says, as if it's the first time he's ever said it, has ever heard his own name spoken aloud. But then, of course, it probably is. That can't be his real name.

"*Verdad?*" I ask. "Like the Incan king?"

"*Sí.*" He dips his head slowly with supreme self-importance.

"*Es verdad?*" I ask again.

His magnified eyes are wet as peeled plums as he says, "If I tell you my true name, they will kill my family." He hangs the words out in the air between us, looks at them, appraises them, tries them on for size, appreciating the story he's building. Something makes me think he's lying.

"Who?" I ask. "Who would kill your family?"

In Nicaragua, he says, he was persecuted for his politics, not by the old dictator or by the Sandanistas but by the current, freely elected government, who framed him for a murder, he says, that they themselves had committed. As he speaks, his eyes jitter over my face as if he's trying to gauge the success of his story.

"But why?" I ask. "Why would they do this?"

Atahuallpa shakes his head. "Politics," he says, sighing loudly, as if that explains it all.

"What *are* your politics?"

His hand falters in the air between us like a wounded bird. "The kind that gets you killed," he explains.

From the doorway, Sister Caroline says that, in order to win the right to stay in the U.S., an illegal immigrant has to produce evidence that he or she is fleeing from danger in the home country—political danger, danger of being murdered. It takes a month or so for a merit hearing to consider the evidence. While they wait, immigrants are held in places like La Posada. Here in Harlingen, 50% win the right to stay in this country, a much higher figure than most records of success in immigration law. This is largely due to the vigilance and energy of programs like La Posada, Projecto Libertad, and other safehouses and coalitions of lawyers and political activists.

"Atahuallpa," she says, "is hoping for political asylum, but proving political persecution is hard to do, especially against a friendly government. So that's one strike against him. And the claim that he'd been framed for murder is the second strike. The court is likely to think he's seeking asylum only to avoid the murder charge, not reason enough to grant asylum. Proving your life is in danger if you return to your home country is hard enough; proving the murder charge against you is false, harder still."

Sensing that his story isn't working, Atahuallpa kicks his chin at me. "My country, Nicaragua, is more beautiful than yours. More peaceful, too, before the gringos. Yes, we had a dictator, but we ate!"

Sister Caroline is gone again, so I thank him for talking with me and stand up, ready to leave. If Captain Fanshawe is dead, there isn't much point to my staying around. But Sister Caroline reappears, pushing someone else into the room in a wheelchair.

Oscar stares straight ahead as he tells his story, almost as if talking to himself. In his thirties, he wears a pale green striped shirt that I later realize is a pajama top. A small man but strong, his curly black hair keeps falling down his forehead, but he patiently forks it back with his fingers. His face is deeply creased around the mouth, under the eyes. His voice is quiet, almost a whisper, a mixture of pain and shame.

The long, sleepless night in the desert was very dark. He spent most of it sitting on his haunches, watching the river. All night people crossed back and forth, with no sign of La Migra. Finally, he stripped down to his underwear and rolled up his clothes and few belongings, tying them up with his belt and heading into the River, half walking, half swimming, holding the bundle over his head.

He was a couple-hundred yards on the other side, crab-walking from one mesquite tree to the next, the night moonless and silent except for a scraping wind, when he heard the sound of an engine roaring to life. He couldn't see where it was, but he ran, keeping the river at his back. The engine's roar came from everywhere at once, a metal scream in the darkness, then swung in a wide arc to his right. Headlights set fire to the dark, caught him, threw his long shadow across the desert floor. He ran, the flailing, elongated shadow mocking him as it followed wildly by his side, sailing over cacti and mesquite, plunging up and down gullies, heading north, north.

At first the wall of slowly moving boxcars crossing his path seemed like the end of everything he'd hoped for, then like a steel blessing. He ran up the grade, within inches of the moving train, pausing for breath. The headlights were behind him now, bouncing over the rough desert floor, now impaling his shadow on the side of a boxcar, now lancing up into the star-strewn blackness. Somehow the train lumbering past him—inches from his face, cars swaying, wheels clanking against the sagging rails—seemed to be the answer. He could see the end of the train now, some eight or ten cars away. He had to make his move or be caught. He leaped for the rung of a ladder on the nearest car, but somehow missed, the train faster or slower than he calculated, and now he was grabbing at nothing, at corrugated steel that gave no purchase.

The last thing he remembers, before his legs fell under the wheels, is the feel of a bolt head cutting down his cheek. The first thing he remembers after is lying on his back, the hard stars above him, the headlights bouncing over him, but no shadow on the side of the boxcar, just the sight of his legs jumping like live things under the belly of the train. And it was so strange, he says, his legs all the way under there when he was out here lying on his back, the rolled-up bundle of clothes still clamped under his arm.

When the train passed, when the headlights finally stopped, two men stepped out of the pale green Bronco and leaned over him, their hands on their knees. One of them, he remembers, had a thick chew of tobacco in one cheek that browned his lips.

The legs now, odd things, were no longer moving, just lying there between the rails, the stumps bloody, the feet clad in cheap leather work shoes. He remembers feeling shame. Only a very poor man would wear such shoes, the soles worn through, the leather torn and sewn and torn again.

The next thing he remembers is the burning, his skin on fire below the waist, and the border agent—the one with the wet brown lips—leaning over him to pluck the bundle from under his arm, undoing the belt, letting the clothes unroll, the legs of his worn jeans unrolling, useless, the agent reaching into the back pocket of his jeans for the hand-tooled wallet his wife had made him "*por el dinero d'el Gigante*," for the Giant's money, the wallet empty now, empty forever, like the leg sockets of his jeans. By now the burning had stopped and a coldness had begun to spread from his toes clenching between the rails to his quivering thighs outside the rails, to his waist, his stomach, the cold hand closing over his heart.

The agent turned to the side and spat a brown stream into the sand, then leaned over him again and said in schoolbook Spanish, "*Oscar, mi amigo, no necessidad por los pantalones de acquí en adelante. Solo calzón, no es verdad?*" No need for pants from now on. Only shorts, right?

Sister Caroline wheels him away. Before I'm fully recovered from Oscar's story, she brings in someone else. I feel battered, helpless.

Like Atahuallpa, she won't tell me her name, afraid if she speaks it aloud her tormentors might find her. I believe her. I feel the fear rising off her like heat. She's dressed in jeans and a blousy white top with an elastic band at the waist, the kind of thing that would fit many women, institutional clothes. Brown face, black hair, downcast eyes, a pale white line around her pursed lips.

I try in many ways to get her to talk about life in her village in Guatemala, but all she'll say is "Life was hard." I look to Sister Caroline, who has stayed in the kitchen this time, sitting in the chair next to hers, but she only shakes her head.

"We don't get many women at the house," she says. "She just arrived last night."

I try again. "*Hay soldades?*" My crude effort to ask if there were soldiers.

She glances up briefly, shrugs. "*Claro.*" Of course.

"*Aflicción?*" Trouble?

Scornful of my bad Spanish, she begins to speak in English. "The soldiers camed down from the mountain and bothered me."

"How did they do that?" I ask. "Bother you?"

"They bothered me. *De noche.* They bothered me."

Sister Caroline leans toward her and touches her knee. She speaks in a low soothing voice. She says the word *violación*, her voice rising in question. The woman's eyes go away when she says that.

Quietly, Sister Caroline says, "I think she means they raped her."

Then, stupidly, I ask, "*Es verdad? Violación?*"

The woman looks up, angry, ashamed, a bloodless white line around her pursed lips. With a slow, sharp hiss she says, "*Claro que sí,*" It's so self-evident. What is your problem? And in English, "That's what means *bothering.*"

For a long time there were rumors of soldiers, then stories from neighboring villages, then the soldiers themselves. Boys, really, barely taller than their rifles were long. There were other rumors—that the army couldn't afford to give them bullets for the guns, or that they could afford it but were afraid an armed army might turn on them. Still, no one tested the rumor, not even when the soldiers showed up one night at their door, two of them standing guard outside, as if they were on official business, while the third, barely old enough to shave, cleared everyone but her from the house, then pointed his rifle first at her face then at the hem of her nightgown, hooking the edge with his gunsight and lifting it slowly. She fought to hold it down, stepped back and back again, but he came forward each time, pushing the muzzle of the gun up between her legs, pushing it harder, until she raised her open palms to him, appealing for patience, and raised the nightgown herself, pulled the nightgown over her head, it never once occurring to her to speak to the man, not in Spanish, not in any language, not to this man, this *demonio*, who must surely have been *extranjero*, from away.

All night the soldiers took turns guarding the door. By first light they were gone, promising to come back that night. Slowly her family came straggling back from the jungle to find her sweeping the dirt floor, the cook fire already started in the center, the ocote in flames, the green mesquite branches already popping. And no one said anything. Not that night. Not any night.

But eventually, when they could stand it no more, they sent her away with the little money they could find. The soldiers would return, they knew, *venganza con extremo*, with extreme vengeance, so they continued to sleep in the jungle, returning to the house only during daylight and then only long enough to pray. Eventually the soldiers, frustrated, deprived, feeling as though they'd been taken advantage of, burned down the house and half the village.

In another life, she'd be sitting in a classroom. But here she was, telling her story to strangers, thick with undeserved shame, shame the perpetrators never felt. How is that possible? How is it possible for anyone to commit those acts, turning off the part of the brain that registers shame, guilt, horror?

I'm grateful when she finishes telling her story. I really can't take any more. I say my goodbyes and rush back to the motel, but I can't stop thinking of her. I can't get her face out of my mind, her downcast eyes, the heavy, half-closed lids, the pale line around the tight knot of her mouth. Back in my room, I throw the deadbolt and the safety bar. Protecting what and from whom?

But I know the answer to this question. In his own way, my father was able to do that. He had no capacity for shame or embarrassment. During his first visit after thirty years, I went with him to my local laundromat. Once there, I watched in shock as he stripped off his clothes, the pale blue plaid shirt and khaki pants, in front of everyone, and put them into a washer. I'd spent half my life in laundromats, and not much could shake the focus of the people there, but this did—the old man sitting in a molded plastic chair in nothing but his underwear, reading the newspaper and chatting with me about the headlines.

He had no sense of shame or guilt. This is clear in his *Mexico Log*, where I find reference after reference to people he met along the road. Most of them, I now realize—at least the ones he wrote about—were young women:

> *I had a companion for a few days recently. Tammy is a real smart young gal who's decided to leave her bonehead boyfriend and strike out for parts unknown. More power to her, I say. I'm glad we decided to share a few miles. She was very free with me, and I with her. I have much hope for today's young people.*

Were young women the only hitchhikers out there? No guys whose cars had broken down on their way to work? No ex-convicts trying for a new life? No single moms trying to get to a job interview? No teenaged boys going to the mall? Was every hitchhiker in the world female and between the ages of eighteen and twenty-one?

"Much hope," he says, "for today's young people." That hope isn't for them; it's for himself. Hope that he can still, in his late 50s, bag a coed. Too harsh? What about "Kristelle is keen of eye and firm of flesh" and "Jody satisfied all the human appetites and then some"?

Oh, Dad, you put the "ape" in "appetite."

I'm not saying my father was like those Guatemalan soldiers. That wouldn't be fair. But what son was ever fair with his father? Maybe these women were looking for a little sexual adventure on the road, but it still feels like he took advantage. Maybe what bothers me is the speed and ease with which he came to know these strangers. In a few days he became more personal, more caring, more outgoing with them than he ever did with his own children.

Even after he put the camper up on blocks and took to the sea, he still met "companions" who accompanied him for a few days or weeks, all of them young, all of them women.

I think my father died as he lived, a man with no capacity for embarrassment or shame, a man who could carry off any enormity with a deep-dimpled smile.

Even the beatings. He wasn't a father inflicting pain on a son. He was a father helping his son through a difficult challenge. While I was on my knees in the bathroom, leaning over the cold rim of the tub, puking from the pain, sometimes the rhythmic rise and fall of the belt would pause, and my father would kneel down beside me, a hand on my arm, his voice soft in my ear.

"Take a breath, son. When you go all tense like that, it only hurts the more. All right? You ready to go on? We'll go on."

He was wrong. When I took a breath, my bare back came alive with a firestorm of pain. And then the belt would rise and fall again.

When I think of my father I often think of him as he was that evening in the laundromat, the vexed faces of the customers, the outright stares, and my father sitting there in his underwear calmly paging through the newspaper and reading aloud from any story that caught his fancy, stories about human folly mostly. I remember one about a man who'd meant to poison his wife's lemonade but who'd drunk it by mistake, the day being hot and his thirst powerful.

In the end, Dad, you were the story—your folly, your face, the days and nights you poisoned. And the way you disappeared. And kept disappearing.

He had no sense of the boundaries between people, especially between himself and his family. In one of the bags, among the carbons of letters he sent to friends and relatives, is a copy of a letter to my sister, an old second-sheet, yellow with wood fibers floating in it, the maniacally neat printing blurred from sea water, from time, ink soaking into the cheap paper, the letters trying to get away from themselves, leaving only ghosts. I've found many letters where the words have soaked away completely, no more than blank sheets with vague blue swirls in the center like a summer sky. It's as if, now that my father is dead, his words, too, are leaving, letter by letter, blurring into the void. But this one is still readable, maybe because of the pressure of his pen, the intensity of his thoughts.

I know that something came between my father and my sister in recent years, know that she asked him not to write or call or see her ever again. All I know is that they had an argument of some kind. When I asked him about it, he just shrugged and pursed his lips, shaking his head slightly at life's mysteries. When I asked her, she said, "Believe me, you don't want to know."

But, Sheree, I do want to know. I do. I want to know everything about this man, want to pry up the rock of who he was and discover what lived and died there.

And now, holding this fuzzy yellow sheet filled with fading print, I know. At least a little. My father, it seemed, didn't approve of my sister's first husband, who would die suddenly, of pancreatic cancer only a few months after this letter was written. Do I make it seem as though my father killed my brother-in-law? He didn't. Not as far as I know. Cancer killed Bill. But my father did kill something the day he wrote this letter:

My dearest Sheree,

Does a father dare to tell his daughter the God's honest truth about her life? What if he risks the truth and loses the world? Is it worth it? It is. This man, this husband is not, not, not the man for you. I am as respectful as anyone of the bonds of matrimony—more so! But this marriage was a mistake from the get-go. Do you want to know what I would like, if it were in my power? I would like you to come away with me, to leave him and your old life behind and come away to California, away from prying eyes and family responsibilities, where we can get to know each other's secret mysteries. I want this as much as I've ever wanted anything. And we can have it. All of it! A new life. Together. Just you and me. Say yes. Let me steal you away. Let me raise a ladder to your window and carry you far from that place and that man and the life he has saddled you with. Let me.

Your loving father,
Robert

Amazing. A love letter, of course, not a letter from a father to a daughter. It's true that my brother-in-law was a character. He ate nothing but red beans and rice all the days of his life. He collected guns. A lot of guns. One room of his house was filled with them. I don't mean on gun racks or in boxes. They were stacked on the floor in a huge raw pile of iron—handguns, rifles, assault weapons. And not just guns—grenades, daggers, you name it. If it was a weapon, he had it. When he wanted to show you some new toy he'd picked up, he had to crawl over the pile on his belly to retrieve it. When the kids were born, he had my sister sew each of them a pair of onesies made from camouflage cloth. He'd built a shack deep in a Louisiana bayou where he planned to take his family "when the Russians come over the hill." He was, in short, a strange man. But he was also a good father and a good husband.

And anyway, none of his strangeness would have seemed strange to my father. During one of his visits I gave him a copy of *Soldier of Fortune* as a joke. Later I found the magazine folded open to the Classifieds, several ads for mercenaries circled with notes next to the ones he'd already called. He looked up, his eyes bright, like a kid discovering *Playboy*. "I had no idea there was such a magazine!"

A few years later he hatched a plan to steal a Chinese junk. I was supposed to quit my teaching job and sign on as his first mate.

"We'll take on the Chinese pirates and fight our way out of the hostile waters of Shanghai Harbor."

"Sure, Dad," I said. "Yo-ho-ho and a bottle of rum." I joked with him in order to find out how serious he was, but he wasn't listening to me, his gaze locked on the watery horizon in his mind. And that's how we left it, with no other words spoken, no arrangements made.

A month or so later, I got a frantic call from the San Jose airport. At first no one spoke. All I could hear was the distant, hollow sound of someone being paged, the words bouncing off the impossibly high walls and ceiling. Then my father's voice, close, intense, his hand squeezing the mouthpiece. "Son! Where are you? I'm here with the rest of the crew! We're waiting on you! Hurry, boy! Zero hour is at hand!" And then the line went dead.

What made my brother-in-law so inappropriate was not the fact that he was a gun-toting survivalist or that he came to Christmas dinner with a hunting knife in his boot and what he called his "snubby" in a shoulder holster "just to make sure nobody gets out of hand." No, that was behavior my father would have admired. Bill's great moral failing was the fact that he loved my sister. How dare he?

Everything weird about my father is contained in this letter—the passion to control someone else's destiny, the zealous disregard for reality (apparently she was not only supposed to leave her husband but her children, then ten and eight years old, as well), and of course his incestuous imagination. He would not have seen it that way, as incest, but as a romantic rescue. And he would not have seen her rejection of him as horror but as a failure of nerve. The way he saw my unwillingness to fight our way out of Shanghai Harbor by his side.

Hell, they're only words, right? But with these words, my father killed my sister's faith in her marriage, her faith in herself, her certainty that reaching out to my father after so many years of his silence was a good thing for her, for the family, for my father.

The sexual predator who succeeds is the one who can convey the sense that what he proposes, with a word, with a touch, is completely natural, an extension of his regard for you, a part of God's plan.

My father never met a border he couldn't cross. As a kid, I'd wake up to find his hands on my body, taking my measure, his pale face hovering in the dark, his eyes on me as if I were an experiment that needed his constant attention. And this was the least of it, before the knife. Today, unless I'm careful, I can still feel those hands, the hard fingers sliding under my thigh, the hot palm cupping my genitals. Now, every night, to get any kind of sleep at all, I have to lie on my stomach and prepare my thoughts. Otherwise, he comes into my dreams. His voice carries over water, over stone, on all the edges of the air. "Why don't you love me, boy? Why?"

My day at La Posada has been a long one and I'm tired, tired of everything, of real and figurative boundaries, of lines in the sand and lines we cross with impunity. And besides that, there are no towels in my bathroom.

I go to the desk to get some, waiting while the aged good-old-boy behind the desk watches the last moments of a news piece on illegal border crossings.

"You ask me," he says wiping his nose on the back of his hand, "the army ought to just line up at the border and shoot every damn one of them that comes across."

I want to tell him about how Oscar watched his legs twitch from ten feet away and about the Guatemalan woman tortured night after night only to be found by her family every morning cooking tortillas over a fresh fire, until they could no longer stand her grim gaze and the white line around her mouth. There are many more things I want to tell him, about fathers and about boundaries that get crossed in the dark, but the words, whether Spanish or English, are so difficult to come by, so inexact, so incapable of conveying anything as complex as the truth.

"Fuck you," I explain.

❧❧

Dear Son,

Brent, we were waiting, the whole crew, in the San Jose airport that day, the day ordained for you to join the mission. I had talked you up some bit to the men, who were looking forward to your joining our brotherhood. Hard men, yes, but usually that's the only kind that will do. We were all of us there in the waiting area with our gear. And where were you?

You probably thought I was joking. I assure you I was not. I am reading books on sailing vessels, the techniques of sailing, racing, wind and currents, and such things. I'm on my eighth book. Part of this reading is just to learn all I can so that I can be a better sailor. However, another part of it is in preparation to realize my dream. The dream I spoke to you about. The dream to steal a Chinese Junk and sail it into the free waters of America. You should have come, boy. You should have kept your word. I won't say you've killed my dream, only that you've done it grievous bodily harm.

While we waited for you, I mentally manned the junk's rigging. In my mind we tacked past rocks and shoals and out to the open sea. In all ways except one we were ready. But then, you never showed, did you. I thought better of you, son.

Of course, now I will probably never really make that trip but I keep inching in that direction. I do not hold this against you much. It is a setback merely, a temporary delay. Besides, it has given me an opportunity for additional study.

I am trying to get experience on larger and larger sail craft, listening to lectures, and I have one more course to take here. This week I am applying for a passport (I have used a Geneva Convention passport in the past) and next week, I attend two days of illustrated lectures on China. It is important to know everything you can about the enemy.

Some time in the next few months, I will fly over to China to do a few days of reconnaissance. I have talked to a number of people about the project and most of those I tell about it want to go with me, women included. My hand-picked crew are all ex-Navy men who will not get seasick, who will be obedient, who can take the isolation, and who can and will fight the ship out of pirate waters.

It's not too late for you to join the mission. Not too late for you to prove you're a man.

Faithfully awaiting your reply,
Your Father

❧

6

THE GOODNESS
OF THE WORLD

When my father came back into my life, after three decades of absence, it was to tell me he loved the Navy.

It was early fall in State College, Pennsylvania, an unusually humid day. I was sitting on the concrete front step of the building in which I rented a basement apartment, where it was too stuffy to study. I was reading *Middlemarch*, reading furiously, trying to be ready for a graduate seminar, cursing myself for reading this great novel so quickly, promising myself I'd come back to it someday and give it the time it deserves. I looked up to see a battered blue F-150 with a pale green camper back pull up to the curb. A tall lanky man in khakis and a flowered sport shirt climbed out of the cab and came toward me smiling.

"How do?" he said as he strode toward me, stretching his hand out to shake, a full six strides before he needed to. It was either the gesture of a man excited to see me, or the gesture of a man who wanted to make his intentions clear from the start. I set aside *Middlemarch* and stood as he grabbed my hand. "I'm just so glad to see you," he said, pumping my hand hard.

I knew who he was, but I had no idea how I knew. It had been thirty years, more, since I'd seen him last.

I said, "It's been—"

"A long time," he said quickly, still shaking my hand. "A long time."

"—thirty years," I said.

"Like I said," he said, finally dropping my hand. He was standing on the sidewalk and I was still on the second step above him, making him seem small. A quick flicker of distaste crossed his face, as if he didn't like looking up at people, or at me. He stepped back and turned to look around the neighborhood at the other once-fine houses that had been cut up into apartments for Penn State's transient student population.

"Your sister told me you were a professor."

"Graduate student," I said.

He smiled back at me. "Whatever you say. You're the doctor."

"Thirty years is a long time," I said. I couldn't help myself.

"It is that," he said, pressing his lips together and nodding.

"I mean people live and die in the space of thirty years." Countries change names. Rivers change course. Mountains crumble. Whole species die out.

"Hey," he said, spreading his open hands and shaking his head, "you get no argument from me."

"And here you show up."

"In the flesh."

"Why?"

"Can't a fellow drop in on his first-born to see how he's doing?"

"I'm doing just fine."

A quick tightening came into his face. He said, quieter now, "I can see that. I can."

"I'm sorry," I said, stepping down to the sidewalk. "It's just that I don't get this. Why are you here? Why now? I barely recognized you coming up the sidewalk."

"Yeah, but you did, didn't you. There are ties between us stronger than barbed wire. Blood calls to blood, you see."

"Not for thirty fucking years it didn't."

His face reddened slightly. I couldn't tell if it was my bad language or the reality of what I'd said.

"A few things got in my way."

"Yeah, like a few decades."

"I'll grant you that, but I'm here now."

"But why? Why bother? What do you want?"

He looked off down the street, then back at me. "I just wanted to say something to you is all."

My heart was hammering. I suddenly realized that he might be about to apologize. For the whippings, the all-night Bible readings, for all of it. And I realized that it was something I'd wanted for many years, an apology, wanted it without realizing it, that I wanted it and would accept it. That, more than anything else, I wanted my father back in my life. And I was suddenly ashamed of the tone I'd taken and the language I'd used. This man with thinning hair and watery blue eyes was my father. He'd come to ask forgiveness. And I knew I would give it to him, gladly, at the first sign of his asking.

He was gazing off at the treetops now, talking almost to himself. "I just wanted to say . . . just that . . . in all my years in the Navy I never met a sailor who swore, gambled, drank to excess, chased women, or ever raised a hand to another person in anger."

Wind tugged at the trees. A few leaves, still green, fell to the street and skittered across the dry pavement. Otherwise the block was silent.

There I was—*this close*—to giving him blanket forgiveness, total immunity from moral prosecution, absolute absolution for his sins, and he comes out with this completely irrelevant remark. When I had a moment to think about it, of course, I realized it was hardly irrelevant. It was a protestation of innocence. I'm a sailor, he was saying, and therefore innocent of anything you may remember or think you remember. And those scars across your ass? Maybe you sat on a hot stove.

I was ready to scream, to lay out his many sins in a neat little row that would reach from here to Hell and back.

Who are you kidding? I wanted to say.

But then he said, "Say, do you know a good place for coffee?"

And without a moment's hesitation, I said, "Sure, yeah. The Corner Room is just a few blocks from here."

I was a grown man and knew better, about the Navy and about him, but as we walked to the restaurant, I let myself consider the possibility. Something said with that much conviction, that much simple pride, had to be true. But, in fact, the only one of the vices he listed that I'm fairly sure my father didn't have was swearing, he whose worst expletive was "Crackers!"

Before we joined him in Indiana, in the summer of 1960, he came home only on shore leave, a few days between ships. He was a stranger, the man who'd visit now and then, so tall he had to duck through doorways. He'd been too big for the little world of our tenement apartment in Pennsylvania. My memories of him from those years are fragmentary—a starched white hat above a starched white uniform, a back retreating through a doorway.

But as soon as I'd looked up from *Middlemarch*, I recognized him. No small feat for thirty years. Maybe it *was* the call of blood to blood, or maybe it was the photo my mother schooled us on in the train's dining car so long ago.

He was telling me about his love for the Navy, which was his way of telling me about himself, about the image of himself he wanted me to believe, that he himself wanted to believe, and that, ultimately, I wanted to believe. That he was part of a pure brotherhood who lived by high ideals, that he was a man capable of love. We both knew better, but that afternoon, years ago, drinking coffee in a corner booth of a State College restaurant, we let ourselves believe the lie.

I'm looking at a copy of the photo now, ten years later, sitting on the floor, my back to the bed, in a motel room in Los Indios. The picture is soaked with seawater, as wet as the day it was pulled from the developer, but somehow the image is intact. The face below the starched hat doesn't give anything away. The set to the mouth is dead level, the eyes dark, mere organs, the muscles of the face neither taut nor slack. It's the look of a man trying hard to erase all the rough edges and rude impediments of personality, a uniform of a face. No wonder we kids weren't sure what he looked like. I'm looking right at him, and I'm not sure I'd recognize him if he walked through the door.

But then I remember with a shudder that he won't be walking through this door or any other. Not anymore. He was found face-down in the waters of the Florida Keys. I stare hard at the picture trying to get that fact through my head. This is my father. My dead father. I should feel something about him, about his death, shouldn't I? He was almost completely out of my life for three decades. Still, he was my father. And when your father dies, you're supposed to feel something, aren't you? What's wrong with me? And is what's missing in me the same thing that was missing in him?

I stare hard at the man but all I see is the starched white uniform, the Dixie Cup hat. At the end of the year in Indiana, he'd be promoted to Ensign. Over the years, he'd make it all the way to Commander, the brim of his black cap filling with the tangled yellow braid sailors call "scrambled eggs," the breast of his uniform paneled with medals, ribbons, devices, badges, bars, patches, and insignia, among them the Navy Commendation Medal, the Navy Achievement Medal with Combat "V" and Second Award with gold star, the Good Conduct Medal with three bronze stars, the Occupation Service Medal with Europe clasp, the National Defense Service Medal with bronze star, the Armed Forces Expeditionary Medal, the Vietnam Service Medal with bronze star, the United Nations Korean Service Medal, the Korean Service Medal, the Korean Presidential Unit Citation, the Surface Warfare pin, and the World War II Victory Medal. Compared to his later uniforms, this white one looks strangely bare, no more than a Halloween costume.

After that day on the train, whenever my sister wanted to tease our little brother, she'd remind him of how he'd mistaken a stranger for our father. She'd fling her arms around herself, throw her head back, and call out wildly, her words small rockets of joy: "Daddy! Daddy! Daddy! Oh! Daddy!" She'd spin so fast her blonde hair whipped around her head, and then she'd fall on the floor and roll around. "Daddy! Oh my daddy!"

Mark never reacted when she did this. He'd just stand rocking foot to foot, his big brown eyes darting with confusion.

But what I remember most about that day in the dining car was my mother's question.

"What are you going to say when you see your daddy?" she asked as she held the picture out to me.

It was too much, like asking, "What will you say to God on Judgment Day?" It was the question my father woke me with in the middle of every night, the question he asked over and over during the whippings.

"Come on," my mother asked again, a little more quietly this time, "what will you say?"

I looked at the stern face in the picture, and it was almost as if I *were* looking into the face of God. I looked up into my mother's thoughtful gaze, and said what I knew may father would want me to say: "I am unclean. I have sinned. I am steeped in my iniquity."

. . .

My father pretty much lost it that year in Indiana, in ways that I'm still not sure I understand. It's why I go through these bags of damp papers, peeling them carefully apart, pages so translucent with wetness that I can read the backside through the front, photos stuck together so tightly that faces and limbs tear off, leaving ragged white clouds, no matter how carefully I separate them, no matter how long I let them dry. The truth is I can't wait very long. Each picture, each page, is a clue to solving the mystery of my father. I run my fingers over the Braille-like impressions left on the blank sheets, the sheets the ink has washed off. I look at each sheet carefully, angling it toward the light, studying the furrows and gouges like a hunter cutting for sign. But I keep looking, keep hanging the pages on the walls and makeshift clotheslines in every motel room, keep waking up to stare at the mystery of my father's life. Who was this man? And if I can't figure that out, how will I ever know myself?

Back in Indiana, at eight years old, I was nervous around my father, around the whole idea of fathers. What were they for? I didn't know how to act around mine, who seemed to study me from a long way off, who never remembered my birthday, whose every word to me was about duty and good behavior and the Day of Judgment.

On weekends back then I liked to hide behind the side-window sheers and watch him work on his Whizzer in the driveway. His tools always looked brand-new, and he spread them out so carefully, it was as though he'd measured the space between them on the ground. Sometimes he just sat on his heels for a while, gazing at his immaculate wrenches. He took each one up like a surgeon takes up a scalpel, every movement—every twist of the wrench, every turn of the screw—precisely calibrated. He wore a white dress shirt when he did this work, its cuffs folded back in exact increments, as if to underscore his own careful nature. The motorbike never dared to break down. The white shirt never got dirty.

I had an eight-year-old's curiosity about the world. There were times when I'd stand next to a passing freight train, trying to work up the courage to latch on and let it carry me far from there. By the end of that year, the last year of our life as a family, I had to fight off the urge to throw myself under every passing train.

My father had a desperate need to believe in the essential goodness of the world—of himself—even if that belief flew in the face of simple reality. He was a strange man, a man with a molten core so deeply buried that most people thought of him as a quiet, tolerant, simple man. I knew a different side of him.

Both my parents grew up in stoic Indiana farm families where any show of emotion was considered a weakness, any show of strength a virtue. My father was an intensely rational man who became violent when things in the household failed to run as smoothly as they did aboard ship. My mother spent much of her time trying to calm him down and keep him unaware of things that might upset him. Even our injuries became guilty secrets.

Once a few friends and I were exploring an abandoned garage. It was filled with trash, barrels, old crates, gutted furniture, a mountain of stuff. We climbed all over it until I fell, my shoulder hitting something so sharp it set my teeth on edge. When I struggled to my feet, I saw the piece of pop bottle still sticking in my left arm, just below the shoulder, blood running in a sheet down it and off the ends of my fingers.

"Guys?" I said. "Guys?" I was feeling dizzy and needed help. But they were gone. Somehow I knew they weren't running for help but away from the horror of my bloody arm. I held it in my other hand, a little away from my body, carrying it home like a dead cat, dripping a trail of blood behind me. I was scared but I was also a little thrilled. I knew about blood. My father had taught me about blood.

When I got home, my mother gave me a mean look and said, "Now what have you gone and done?" She took me into the bathroom. "Come on, we have to take care of this before your father gets home." She pulled out the glass, cleaned the three-inch gash, swabbed it with iodine, and put a butterfly bandage on it to hold the two sides of the cut together. "You say a word about this to your father—if he finds out in *any* way—there won't be enough left of you to mop up with a dish rag."

So I didn't say a word about it to my father. I could have. I knew that. I knew he would approve, but I did what my mother said and wore long-sleeved shirts until it healed.

Each day she changed my bandage in secret until a crusty brown scab formed over the wound. On the days my father didn't whip me enough for being a sinner beyond the reach of God's love, I'd pierce the crusty scab with a toy soldier's bayonet, no broader than a blade of grass. I'd watch a bead of blood well up and run down my arm. I knew about blood. Blood didn't bother me. He never found out about the injury. I still carry the scar, just below my left shoulder, the size and shape of an open mouth.

His violence was so ritualized, so tied to his sense of justice and order, that it didn't seem like violence at all but more like a force of nature, evidence of the world's urge to order. I never blamed him for the whippings. My father was in the Navy. He was tough. The whippings were just another aspect of the toughness, an opportunity to show my own toughness.

He whipped me for my dirty fingernails, for getting grass stains on my knees, for doing chores badly or not at all. He whipped me once for fighting and twice if I lost the fight. He whipped me for my thoughts, for my feelings, for the look in my eye and the cut of my jib. He whipped me for what I might have done, could have done, would surely do if I only had the chance. He whipped me for being a sinner before God. And he whipped me for crying while I was whipped.

Like every other kid who lived with a parent who was more force than father, I never once questioned the whippings, never once questioned their appropriateness. I only wondered how I could become the boy my father wanted, the boy who didn't deserve such whippings, the boy who lit his father's eyes with pride. What did it take? What quantity of good behavior and right thinking that I lacked? It never once occurred to me that fathers weren't supposed to whip their children, especially my father, the war hero, the naval engineer. How could this precise man be anything but correct in everything he did? I pitied him for having to put up with a kid like me. He deserved better. The world deserved better. Only what was it again, Dad, that I did? What made me so awful, so in need of correction? It must have been an awful measure of evil for you to have to whip it out and cut it out of me.

He was as orderly with his tools of punishment as he was with his motorbike tools—the shaving strop, the belt, the knotted wet towel, the rope. And toward the end of that year, the knife. Until that year in Indiana, I had been waiting, waiting, waiting for the chance to get to know him, the chance for him to get to know me. But the kid he got to know didn't pass inspection. And so, almost every night after supper, he led me gently to the bathroom, where he had me pull down my pants and hang over the edge of the tub while he swung, his words about God's justice booming between bright flashes of pain. When he used the strop or the belt, I could hear it coming, the way they hissed through the air, could get myself set for the pain. But I hated the towel. It was silent, each blow a fiery shock of pain, the knot like a balled fist against my back and backside. The big, grapefruit-sized bruises were tender for days. When my hands, almost against my will, jumped behind me to ward off the blows, he would kneel and paw the sweaty hair away from my face and patiently explain that protecting myself would only cause more pain.

"One blow from this towel could snap your arm in two. Is that what you want?"

"No, sir."

"Then keep your hands clear."

"Yes, sir."

Over time I learned to hold my hands flat against the inside of the tub and stare myself blind at the enameled iron, the white throbbing brighter at every blow, the pain no more than noise from another neighborhood.

My father was religious in the classic sense. His God was no sissy, like my mother's, something he told me many times as I hung over the edge of the tub. Every Sunday morning they argued about where we'd go to church. She'd end up taking us to the Methodist church while he went, alone and mumbling, to a brush arbor service somewhere deep in the woods.

In some ways, the rare nights when there were no whippings were harder to get through. I trembled on the verge of vomiting, so afraid was I of every move my father made. When he reached for the *TV Guide*, I cowered. When he shook out the evening paper, tears sprang to my eyes. The fear of a whipping was worse than the whipping itself. At least a whipping ended eventually, but the stress of anticipation never ended, except for the hour or so after a whipping, when, curled up on the cold bathroom tiles, my arms tied around the base of the toilet, I was in too much pain to feel much of anything else.

Neurologists say that suffering one act of violence alters the victim's brain chemistry forever. I feel the truth of that, feel it in my deep streak of self-doubt, in my fear of success, my urge toward self-destruction, my strong sense of inadequacy. I will never be good enough to please my father, never be good enough to have earned my place in the world. I will never rise to his standard of behavior. I will always and forever be with Jeremiah in the pit.

"The grave is all about you, boy." Night after night he hissed it in my ear. "And the sides are studded with corpses. Them what descend to the nether parts do not rise except by the grace of the flaming fire." And then, his mouth so close I didn't so much hear the words as feel the wet muscles of his lips work them into the skin at my temple as he pinned my head to the pillow: "Let not the pit shut her mouth upon thee. Let not the pit shut her mouth upon thee. Let not the pit shut her mouth upon thee."

• • •

At the end of that school year, in 1961, our life together ended. I never knew quite why. One day my mother sat me down to tell me they were getting a divorce. She had to explain that to me, what it was. I had never heard the word, never knew such a thing was possible, that a marriage could end, that pain like that could ever stop. And the truth is that not for a minute did the news give me pleasure. I knew in my heart what it meant—that my father had given up on me, that he'd concluded I would never be the boy he deserved, that I had fallen completely and irredeemably into the pit, that I had chosen, over God and him, "the imagination of my evil heart."

The only life that had meaning for me—that *has* meaning for me—was life in the time of his anger. No amount of drug or talk therapy can shake that from me. My daylight mind may know the truth—that he was sick, that he was sublimating, that he was using me to help him polish a small kernel of self-hatred—but those are just words. My night brain knows different. The truths etched there were cut too deep to change.

After the divorce, over thirty years passed before the day I sat across the table from him, drinking coffee at a State College restaurant aptly called "The Corner Room Unusual." Time had mellowed him. For one thing, he'd become a Methodist, like my mother. He was still someone who made a sharp distinction between the good and the bad, the right and the wrong. But now, instead of fixating on the wrong, he seemed to focus to a fanatical degree on the right and good. In his world, all sailors were Boy Scouts, all women were saints, all children were pure of heart. The words were different, but the tune was the same. It made me realize that, for him, the whippings were no more than a form of negotiation, a kind of instruction, a theology of sorts, a laying on of hands.

• • •

Our little ranch house in Lafayette had a screened-in porch at the back that had a shallow utility closet with a sliding door. It was barely big enough for the mops and brooms and buckets for which it was intended. Shortly after we moved there, my father converted it into a tiny study for himself. Among the soggy contents of the garbage bags, I found his old homework from Purdue—the tests he'd taken, the papers he'd written in the little closet. The Navy had sent him to Purdue as part of the Navy Enlisted Scientific Education Program (NESEP) to learn electrical engineering, and he would use the closet to read and do his homework in peace.

When he was inside, I knew I wasn't supposed to play on the porch. I knew it was best to be off down the street somewhere, anywhere, else. Hiding in a cistern and holding my breath was good. A thousand miles away under a stone slab was better. Floating gray and dead in the airless immensity of outer space would have been ideal. I was reminded often that I was never to open the door, never to look inside the little world my father had made.

"This is Daddy's secret place," he said the day he finished it. He sat inside the barely big enough space and spoke to me through the open pocket door. "You must never bother Daddy when he's in his secret place, and you must never ever go inside Daddy's secret place. Understood?" And then he closed himself inside like a vampire afraid of the light.

How could I resist?

One day after school, while my mother vacuumed and my brother and sister were off somewhere and the cat was asleep on the seat of my bicycle and God was answering his mail, I quietly rolled open the hollow core door and slipped inside my father's private world. I wanted to know what his secret place felt like.

Even for a child, the room was tiny, every square inch calibrated for the most efficient use of space. I slid into the seat and closed the door, sure the quiet rumble of the door's plastic wheels in their channel would give me away. I sat in the dark for a few minutes until it was clear my mother hadn't heard me. Then I reached up and pulled the string attached to the bare bulb overhead, yellow light jumping into every corner of the little room. The desk inside, barely big enough for the space that contained it, was just like the desks at school, except the lid of his was made of clear light oak silky to the touch. Above it, my father had built bookshelves that reached from the desktop to the ceiling. They were filled with math and science books set in place as carefully as bricks in a wall. I ran my fingertips over the unmarked desktop. I had never seen one that wasn't cut, scarred, and scribbled on. My own desk at school was similar, except a few decades of grime had been ground into it. Someone had gouged "JoAnne does it with dogs," and someone else had gouged "I hate hellth class." I myself had corrected the spelling of "health" by turning the extra "l" into an "A". But since I didn't know what it was JoAnne did with dogs, I didn't know that there was anything there to correct.

I lifted the lid of my father's desk and saw his neat stacks of tablets and bluebooks, his tin box full of pencils, each one chiseled stiletto-sharp. Inside also were unlined sheets of paper covered with preternaturally careful printing. My father's school essays. He hated lined paper, preferring to follow his own invisible lines. Every word on every page was written in a dead-even straight line. Every letter in every word was squared off perfectly, as if he wanted you to believe a machine and not a man had made it. The writing was the most magical and the most frightening thing I had ever seen. It still is. These are the same papers I'm looking at now, thirty years later, water logged, the staples gone to rust, but still readable, even the teachers' scribbled comments:

A nice conception. If you get the chance, drop in to my office. I want to go over your file with you and decide which themes we might use—either for Kneale Awards or Trial Flight.   B+

When I lifted the lid higher, I bumped something on top and quickly lowered it. I had almost knocked off the ashtray perched on the back of the desk. I reached out to pull it back a bit from the edge, studying the three blond butts that stood in it like tiny tree stumps. In the pencil tray at the back of the desk lay a beautiful blue fountain pen, the blue swirled with black. I unscrewed the two halves, revealing the scalloped nib etched with black scrollwork. I touched the point to my finger. It was sharper than I thought, and when I pulled it away, a drop of ink fell to the desktop, where it lay like a tiny blood dot on the clear blond wood. I wiped at it with the side of my hand, then with my sleeve. It was clean now, wasn't it? Or had I just smeared it into a pale gray cloud? I rubbed at it more, rocking the desk slightly, the ashtray edging toward the back of the desk again. I lunged, saving it from toppling over the back. I set it down. I tried to catch my breath.

It was then that I noticed the real damage I had done.

My father's blackboard, at my right shoulder, had been filled edge-to-edge with a long equation, rows of white numbers, letters, and symbols standing out starkly against the black background, all clinging together with plus and minus signs, brackets, parentheses, all written in my father's neat, squared-off printing. In lunging for the ashtray, I'd rubbed my shoulder against the board, erasing some of the equation, nothing there now but a smear of chalk. I panicked. The idea was to sneak into my father's secret place so he would never know. I pulled the cuff of my sleeve over my right hand and carefully wiped at the chalky haze until it was more or less gone, leaving nothing but a black hole in my father's field of figures. I picked up the bullet of chalk and copied numbers and symbols from above into the blank hole at the bottom, imitating the machine-like precision of my father's hand. But as I wrote, my sleeve and the edge of my hand smeared other letters and numbers. I traced them over, guessing at the ones too smeared to read. The more I tried to correct my mess, the more mess I made. But somehow I fixed it. My cunning and dexterity surprised me. When I was finished, the blackboard looked as though nothing had ever happened to it. At least to me.

But something had happened to it. And though my father didn't notice it at first, the *way* he noticed it made my offense even worse. It would have been bad enough if I had rubbed out some of the formula, which turned out to be part of a semester-long project. But my imitation of his handwriting was better than I thought. He hadn't noticed the damage, copying everything onto his careful white pages and handing it in to his teacher, complete with my childish guesses at what I had erased.

A few days later, in class, his teacher humiliated him. It wasn't that the answer was merely wrong, he'd said, or that his process was flawed. It was that the answer was so unspeakably stupid, as if a child had merely scribbled numbers and symbols at random.

I hadn't simply disobeyed my father; I had made him look like a fool. All this I learned between blows from his doubled razor strop, the only whipping I ever really understood. No amount of apologizing could undo the harm I had done. It was the kind of crime only pain could erase. Mine.

"Why didn't you just *tell* me?" he said at the end, wiping away my tears with the rough edges of his thumbs. The answer was obvious, though I pretended not to know. Because either way I'd be whipped. The whipping was my father's métier, his forté, his pleasure. This way, I thought, my mistake had a slim chance of going undetected.

I never went into his secret place—or any other secret space—again. Until now, I guess. Until going through his papers.

I don't think my father liked himself very much, despite his many achievements. I know now, from his papers, that during the course of over thirty-one years of service, he served in Korea, Vietnam, Lebanon, the Dominican Republic, Latin America, and several other parts of the globe. After he graduated from Purdue, he was sent to Annapolis, graduating with the rank of Lieutenant. For a few years he served as a gunnery officer or engineering officer on a variety of ships. One of his jobs was to convert World War II-era destroyer escorts into missile launchers. His success led to a promotion to Lieutenant Commander. At various stages of his career, he represented the Navy at White Sands, worked as a test engineer in the Pentagon, and later studied lasers, becoming Professor of Laser Technology at the Naval Postgraduate School in Monterey. After a three-year stint there, he was assigned to Fort Ord, where his work was classified.

The blackboard whipping, as I say, made sense to me. The others usually didn't. To him they weren't whippings at all but correctives, lessons, waker-uppers, something to think about. Each whipping came with appropriate Bible passages. Sometimes the whippings wouldn't start right away. I'd hang over the edge of the tub waiting while he read from the Bible. Sometimes an hour would pass, and I would be asleep from the sound of his voice booming against the hard walls. And then, when the whipping began, it was like the very hand of God. It would be easy to blame my father, to feel nothing but rage. And I have felt that. But it didn't get me anywhere. Rage begets more rage, not understanding, not change.

And besides, in the end I think the whippings were a form of self-flagellation, a form of self-hatred that spread to those he was close to.

There are many photos in the bags I'm dragging around, many of them blotchy with sea water. But there's only one of my father as a child. He's sitting on the running board of a truck. He's eight years old, the same age I was in Indiana. His older brother, Carl, sitting next to him, is ten. Carl, wearing overalls and no shirt, has the grimace of a troublemaker, a thick hank of hair in his eyes. My father, a slight boy with spindly arms and legs, wears a double-breasted sailor shirt and plaid shorts. His head is turned slightly to the side of the picture, his mouth open. I can't tell if he's about to smile or wince. Maybe it's a wounded look in his eyes. I can't really tell. His blond hair hangs wildly on his forehead. Sitting on the running board between them is a plaster dog with a Cheshire smile, its sly eyes turned up toward my father. His "chessy dog," he called it. This toy seems to know more about my father than I ever will. What was it, Dad? What were you thinking? Who were you? What did you become? And why?

His *Mexico Log* is filled with glowing accounts of the people he met along the border. Even the unpleasant ones are described in playful terms:

> *At one point, the bus was stopped by about twenty policemen at a roadblock. They were armed with machine pistols. The bus, all luggage, and some passengers were thoroughly searched. One of the officers played macho with me for his fellow citizens. I played the game and we had some laughs.*

It's downright Hemingway, this passage. Maybe he idealized others in order to give himself something to shoot for, a model of another way to be. Maybe he was so afraid of what he would become that he kept his eyes locked instead on what he *could* become, what he *might*, with luck and will, become. Maybe the possibility that he could perceive goodness (whether it was actually there or not) made him feel that he himself was good, keeping his bad animal at bay.

But it was my father's bad animal I knew best. And strangely, it was the bad animal I was proudest of. I was proud that my father was, even if he showed it by whipping me, maybe especially then. It meant he wouldn't accept anything but the best. I lived in that strange whirl of fear and pride without realizing there might be any other way to live. I felt toward my father what I felt about the solar system, pictured on a poster taped to the ceiling over my bunk. After each night's whipping, I'd gaze up at the bright pinpricks of the universe, terrified by its vastness, its heartless power, its frightening beauty.

❧❧❧

Pattern for Effective Study

I enjoy studying more than anything else. Studying has come to be enjoyable to me because of the knowledge which I gain from it. Knowledge is the one thing in life that is indestructible, and knowledge can only be assimilated through study. I would like to impart to you the manner in which I have found study productive.

First, I have carefully prepared a place to study in a room used only for that purpose. I have secured myself a comfortable straight-back chair and a desk of adequate proportions. I have installed a desk light which illuminates adequately without glare and have located it so that its light falls only on the desk, thereby reducing distractions. I have located my bookcase so that it is unobtrusive yet provides for all my books to be at my fingertips. I have posted the necessary charts so that I need only turn my head to see them. My blackboard occupies the wall adjacent to my desk.

The second factor of successful study which I will discuss is the manner in which I prepare a homework assignment. I have found that the most important point about this preparation is the necessity for complete concentration. I first read the chapter summary and the study-questions provided. I next read the entire chapter rapidly. Beginning again at the beginning of the chapter, I read each sentence slowly, attempting to assimilate every fact therein. After the completion of each paragraph in this manner, I write a summary of that paragraph. I pause often to state facts aloud. After the completion of a chapter in this manner, I study sections relating to the same material in the other books at my disposal. After assuring myself that I have command of the knowledge contained in the assignment, I proceed to perform all exercises provided. If I experience any difficulty in the performance of an exercise, I restudy the material covering that particular point until I have mastered it.

Several other points are important to me in my endeavor to acquire knowledge. I sleep at least five hours every night so that I am always alert and attentive. I attend help-sessions whenever possible. I talk to my classmates about any points which are not clear to me. I utilize short periods of relaxation to contemplate the knowledge which I have acquired, and I find that this contemplation makes the knowledge more meaningful to me.

By following this method of study, I am able to absorb the maximum amount of knowledge of which I am capable. I find that I am never more content than when I am learning new things—doing research, working a problem, stretching the limits of my mental faculties. It is the thing in life that matters to me most. Stepping into my study is like stepping out of the world. My study is the place where I am by far the happiest that I have ever been or ever shall be.

Robert C. Spencer
Theme for Freshman English
Purdue University, 1960

∽◌∾

7

"BEST OF LUCK TO A SWELL BOY IN THE FUTURE"

I pull into Nuevo Progreso, just east of Reynosa on Highway 281, completely exhausted from a full day of Rio Grande Valley heat. The town seems to have more than its share of elderly tourists. Oldsters are everywhere. Plaid shirts and white pants walking indifferently with each other through the silver shops, the glass shops, the leather shops. The sidewalks are wider here than in most border towns, and many shop owners have extended canopies over them to keep the sun off all those bald heads. Nevertheless, for some of the tourists, Progreso is only the stopping-off place on their way to the *super mercado* in nearby Rio Bravo. All this way for a Walmart. But many are here for Progreso's pharmacies, where prescription drugs can be had for much less than north of the border. Before checking into the Hotel Pitayas, I buy a six of Corona from "Uncle Sam Liquor Store" and hope the desk clerk doesn't think I'm just looking for a place to get loaded. After checking in, unable to resist the bad joke, I hoist up the six and say, "*Mi equipaje*." My luggage.

The clerk gives me the no-nonsense look of a man pulling a double-shift and says in startlingly unaccented English, "Hey, whatever floats your boat."

The room is mercifully clean and quiet, the swamper pumping a good imitation of chilled air. I've been hoping for an opportunity to look through the two high school yearbooks I found among my father's things—*The Log* from Columbus High School, Columbus, Indiana, for 1946 and 1947. My parents were classmates and, in fact, lived on neighboring farms not far from Columbus. They must have shared the bus to school every day. So the books represent a record of both their lives, from a time I know very little about.

The burgundy and gold cover of the 1946 book is embossed with the outline of a male figure leaning over an old tripod movie camera, the theme of the year being "Scenes of the Teens." The figure is supposed to be wearing an artist's smock, I guess, though it looks more like a hospital gown split up the back. On the flyleaf is an inscription from what must have been one of my father's teachers. "To the best kid that I ever worked with." High praise for my father, though when I check I can't find the man in either book's list of faculty and staff. Some kind of joke? The students look painfully older than their years, their hair tortured into slick shells. The opening pages show them performing a scene from *The Doctor Decides*, setting type in the print shop, working in the machine shop, learning to use a Dictaphone, and parading with brooms and signs that read, "Your job is to clean up the victory loan!" It's the only reference to the war in either book.

As I search for pictures of my parents, carefully peeling the damp pages apart, I make the sad discovery that neither book covers my parents' senior years. My father isn't even in the '46 volume, and he's a sophomore in the '47. It's just like my father to keep the wrong high school yearbooks close at hand, always carefully documenting the wrong thing. More and more, I wonder if this is the fate of my trip—wrong leads, dead ends, bales of paper documenting nothing.

Still, the books are heavily inscribed with the usual good wishes. I envy his classmates' easy familiarity with him, their intimate knowledge of his daily life. "To a swell kid," "To a good guy," "Best wishes to a swell guy. Good luck to you." In many, the operative word is "swell," the word of the day, reaching its apotheosis in June Lewellen's inscription: "To a very Swell Classmate who has been swell to me. Best of Luck to a swell fellow."

One inscription seems strange, coming from a fellow student: "Be good this summer." Was it the moral uprightness of those days, or did my father have a reputation?

Some of the inscriptions are downright strange. One reads, "Lots of luck to a pal and the big freek in CHS." Clearly from a crony, someone who probably knew my father better than anyone, a co-conspirator, a fellow traveler, a homie.

Another reads, "The very best wishes to a fellow geometry." At first I think his classmate must have gotten distracted while writing his message. But then I wonder whether he knew more about his friend than most, that my father was more geometry than man, more an orderly intersection of lines and planes, a concatenation of equations and formulae.

And another inscription, made strange by syntax: "Best of luck to a swell boy in the future." I love this one, how the misplaced phrase makes it seem as though my father isn't yet, but may someday be, swell.

Was my father lucky? It's a good question. The answer is yes if I think of how he came through a lifetime of military service with hardly a scratch.

Besides the USS Danning's near-fatal collision, he was a gunner's mate in Korea. He was caught in a violent uprising at the start of the Moroccan Revolution. He was an officer in the Shore Patrol whose beat was the Casbah. He served on destroyer escorts in the Black Sea during the Cold War. He was a Beach Jumper in Vietnam, a Raid and Reconnaissance Team Leader who co-piloted swift boats up the nine dragons of Cuu Long, in the Mekong Delta. Somewhere in his long career, he slept with cannibals in the jungles of Latin America. All this I've been able to piece together from the papers, which include a number of official and unofficial service records. And through it all he broke no more than a sweat, a touch of malaria he picked up in the jungle. All in all, I guess I would say he was lucky. In war at least.

In love, not so lucky. He was married and divorced twice, which I guess makes him no luckier than many other men. I peel through a stack of old documents—tax returns for twenty years ago, statements from long-dead bank accounts. And this. What strangely firing synapse in the brain makes you keep the marriage documents thirty years after your divorce? Yet here they are, the license he took out when he married my mother and the certificate of marriage from the Army chaplain who married them: "This certifies that on the 11th day of April in the year 1951, Robert Spencer and Patricia Pittman were by me united in Holy Matrimony at Columbus, Indiana, according to the Ordinance of God and the Laws of the State of Indiana."

But then I find something else. At first it looks like another copy of the license. But no. Another license. But not for his California wife, the only other wife I know about. For someone else, someone in between. The license is from the State of New York, Nassau County, authorizing "any person empowered by law to solemnize Marriages" to join together as husband and wife my father and another woman, a third wife, one I never knew about.

After the initial shock, I tell myself there are probably lots of things I don't know about my father, a man who stayed out of my life for over thirty years. My father never shared many of the facts of his life with me, but this makes me ashamed. Surely I should know about a third wife.

And before I can adjust to this new fact, I find something else. Another birth certificate, for a child I don't know, a child who would be a few years younger than me now. How strange. Stranger still that the name on this license is "Bob Cornelius."

The date on the marriage certificate, the 21st day of October 1959. I dig out the divorce decree and lay it beside this new license. I can hardly believe it: my father was married to another woman at the same time he was married to my mother. It can't be. Not a man so moral. Not a man so careful and frugal that he portions out his toilet paper. But after double-checking the dates, I see it's true.

It's as if the four walls of my motel room have snapped up like window shades. Every surface in the room—from the nubbly brown spreads on the two single beds to the chocolate shag carpeting to the fake mahogany dresser edged with cigarette burns—is covered with damp documents, most of them meaningless. But this one. I can hardly believe it. I mean, my God. My father was married to two women at the same time. The word is too silly-sounding to account for its impact on me. My father was a bigamist.

Suddenly so many things make sense that never did before. How my father was gone as much as he was home. How he planted us in northeastern Pennsylvania, he said, to make it convenient for him to commute to the Brooklyn Naval Yard, where he was stationed, in those days a good five-hour drive. Convenient for whom? More convenient than—oh, I'm just pulling a location out of a hat here, but, say—Brooklyn? Conveniently far, I realize now, from Nassau County, the scene of his other life. He must have been making sure the circles in the Venn diagram of his life didn't overlap.

"Your dad has to ship out again," my mother would say, kneeling down to us while our father stood tall next to her, more a cardboard cut-out of a father than the living, breathing kind. As the oldest, I'd stand tall and hold my hand out to shake his.

"Happy hunting, sir," the send-off my father had taught me to say. Hunting Russian trawlers on the Black Sea. Secretly, of course, I was glad to see him go. Now my bruises would have time to heal. But beneath that feeling was a stronger one, of failure and self-hatred. I was the cancer on my family. I'd stand there with my hand out, ready to shake, and he'd give me the look you'd give the goop in a Petri dish that was turning out terribly wrong. Only after a long moment of grim appraisal would he place the fingertips of his right hand into mine. And then he'd be gone.

He'd ship out for months at a time, and when he came back he'd often be surly, taking out his anger on me. But maybe his two lives were colliding, and I was the easiest focal point for his frustration and confusion. Another woman, another child, another life. When he shipped out for six months at a time, it probably wasn't to the Black Sea but to his Long Island family. And then, after a few months there, did he tell wife-and-child #2 that he had to ship out again, stealing back to us? Amazing.

My God. I can't help wondering if some of his violence and weirdness had something to do with the force of his two lives pulling at him. Bigamist. I'd always thought the word a kind of joke, the silly sound of it, the wild improbability of someone carrying on two lives, with two different wives, at the same time. Who had the energy for that kind of drama? The money? The time? There weren't enough Russian trawlers in the world to sustain that kind of double life.

And why? Was one woman not enough for him? Did they have different qualities and talents? I think of the cliché about sailors—a woman in every port. Married to two women at the same time, though, was taking things a little too far. In some ways it makes perfect sense. My father was a deeply religious man. He probably couldn't imagine "having relations" with a woman unless he was married to her. I wish I knew what happened, whether one found out about the other, whether he confessed. All I know is that suddenly, when I was eight, he and my mother divorced, and my mother took us as far away from him as she could afford to take us, even though it was back to Wilkes-Barre, Pennsylvania, the place he had stashed us. Of course, I thought I had caused it, the misfit son.

I reread the carbons of the letters he sent me, the ones about the hitchhikers he picked up. Were they more than traveling companions? You can't picture your father having sex with your mother, let alone with women less than half his age. Maybe he was addicted to sex, or maybe he just liked the company of women. All I know is it makes me question how much of my own failed marriage, failed relationships, commitment-phobia, and preference for the company of women are a result of my genetic inheritance. Or maybe I'm just looking to blame Daddy for my shortcomings.

It's then that I remember something he told me during one of his visits. I'd asked him about my half-brother, the son he'd had with his last wife, who was sixteen at the time. He told me he was a talented boy who wanted to go to a Bible college in Los Angeles. When I pressed for more information, he said, "He doesn't speak to me much these days. He's renounced me as his father."

A strange sympathy filled me, even though I could have provided a hundred reasons myself for renouncing him. In fact, in some nonverbal way I had renounced him.

"Why?" I asked. I know the answer, but I want him to say it, to admit that he beat his other son the way he beat me.

After some hesitation, he said, "He thinks I'm a sinner because I was . . . married before."

"Because you were married before? Married to Mom? What's wrong with that? Everybody gets divorced these days."

He hemmed and hawed a little, then said, "Yes, I suppose, but it's not that simple." I thought he was talking about the complexity of their fundamentalist faith. I didn't realize he was talking about the complexity of his life.

Now I realize his son must have found out about the other wife. What else would explain it? I remember at the time thinking the kid must be a very fundamental fundamentalist to reject his father because he'd been divorced. But this, this makes more sense. How long had the secret marriage lasted? Long enough, I guess. And for that matters, which marriage was the secret? Both, I guess.

I can't help myself. I pull the flesh-colored phone off the night table and onto my knees. It looks too large, too heavy, an ancient weapon of some kind.

I call my mother, his first wife, but when I tell her about my discovery, all she says is "Oh, I know all about that." Old news. Bygones.

"But Mom, he betrayed you. I mean, how did this make you feel?"

After an uncomfortable pause, she says, "Your father," she pauses again for a long moment, "was a real character." And that's all she'll say.

The phone seems to be getting bigger by the second, growing in my hand. It's the size of a suitcase now. I study the name on the marriage license. After a few calls to information, by some miracle, I reach her. And before I quite know what to say, I'm talking to her, to his second wife, the Long Island wife, his backdoor wife.

"You don't know me," I say, "but I'm Bob Spencer's son."

Silence on the other end, then "Yes?"

"You knew him as Bob Cornelius, I think. Your former husband."

"I know who he is." A hardness has come into her voice. "What's this about?"

"Well, I don't know if anyone has told you," I say, "but he died last week."

For a while she doesn't say anything. All I can hear is her breathing. Then she says, her voice aching with bitterness, "He died long before that," and hangs up on me.

I remember him telling me that his last wife once called the state police on him, fearing for her life. "She's a funny gal," he said. Yeah, right. A laugh riot.

In the last ten years of his life, I thought he'd given up on marriage. He spent it alone on the road, living in a camper and then, in the end, on a forty-six-foot cutter rigged sailboat. But as I read through the Coast Guard accident report my sister faxed to me, and the local news accounts, I see that he wasn't quite finished with marriage.

His fourth try was the unluckiest of all. It turns out that a woman died with him in the accident. Not lucky in love, I guess. No, not lucky at all.

At least the woman was his own age. She's described in news articles as his fiancée. But I don't know how they'd know that. None of his children knew he was getting married again. Maybe it was true. Maybe he had finally settled down. What a cruel joke if that were so.

When I peel apart the next soggy pages of the yearbook, another surprise. A book is a time machine, of course. Even a yearbook, with its studied poses and careful tableaus. But suddenly it's as if I'm being swept backward on a great wave of time, a time-tsunami.

There, in her neat script, I find my mother's inscription:

Dear Bob,
Best wishes and loads of luck in your coming years.
Patricia Pittman "50"

Something more deliberate about her words than those of her classmates, more formal, more lasting. She's written it with a fountain pen, for one thing. And hers is the only inscription framed like a letter and signed with her full name, not "Pat," "Patty," or "Patsy." The reference to "your coming years" refers to his decision to drop out of school to join the Navy. But this and the use of her full name also indicate the distance between them. Obviously they have no plans to marry at this point, unless my mother is the supreme ironist wishing herself and their marriage luck. The placement of the inscription suggests that this may be true—upside-down in the lower right corner of the title page, the only upside-down inscription in the book. But irony isn't my mother's stock in trade, the straight-talking farmer's daughter. From the sound of her inscription, they don't seem to know each other all that well. He didn't even turn the book to offer it for her to sign.

I'll bet he didn't even ask her to sign it. I picture him sitting at a cafeteria table with the open book, studying his friends' good wishes, while she sits down on the other side of the table, just long enough to reach across the open page and sign it in the corner. She was a year younger than he, and maybe she didn't feel she had the right to sign the book properly. Like I said, strangers. And yet, in a few months, the death of my mother's father will trigger a correspondence between them that will bring them closer. And within two years they will be married, off on Mr. Toad's Wild Ride.

All this history. Not history with a capital h, maybe. Lowercase history. But the signers of a yearbook are as much a part of history as the signers of the Declaration. And surely these photographs are valid historical documents in their own right, documents of days gone by, of a culture as nearly lost to us as that of the Anasazi, remnants of the people we once were.

Among my father's things, a copy of my mother's high school graduation picture. She must have mailed it to him overseas. She's standing beside a small frame house, between two shoulder-high forsythia bushes, wearing a homemade dress and a mortarboard, tassle in its pre-graduation position. I like the look of determination on her taut face, her slightly knit brows, her mouth set, her gaze direct. Or is it just the sun in her eyes? Determination, I think.

I see it in the photo of her at four-years-old, the same sun in her eyes, standing next to the same small house, its raw siding curling away from the studs, no sign of the forsythia yet, just a splash of blossom in an unpainted window box. This dress, too, is homemade, from a flour sack, but her mother has sewn three perfectly useless buttons near the left shoulder, a touch of style.

My mother's hand is resting on the scruff of her dog's neck, a mutt she named "Red Rover." Even at that young age, my mother already had those deep soulful eyes. And a touch of fear or anxiety, the prelude to determination.

Everything in these pictures—the cracked siding, the flour sack dress with its three jaunty buttons, even the look in her eyes—all these things are pieces of history. And not just family history or personal history, but the history of a people, my people.

In the next picture, from years later, she's married. You can tell, even without the inscription on the back, "Mrs. Patricia Spencer," her new name, her address, and her age, nineteen. The earlier pictures show her standing stiffly before the camera, the posture meant to please a parent. In this one, she's lounging in an Adirondack chair. She's wearing an untucked plaid blouse and jeans rolled up to look like pedal pushers. One knee is raised, a loafered foot resting on the seat of the chair. The sun is still in her eyes, but she's found a way to deal with it. Now her gaze is direct, her hair permed, her smile scandalous. A starlet's pose, a pose meant to please a husband. It's January 3, 1952. Does she know she's pregnant? Though the picture was taken next to the same Indiana farmhouse, it's a completely different world, a Riviera of the mind. And this, too, is history.

My quiet, self-reliant grandmother put that Adirondack chair together from a kit. She was like that. When the engine on her Model A pickup went out, she ordered a new one, bought a manual, and installed it herself. For years I've looked at the picture of my grandmother, my mother, and aunt standing in front of the pickup and only thought of it as a picture of a proud family showing off their wheels. My aunt, at three, is actually climbing up on the front bumper. Now I realize it wasn't the truck they were showing off, but what was inside, the working engine. It's almost as though my aunt, realizing the potential misunderstanding in generations to come, wants to flip up the wings of the hood to show off my grandmother's handiwork.

Surely this is history, too? And of a very important kind. These photographs remind me that not all historically important figures wear suits and ties or lead armies or head up countries and corporations. Some of them build Adirondack chairs and teach themselves to install truck engines.

If I were to guess which classmate my father would end up with, it would be the one I find later in the yearbook, the one who wrote, "Best of luck to a very nice boy who I like very much. Love, Doris." Most of his friends have written their inscriptions on the flyleaf. A few have written next to their pictures. Doris's message is written on the page showing a cartoon of a young couple holding hands under the legend "To Find Our Personal Place . . ." Hers is the only one that says "love," a word not tossed around then as lightly as it is now. She doesn't need to add her last name. This is more than flirting, I think. There's a bond between them. Doris might have been my father's high school girlfriend. Did he sleep with her? Did he sit in the back seat of somebody's DeSoto fumbling at the strange armory of her underwear? But maybe her message is not meant for him, but for others who might see the yearbook, a way of putting her stamp on him.

Elsewhere in the book there's evidence of Doris's passion. A cartoon of a young man in a roadster with two women. Over one woman is written "Doris." Over the man, "Bob." And over the other woman, "Pat." Then this third name is crossed out savagely, jealously, first in pencil and then, perhaps at a later time, in ink, for good measure. So my mother and father must have known each other a little better than her inscription suggests. Maybe my mother was taking the high road, not stooping to use the public space of a yearbook to show her feelings. Or maybe Doris was just taking aim at the woman she imagined as her closest competitor, a mere freshman.

Doris's overlit picture makes her features seem more delicate than they probably were. Her eyes are hooded. Her chin comes to a bony point below her predatory overbite. Her gaze has a calculating directness as opposed to my mother's honest directness. This is not just the dutiful son talking. No, it's there in the picture. Doris's mouth is a hard line, a rock overhang sheltering a nest of snakes. And how much do you have to pay to get that Medea perm? Maybe I'm exaggerating. Maybe I'm just defending my mother. But still. What a tramp. I'm sure glad I didn't end up with her as my mother.

In the picture of the freshman class, my mother's wearing the shortest dress. I'd think it a little racy if not for her pigeon toes, knobby knees, and wrists crossed discreetly in front of her cardigan. Even then she had the steady, thoughtful gaze I would come to know so well.

As carefully as I pore over the pictures and inscriptions in the yearbook, they don't tell me much. Was my father really as well-liked as the inscriptions suggest? Or was the warm language—even my mother's—just evidence of good breeding? One student who clearly didn't know my father at all but didn't want to be rude signed the book anyway, writing, "Best of luck to a future friend!"

The 1947 edition of "The Log" is padded in brown vinyl that's been textured to look like tree bark. Such a contrast to the picture of my father with his sophomore class. He's off in the back row, his big ears flapping, his mouth locked in a smirk as though he's trying to keep from laughing, his eyes gone to dark slits from the strain. None of the boys around you was laughing, not Milton Snyder, Kenneth Stoughton, or Ronald Spaulding. What was the joke, Dad? Tell me.

❧✦❧

The long trip into the wilds of Peru was by motorboat, partway with an escort of dolphins. My indian guide called them "bufeos," which I like to think means "buffaloes," as if they are the bison of the sea. Upriver we passed birds of every color and description. The jungle was a continuous, unbroken wall of green. How my guide knew where to put in I couldn't tell. But as soon as we did, villagers appeared from nowhere, rushing to the boat, helping me out, gathering some too close for comfort. One young boy of about eight, his hair in muddy braids and otherwise nude, insisted on touching my khakis, pinching the cloth, asking my guide what had made my skin so loose and dry.

I was not prepared for nudity. That was certainly different. Though missionaries had persuaded them of the virtues of the grass skirt, many of the villagers continued to walk about in the altogether. I was not bothered overmuch by the males all at a dangle, but the sight of the native women walking around with their dugs exposed was disturbing. Still, in order not to show disrespect for their culture, I stripped down to my skivvies. The villagers took great interest in the way my "grass skirt" was fashioned, by which they meant my white cotton B.V.D.s.

I came to know the villagers fairly well. Their leader was a small man who also wore his hair in muddy braids, apparently the fashion of the day. He was much addicted to dancing, as I found out that night during a feast they held in my honor. Here men dance with men, and he danced so close to me at times that I thought maybe we'd become engaged while my back was turned.

As far as daily activities are concerned, they farm, they hunt, they fish, and they eat people. I was assured by my guide that cannibalism was all a part of their past, but when he added a quiet "mostly," I admit to becoming a mite concerned.

❧✦❧

8

————

CITY OF GHOSTS

I woke up today sick to death of the wet bales of my father's life, the sour smell of his damp documents, sick of his machine-like printing on scores and scores of letters, with not one crossed-out word, sick of the pages I've laid out to dry one by one, sick of the yellowed leaves curling up from each other like the ancient parchments of some cloistered monk. But that's just what he was, my father, driving the line in his camper, closed up inside its tin walls, his monk's cell, a rolling tomb.

I find nothing in his notes about the next stretch of border, nothing until White Sands, where he was stationed on and off, attached to various missile projects. I find an embossed nameplate identifying him as part of the High Energy Laser Test Facility and a number of notebooks and loose pages filled with cryptic notes and drawings with names like "Hermes" and "LOKI" and phrases "electrostatic discharge," "hypervelocity bundles," and "kinetic energy weapons." Printed in large block letters filling one page edge-to-edge are two words, one on top of the other: "God Rods." And an old T-shirt printed with the words "Get Your Rockets Off at White Sands Missile Range."

I call the missile testing site and ask to be connected to the post office, explaining that my father, who served there, has just died, and I'm wondering if there's any mail for him I should pick up.

"I'm not at liberty to give such an indication, sir," the orderly replies, "not without proper authority."

"Assuming I have the proper authority, can't you just look into his box and tell me if you see any mail?"

"I cannot make that assumption, sir."

"OK, let me just ask you a hypothetical," I say. "If I go to the trouble of getting the proper authority and driving all the way there, would I be wasting my time?"

There is a long pause during which I think our connection is broken. Then he says, "No, sir."

"No I would not be wasting my time?"

"That's affirmative, sir."

I give him my name and all my contact information, insisting he write it down. And he seems to do just that. I tell him where I am and when I expect to arrive at the range. And I make sure to get his name and rank. At least someone will be expecting me when I arrive, making it more likely that I'll get through the gate. What will I find there? I want to know.

I call Sheree to ask her to mail the death certificate to me general delivery at El Paso. She's not there but I leave a message. Proper authority. This is good. This may be something. Something that helps me fill in the blanks. He used to tell me he worked on missile projects at White Sands and other places. He said he worked on one project so secret they had to situate it out in the desert far away from any power source. It was his idea to generate electricity for the entire compound with a jet engine bolted to the desert floor. But mostly he had nothing to say about White Sands, not in person nor in his letters and notes. Nothing that makes sense to me anyway. Maybe I'll learn something new about him there. There may be something in his mail, maybe even a member of his team? For a while he was loosely attached to a group that called themselves the "Broomstick Scientists." What if I can find one of them? Find out what he was like? How he worked and played, what jokes he told, what people said about him behind his back.

I'm feeling strangely elated now that I have a goal, however amorphous. In celebration, I decide to make an unscheduled stop, one that has nothing to do with my father. A border place I've always wanted to visit, a haunted place. I need to get away from him, from the constant analysis of his papers, the constant memories, the dead face locked inside the envelope that I'm afraid to open.

I drive to the ghost town of Guerrero Viejo. The history of the border is the history of so-called "deserted" places. In 1953, the town, which had survived stylishly at the junction of the Salado and Río Grande rivers since 1750, was submerged to make way for the Falcon Dam and its sixty-mile long, 87,210-acre reservoir, making it the main source of water for the Lower Río Grande Valley. Once teeming with 15,000 people in its heyday in 1900, a center for culture and commerce straddling both sides of the border, Guerrero Viejo is now most often described as "abandoned," suggesting that the 2,500 people who lived there simply chose to leave town that day in 1953.

In fact, at least according to some environmentalists, the town was obliterated in an act of environmental racism. According to them, Guerrero Viejo represented too much commercial competition, its obliteration justified by a water project that had been in the works since a 1944 treaty.

I've wanted to see the city ever since I heard that the drought was revealing so much of the old town and that Mexican-Americans from Zapata, San Ygnacio, and Río Grande City were making pilgrimages to the city of their ancestors, all these people coming back to find the ghosts of their people in this ghost of a place.

I head west on Highway 2, across Falcon Dam, west of the current town of Guerrero Nuevo. Trying to avoid the rubble of the steadily decaying road nearly makes me miss the turnoff to the old road. Ten miles or more past grazing goats and bulls, cacti, and parched strips of faded mesquite, *huisache*, ebony, wild olive, cactus, and native grasses, the road becomes impassable, lined and choked with boulders. Eyes stinging from the white dust carried on the wind, I hike the rest of the way into Guerrero Viejo.

I'm visiting during the worst of the drought that has plagued the Río Grande Valley, with rainfall five to ten inches below normal and the reservoir's storage level about 40 feet below normal. As the water in the reservoir continues to recede, sometimes by as much as two feet in a month, the ruins of the once-proud town continue to rise and more and more people return.

The first thing I see in town is Nuestra Señora del Refugio, the decaying church that once again dominates the *zocalo* of Guerrero Viejo, having risen from fifty years of mud and water. The walls are choked with scrub brush, mesquite trees. Lichen-scarred stones balance upon each other precariously, much of the stucco and mortar soaked away long ago. It's impossible not to see the place as an architectural version of a figure from a George Romero movie, a skeleton of a city, a city of ghosts, all its doors and windows and roofs thrown open to the air.

Everywhere the once beautiful stonework has fallen into the streets. Every step is a climb. I make my way across a rubble of bricks and suitcase-sized boulders—all that's left of the fence that once surrounded Nuestra Señora. I scramble through snake-infested rocks, trying to get a good look at the flaking stucco, at the crumbling stone and tile-work, at the rotting timbers. The windows and roofs of the city are long gone, the doors gone to rot. But the stacked columns and archways the city's artisans were famous for mostly remain, except for a few broken capitals and carved cornices that sometimes line the streets.

The front wall of the church stands more or less as it used to, ignoring the utter collapse around it. Only the town's bandstand and concrete benches seem untouched. The Hotel Flores, the public market, and the Palacio Municipal lie in ruins, their sandstone foundations having dissolved to a humped border of grit. Everywhere I look, the town is like a sugar-candy sculpture that has been rained on, washed away, soaked, chewed, and left to rot. In places, the limestone tablets of the Palacio's archways have dropped neatly and ironically to the ground in almost the same pattern in which they stood. Near the center of the plaza stands a spiral staircase leading up to nothing, to empty air. But the church is still standing, more or less, still waiting for life to start up again in the old town. Squared off around the plaza are the three most important buildings of the city—the church, the palace, and the cinema, all of them in ruins. Still, it's hard not to love a city that sets its priorities so clearly.

But the city is no longer abandoned, not really, though I wouldn't exactly call it inhabited. Some of the descendants of former residents have moved back into the more habitable buildings, despite the fact that there's no electricity, no water, no services, and no law hereabout, except for the occasional Federale. Near an ancient wall recently tagged with graffiti, a team of architecture interns has set up a surveying station, earnest young men and women in GAP jeans and polo shirts. There is talk of restoration and return. In fact, the church—or at least its shell—has largely been restored. And at least one former resident never left. Doña Julia Zamora simply moved to higher ground and still lives there, giving tours and letting her goats run freely through the old town. All this despite the certainty that the water will someday return, flooding the streets once again. Until then, we walk the streets, students, descendants, and men like me wandering the streets as if we're looking for the address of a house we never lived in.

Except for the leader of the architectural team, I'm the only gringo male here. But that's not quite true. I keep seeing a guy in a blue Hawaiian shirt, khakis, a ball cap, and sunglasses. He's down the street a ways, gazing at the water-worn ruins. A developer, probably. The next generation of people trying to rip this place off.

You can tell yourself that the need for water is so great in the region that some sacrifices must be made. But why, you wonder, is it always brown people who are made to make the sacrifice? And the flooding of the city was not even complete, only enough to make it uninhabitable. Before the drought, if you took a boat to the site, you came upon the city through a stand of mostly submerged trees to find Nuestra Señora floating on the water like something out of a film by Werner Herzog, a monument to the lost. From overhead, the elegant plaza and neatly laid-out city blocks would have been barely visible through the water, like the raised beds of rice paddies, enough to make the former residents remember vividly what they'd once had, too much to allow them to forget.

What was lost here was not a place of military or political importance, not a rich repository of culture. What was lost here was a way of life. Ordinary life, that sacred thing, was taken away from these people. You get a glimpse of it every so often walking the rocky streets. A tree shading a stony wall reminds you of the pleasant spot this must have made. A worn limestone threshold marks the passage of thousands of footsteps, thousands of lives. How are these ruined homes, this abandoned cemetery, different from sacked Egyptian tombs? The answer: they're not.

The sight of this orphaned place—the dusty streets going nowhere, a single stone archway opening onto a pile of rubble that was once a building, the enduring concrete benches of the *zocalo* poised to look on nothing, the scrub-choked cemetery (did no one even offer to move the bodies?), the sight of an old man carefully unwinding a skein of old fishing line from a mesquite thicket onto a spool—just breaks your heart. You can't help feeling a mixture of sadness at what was lost and joy at the indomitable old town defying its fate, at least for a little while longer. Nearby, the man in the Hawaiian shirt watches.

Despite its shoulder-high water line across the scalloped façade, Nuestra Señora still stands as graceful as ever. More graceful, in fact. Its roof and windows have rotted away, it's true, but now they open onto bright blue sky. If anything, its spiritual quotient has increased.

But I can't help wondering what I'm doing here. In this place that doesn't belong to me, a place to which I have no ties. I can't even find a reference to it in my father's journal or notes. So why come? Why does it matter to me? Still, I'm glad to have finally seen the place, which has lived in my imagination for so long.

As the afternoon fades and I walk the cracked and rubble-strewn streets back to the edge of town, I see him again, about halfway down the block, the man in the Hawaiian shirt with his hands locked behind his back, gazing at the rooflines, his face in the shadow of his ball cap's brim, his jaw a white blade. He's only doing what I'm doing, but he's been like this all afternoon, just a block or so behind me at every turn. He makes me think of my father, with his Hawaiian shirt and khakis short enough to show the bony white ankles above his penny loafers.

The cemetery again, its stones so crusty with old lichen that they're unreadable. I can't get over the fact that no one bothered to move the graves.

It's then that I realize today is my father's funeral. The day they wrap his coffin in the flag and put him in the ground with prayers and tears. The realization catches me so completely off-guard that I sit down suddenly on the cemetery's low stucco wall. I'm flooded with a feeling of loss, painful gut-hollowing grief. Stinging tears, hot tears, the works. I hate myself for it, but I miss him, miss the man I never knew, the man who never knew me.

Somehow, amazingly, my cell phone gets a signal and I call my brother, who's in Indiana for the funeral. By now it's over and everyone's at Uncle Tom's.

"The food, Brent, every different kind of thing. All you can eat." He makes the funeral sound like a birthday. I can hear voices in the background. Someone laughing. It almost sounds like a party.

I say, "What about the funeral?"

"Hmm, good. Simple but tasteful. Lots of flowers. I guess yours got lost in the delivery truck." He's joking. Isn't he? Neither one of us knew the man. "You should have seen the—you know—the burial. Flag, twenty-one-gun salute, the whole shebang." He's starting to sound like my father, as if going back to those southern Indiana cornfields has infected his speech patterns, his thinking.

"Really? Twenty-one-gun salute?"

"Yeah, three guys from the Armory—"

"—*Three* guys? Not twenty-one?"

"Three guys fired their carbines seven times. Equals twenty-one."

A pause.

"Is that the way it's done? I mean, is that even legal?"

"Don't know, but that's the way they did it. Quite a show. I cried. So'd Sheree. I better get back. You want to talk to anybody? No, of course not." And then either we lose the signal or he hangs up.

My brother's right. What kind of son am I? He was my father. It doesn't matter what he did or didn't do. He was my father. I should have been there to put him in the ground. If not out of respect, then to make sure he stays dead. Now, because I'm not there, I'll never really believe he's dead. He'll always be alive, a pair of eyes at every window, a word turning on the air, a breath under the door, a figure at the edge of every shadow.

Then it becomes clear why I've come here on the day they've lowered him into the ground, firing guns over his grave. Here to this city of the dead, city of my father, the dead who defy the odds, time, and wicked fate. Here where the dead leap back to life, where the years roll back, where the photos flip from full dress Commander's uniform to swabbie whites, and all the way back to the double-breasted sailor shirt and plaid shorts he wore as a child.

"Some people just can't leave well enough alone, you know?" He's here again, the man in the Hawaiian shirt, standing right behind me. I don't know whether he means the people who flooded the town, the people trying to reclaim it, or something else entirely. I look over my shoulder at him, but the sun is in my eyes and I can't really see him, only a sun-carved silhouette.

"Excuse me?"

He shrugs. "Sometimes you have to leave things the way they are." He resettles his ballcap and turns to go.

I'm up on my feet now, following. "What are you saying? Who are you?"

He turns back to me but doesn't say anything. He has my father's firm set to his jaw. It's not him. It can't be him. It's the expression I recognize—a father's disappointment.

As he turns away again, I yell, "You don't know me!" The architectural interns look up from their work. Who is this crazy person? But I don't care. "You don't know me!"

He turns back to me, says, "Oh we know you, sir. Do not doubt this."

I step closer but am afraid to get too close. His short-cropped hair is so blond it looks transparent. "Is this about my father? Is this about White Sands?"

He takes a breath, removes his sunglasses, and looks off down the dusty street. His eyes are a dark mineral blue. "This matter, sir, is about you. Do you comprehend my meaning?"

"No, I do not comprehend your meaning." I mean to wither him with scorn, but even to myself I sound like a spoiled child.

He steps closer, close enough now for me to see the pale white crescent of an old scar at the corner of his right eye. "Let me explain. You are about to step into some deep shit. And once stepped in, it cannot be unstepped in. I hope that provides you with the clarification you require. Good day, sir."

He puts his sunglasses back on, turns sharply, and is gone, down the street, into the glare. Gone. The interns, realizing that the show is over, go back to their work.

Just some stranger. Not my father. My father's dead and in the ground by now. And anyway, I'd know my own father, right? Even after so many years? It's some crazy man. But for me, from now on, every night the dead will rise from the dark water of my dreams, wet and heaving with a new and terrible life.

❧❧❧

At times I have been pleased to see rich agricultural lands but not much of it is farmed. In fact, most of Mexico's natural resources are undeveloped. With exceptions, much of the Mexico I saw was like the U.S. West must have been around 1840. This goes double for the border towns, which are as wide open as any town of the Old West. As I travel along the border, I am most impressed with the freedom enjoyed by the Mexican people. U.S. Law would forbid much of that freedom. In fact, most of Mexico would be against U.S. Law.

In the interests of sociology and understanding the workings of sin, I stopped by a village called Boys Town, just south of Nuevo Laredo. It is extremely run down, like most places in Mexico, and though the ladies there are all streetwalkers, I was some surprised to find they are also pleasant company. I suppose "streetwalker" is inaccurate terminology, since in fact the village belongs to them, a city of sin if there ever was one. I spent a pleasurable evening there, talking with them about their lives and their choice of occupation. I felt it was only natural that I pay them for their time, though I, of course, did not partake of their services. They are all of them good girls: Claudia, who's no bigger than a minute; Marisel, the jokester; Jacqueline, the best dancer by far; and Sonya.

9

RED-EYED DOG

The radio throbs with salsa, and the announcer's in love with the reverb effect. "THE GREATEST TEJANO HITS IN THE RIO GRANDE VALLEY!!" Every word has the hollow ring of a national emergency.

I'm heading to Laredo to sort out a mystery. At first the references in my father's Mexico log to "Boys Town" made me think of the famous center for troubled kids back in Omaha. I had a quick flash of my father as a philanthropist, making up for his bad parenting by helping other kids. But no.

According to his journal, my father was a friendly guy, stopping and talking to strangers everywhere he went. But after reading his journal for a while, I realize it wasn't just anybody he'd stop and talk to. There's no record of him talking with an old man seining for carp in the river or a harried mother shopping for groceries with her kids or the road crew worker taking a break. Almost all the people my father spent time with were young single women, some of them prostitutes, and several of them in and around Laredo and Nuevo Laredo.

I stop beside the river, just short of town, to watch an old refrigerator truck try to cross to the north at a shallow spot. The truck rolls slowly down the bank and enters the river like a fat man stepping into a cold lake. Not shallow enough, I guess. The truck makes it halfway across before the engine drowns. The driver tries to restart it. Nothing. The truck leans and twists slowly to the side until the windshield hangs just a few inches from the water. I can see the little ornamental saddle and lariat dangling from the rear-view mirror. I can see the driver's frightened eyes as he leans into the ignition, hoping for a miracle. But nothing. The river nudges the nose of the truck a little farther downstream. He gives up, laying his forehead on the steering wheel before climbing out and wading back to the Mexico side.

People come from nowhere, gathering around him, calling out suggestions: "Tow truck!" somebody yells. "Winch!"

Miraculously, a man shows up with a team of burros, which he hooks up with ropes to the rear of the truck, trying to pull it back to Mexico. The truck rocks once, twice, the burros loudly honking in complaint, then sinks more deeply into the muddy river bottom. The man and driver, with remarkable patience, unhook the burros and lead them through the river, hoping to have better luck pulling the truck up the north bank.

But as they haul the dripping burros out of the river near me, the people on the Mexico side wade to the truck, popping the back doors. Laughing men, women, and children fill their arms with frozen chickens and wade back to shore. An old man steps out of the river, raises a bird over his head and says, "*Hola, Señor Pollo!*" Then he kisses it and makes for home, the chicken tucked under his arm like a football. Without a word of complaint, the driver and his helper sit down on the north bank to watch the show with a shared cigarette. I can't help thinking of my father's boat hung up on the jetty. Pretty soon all the chickens and people are gone. Nothing left but the truck nose-down in the brown swirl. That and a dozen frozen chickens bobbing toward the Gulf like severed heads.

• • •

In town I park at the shopping mall right on the line and walk over to Nuevo Laredo, past ramshackle shops leaning against each other selling jewelry, *ristras*, *pâpier-maché* fruit, stuffed and shellacked singing frogs, watered-down margaritas in plastic cups, "Air Nice" running shoes, bright frilly dresses and *Saturday Night Fever* shirts, the owners yelling from doorways, "*Amigo! Amiga!*," the old American couples walking wearily past it all, wondering why they've come, why they even bother. The only thing missing are the *chicletistas*, the kids selling Chiclets from grimy cardboard trays.

I guess I should have figured that a place like Boys Town wouldn't be on a main street. After wandering around for a while, I decide I need to ask directions. As I step into a restaurant, a little girl with eyes the color of skinned chestnuts offers me a crocheted cross for a dollar. I buy it for luck, a kind of blessing, a protection against broken dreams and bodies floating in dark water. The cross is beautiful, with delicate turns of bright red and black thread. I will find many more of them from here to Tijuana, and I will buy them all, but the farther west I go, the more misshapen the crosses become, the more crude the crochet work. Broken blessings.

Inside the restaurant, every color, texture, object, and vista is calculated to give pleasure—from the ruddy saltillo tiles to the cobalt bar to the salmon walls. I came here for directions, not food, but I'm suddenly hungry. Or maybe I just want to delay asking my embarrassing question. Either way, I have an incredible lunch of trout steamed in plantain leaves. Then I sit at the bar for a couple beers, enough to build up my courage (and my Spanish) to ask. After a while, the bartender wipes his way down toward me.

"Sir," I ask in my broken Spanish, "do you know Boys Town?"

"*Sí.*" I've been worried about offending his sensibilities, but nothing registers in his eyes, not distaste, blame, or delight. I might be asking directions to the men's room. I'm worried about one thing in particular.

"*Yo voya Boystown,*" I ask, not at all sure of my Spanish. "Do you think that I will be harmed if I go there?"

"*Sí.*" He keeps wiping the bar until the blue tiles gleam. He couldn't have understood me. Why am I trying to say things in the conditional tense?

I try again. "What I mean is, will they kill me?"

"*Sí, te pueden chingar,*" he says in the same placid tone. *You could get fucked up.* And then he works his way past me with the bar rag.

My heart gives my ribs a swift kick. I'm ready to go home right now. I miss Nebraska, where nothing bad happens, where nothing at all happens. What am I *doing* here? Is this whole trip no more than some twisted effort to join my father, a tricked-out death-wish?

Along the border, "Boys Town" is code for any free-standing community of prostitutes, and the one at Nuevo Laredo is the most famous. My father, I knew from his log, had been to this one, the grandmother of them all, just south of Nuevo Laredo. What I think I'll find there, I don't know. His journal entries seem innocent enough, but why come here at all? Did he think of himself as some kind of missionary? Or was it some more primary need that drove him?

I want to see behind his veneer of moral uprightness, to find out that he could be as corrupt as any, more corrupt. I want to know the extent of his moral degradation. But what do I think I'll find? A monument, a police report, a DNA sample?

But the deal's off. No way am I going to get myself killed over him. He'd love that, a little company in the grave.

I'm on my way to the men's room, planning my route back home, back to hot, flat, lovely, uneventful Nebraska, when I overhear the bartender laughing with the kitchen help.

"'Will they be killing me?' he says, mimicking my bad Spanish. "'Oh yes,' I tell him. 'They will most definitely be killing you.'"

That's when he sees me, my mouth hanging open so wide he could do a dental exam right from where he stands, my eyes aslosh with shame and rage.

I want the Wild Bunch to step out from the shadows and stand beside me. I want to get all western on his ass. I want to do some damage. At the very least, I want to mutter, "*Vete a la chingada*," which translates loosely as "Go where the fucked go," except that's exactly where *I'm* going.

• • •

"*Quanto cuesta à Boys Town?*"

"Ten dollars American," the driver says flatly and takes off like an ambulance, turning the two-lane road into three lanes, passing in the middle, on the shoulder, wherever. I suck in my gut as if I can make the car thinner. He shoots through any opening—every driver here does—blowing each other's ears back. But they never drive so fast that they forget to raise a forefinger from the steering wheel in salute to the passing driver. It's obvious that the speed limit around here is "hell-bent." I can tell because there's no sound but the screeching of tires. No one leans on the horn, and the only person screaming is me.

By the time we reach Boys Town, southwest of the city, I'm grateful to fall out of the car onto solid ground.

Even the late-afternoon light does nothing to soften the place, a ten-acre crumbling cinderblock compound topped with rickety neon spires. The cab driver has parked just inside the main gate, in front of the little adobe jailhouse. Out on the stoop, two private cops are asleep in their chairs. But when I get out of the car, I see that they're watching me through half-closed eyes. And they may be real cops. I can't tell from the gaudy uniforms, the epaulettes, the gold braid, the shiny mismatched buttons. They look like extras from a Mack Sennet short, but they're probably the real thing. City cops in Mexico are allowed to improvise their own uniforms. Whoever they are, I hope I don't seem worth their trouble.

The whole place looks like twenty rundown one-story motels that have been shoved together and hammered on for ten or twelve years. They're painted pink, blue, and leprous green, but not in recent history. Young Mexican guys— sweaty, unshaven, hollow-eyed—step part-way out of the shadows, watching, taking the measure of my need, of their opportunity. A red-eyed dog with its hackles up steps side-wise out of the shadows. I'm tempted to jump back into the cab, but my stomach hasn't settled yet, and my pride won't allow it. I run into the closest place.

That place is Papagayo, the most luxurious brothel in the compound, which, of course, is relative. At the front door, a large sign warns patrons, in English, to leave their guns in the corner. Inside, the main room is deep and dark, with pale blue spills of light from a few fixtures in the ceiling. I can see figures sitting at the bar, moving through the shadows, sitting at tables. Scratchy *musica romantica* grinds from a few hidden speakers. My eyes haven't yet adjusted, and the armory of handguns and hunting rifles in the corner is freaking me out.

"Got-dammit! Sit down or you're going to get yourself killed!" The voice comes from a nearby table against the side wall. As I move closer, I see a big man in a Stetson and a silver suit that makes him look like a chubby alien on vacation. He's surrounded by several women in shabby negligees, all of them in shadow, lit for brief flashes by a blue strobe in the ceiling. I sit down in the only empty chair at the table. Better than drawing so much attention to myself.

"Now that's more like it," the man says without looking at me. He's got each arm around the bare shoulders of a woman. He's got a big jowly face with dark pouches under his eyes and a veiny nose.

"You walk in here like that, you're apt to get your ass handed to you," he says. "You want to know why nobody hassles me?" When he leans back, the back of his Stetson taps the wall behind his head, raising the brim in front. "By day I'm Mr. Business in my silver suit and my short hair. I go around grinning with a six-inch pig-sticker. 'You got a problem?' I say. And you know what? Nobody does. They see this big ole boy with this shit-eating grin and a knife 'bout yea-big. *No es problema.* They see this crazy man and they leave me alone. It's a custom followed the world over." At last he looks at me, studies me. "So what're you looking for, a hot-'n-spicy *sin*orita?"

"No," I say. "Actually—" But I have no idea why I'm here.

He leans forward, dropping the front legs of his chair to the floor, and peers at me through the blue strobing darkness. "Jesus H. Christ on a crutch! You're nothing but a blue-peckered boy!" He leans over the table and thrusts a pale meaty hand from the end of his silver sleeve. "Willy B," he says.

"Hi, Willy," I say, shaking it.

"Willy B," he corrects, leaning back against the wall. "Willy's the mangy critter between my legs."

For the next two hours Willard B. Hayes talks non-stop about his favorite subjects: sex, drugs, and money.

"Beer's about all I do now," he says. "Got tired of cocaine. Took me too damn many days to recover. Sure there's other bars in Mexico, and there's good bars on the other side, but there's two drawbacks: 1) the beer is more expensive and 2) they don't let you fuck the waitresses!"

The woman next to him reaches for his belt buckle, but he waves her off. "I'd like to, darlin', but you already mangled my *morrongo* enough for one trip."

Then, as if taking a cue from the other woman, the one next to me starts to stroke the top of my thigh. She may not be as young as she seems. It could be that she's just small, that the black negligee just seems somehow too old for her. Or that her tiny, heart-shaped face only makes her seem young. Hard to say. She keeps rubbing my thigh, and when I don't respond, she says, in English, "You buy me a drink and think about." After our drinks come, we take a sip and she turns her eyes up at me. "You want to go room now?"

"No," I say. "No thanks."

She nods, tries another tactic, her eyes going sly. "You want Mexican sandwich?" Only five minutes in town, and I'm already sophisticated enough to know that she's not talking about something on the lunch menu.

There is no prostitution in Mexico. At least not according to the government. If this seems like a willful disregard for reality, it is. If, on second thought, it seems like an open-minded effort at tolerance, it's that, too. On the border, the fact that two things contradict each other doesn't prevent them from both being true. It's Keats's Negative Capability, the ability to hold two contradictory ideas in the mind at the same time. What some refer to as the "wisdom" of "adulthood." That is, prostitution is not regarded as a crime but as a private matter between people, requiring just the merest bit of regulation, if that. The key word is "private." Sex for hire on a public bus is illegal. Sex for hire in a private room is OK, as long as the practitioner's health card is current (in some states, anyway, some of the time). Problems arise where the rough edges of these contradictions rub together. Though prostitution is, to be more accurate, not *recognized* by the government, crimes against minors (exploitation, abuse, corruption) are, and yet there is no regulation setting the age for legal consent. Is it a crime to put a fourteen-year-old to work as a prostitute? Not by the letter of the law.

Drinks served at Papagayo: Amoretto Extasis, Slippery Nipple, Mind Eraser, Vampire, Windex, Blow Job, Zima.

Willy B describes himself as a "facilitator."

"I started out as a dozer driver in the Guat." The flash of the blue strobe must show my confusion, because he says, "Bulldozers. Guatemala. Get with the program, buddy! I's tramping through the jungle. I's moving dirt here. I's moving dirt there. Dumb! Then I got it through my head to let go of the shitty end of the stick and grab the executive end." He leans back against the wall, the front of his Stetson rising. "Now I *facilitate*. Thirty thousand here, a hunnert ninety thousand there. Down here, I'm the big wienie . . . in more ways than one."

He's stopping off here for a little relaxation after a big business deal—a ten percent commission on the sale of a million dollars' worth of beer trucks. Says he plans to stay a month in Boys Town, "spending pesos like play money, which it is!" Says he doesn't want to go home to the ball-'n-chain just yet.

"You're married?" I'm so stupid somebody ought to shoot me.

"Sure! Twice over! Once for practice and the second time for keeps. Hell, my first wife pushed me around. You know why? Because I let her—let her open her mouth, that is! Big mistake! Met my second wife right here, and I ain't looked back since day one. No sir. Prettiest little thing. She knows where I am. Sex ain't the big deal south of the line as it is up north. Here it's just something a man needs now and then, like food and water. She knows that. Does anybody make a fuss if you get hungry and buy a sandwich instead of going home for lunch? No, they do not. Same difference."

He drops the front legs of his chair to the floor and lays his rumpled silver forearms on the table, looking out at me from the shade of his Stetson's brim. "I'll tell you what. Only way you're going to understand this place is to hoist your mast, dip your doodle, dangle the old bangle, bury the one-eyed snake. You got to *feel* it. You got to *be* it." He waves his hand at the women around the table, who are mostly gazing around the room and whispering to each other. "Let me tell you, there's things I could tell you, and the main thing is just to take it easy. Comin' in here you was all nervous and shit. That ain't the way to do it, man, you know?" He opens his arms wide to take in the women around our table, who perk up like a pack of dogs. "These people treat you right. They're not gonna fuck with you unless you fuck with them. This place is special. I been to Malaysia, Thailand, Ecuador. I been everywhere, you know? Hell, I'm an international nooky expert. And nobody can touch these girls. Up there over the line, it's all Puritanical. Down here whoring's respectable. These are good conservative country girls. Anybody tells you different is a lying lump of pigshit. Take your little girlfriend Sonya there—"

Sonya. One of the names in my father's log. A common name. Not unusual, anyway. Not down here.

Sonya, Sonya, Sonya. What can I say about Sonya? Child-vixen, temptress, a woman to make you forget your higher purpose. We sat talking one night for many hours, our chairs face-to-face. I held her knee between mine. She took me very far away from God.

"Your name is Sonya?" I'm stunned. Now I'm the dog, a dog on a scent. Quietly, before I realize how ridiculous I'll look and sound, I say, "Maybe you knew my father?"

As if in answer, Sonya looks up at me and lets her lips part, wetting them with the tip of her tongue. She smiles. She wedges her hand between my legs, an offer, a promise, a placeholder, a bookmark, a claimstake.

Willy B's sales pitch drones on. "She got herself a little *casita*. She got herself a couple of kids. When she wakes up in the morning, she pulls her little crotchless panties on one leg at a time, just like your mama and her mama before her. She takes her kids to school. She goes to work. Same as you, same as me. She's in business. She's a businesswoman. Hell, she's a goddamn entrepreneur! I been with ever' dang one of these girls, and they're the best. You won't regret it."

But I want none of it. I'm as prone to sin and stupidity as the next man, but sex without love is no more than aerobics. And anyway, this is just too weird. My father may have been with this woman. Too Oedipal for me. But Sonya raises her heart-shaped face, her lips wet, her eyes bright. I can see down the front of her black negligee, can see her soft brown nipples. It occurs to me suddenly that I could reach inside and cup her bare breast, and in this place, at this time, it would be seen as no more than sampling the merchandise.

"G'wan, look," Willy B says. "You can see all the way from her howdy to her hoo-ha."

I look away from Sonya's bright eyes and drain my beer in one long, desperate swallow.

He shakes his head. He pushes the brim of his hat up and wipes his face. "Shit, 'migo, I just can't figure you the hell out. What're you worried about? You worried about AIDS? Well, don't. That's not the problem down here it is up above the line. These girls are clean. They get a check-up every week."

"An AIDS test every week?" I ask.

His face knots up in frustration. "I tell you, they're *regulated*!"

Sonya honks her chair closer to mine and hugs my arm to the side of her breast. Dark ringlets of hair frame her face, her shining eyes. I smell coconut shampoo. I smell curling iron. I stroke the side of her neck with my thumb. She nudges her face up toward mine and opens her mouth a little more. "*Imposible,*" I say, but my thumb finds the soft shallow at the base of her throat, and I lean down and kiss her soft, full lips and feel the small, darting tip of her tongue. What's lust but hope?

The table has gone quiet. Self-conscious, ashamed of my textbook accent, of my desire, I say, "*Te quiero. Eres muy bonita. Cuanto cuesta?*" I like you. You are very beautiful. How much?

"Sixty dollars," she says.

I feel my eyes go wide. I sit up straighter. "*Eres casi demasiado bonita.*" You are almost too beautiful.

"G'wan 'n git up on that filly," Willy B says. "My treat!"

She doesn't speak. She doesn't have to. She stands and leads me by the hand. For once, Willy B doesn't crack wise, and I'm grateful.

As we walk across the barroom, I come to my senses a little. "I only want to talk," I say to her. "No sex. But I'll pay." I feel a sudden stab of guilt as I hear the echo of my father's words.

But she ignores my words, taking me by the hand through a doorway that opens onto a hall lined with small rooms. Cubicles, really. Spaces sectioned off with whitewashed plywood panels. Each room is hardly bigger than the single bed inside it, and none of them is occupied. It's early, I guess. "No sex," I say again. "Just to talk, OK?" Now even my English is broken.

Sonya pays no attention. As soon as we're through the doorway, she turns and stops me with a hand on my chest.

I don't get it. "*Qué?*" I ask her.

She looks up at me with those liquid eyes. I can see all the way down the front of her negligee.

"*Qué?*" I say again. Something's wrong. "*No hay es un cuarto?*" *Isn't there a room?* She has stopped just inside the doorway, where an old woman is sitting at a card table watching a *telenovela* on a little beach TV. Sonya moves me to the side of the table. The old woman sits hunched over, taking almost no notice of anything but the screen. Her eyes are pinpricks of black in a withered brown face. She has no teeth but her jaws work constantly. Standing at her feet is a soda bottle partly filled with brown tobacco spittle.

I look down at Sonya, a little desperate now. "*Qué?*" I say again, the word spiky with panic. Is she trying to hand me off to this crone? "No!" I grab Sonya's wrists. "*Tú,*" I say, shaking them, "*tú es mi cuarto.*" *You are my room.*

But now the old woman has me by the belt buckle, and now she's undoing my pants, all the while keeping her eyes on the TV, except for the moment she fishes out my shrinking *chuperson*. Sonya stands next to me patiently, equally absorbed in the *telenovela*. I stand there feeling eleven different kinds of shame. The old woman lifts me to see the underside, turns me left, right. She's looking for signs of disease, I guess. "I just want to talk," I say weakly, forcing my thoughts beyond the moment at hand, so to speak.

Did my father stand where I'm standing now, with his *chilé* in the old woman's leathery palm? The thought horrifies me. I pull away from her and zip up as discreetly as possible.

The three of us stand there, unable to take our eyes off the screen. A woman meets her lover on the beach, the waves falling listlessly behind them. She tosses her wind-blown hair, this child-vixen, the model for the women here in Papagayo. She laughs and twitches the hem of her flimsy cotton dress. Her fluffy little dog makes one of his mental remarks. The lush strings of the orchestra swell. A few contemplative notes are stuck on the piano. Halfheartedly, her eyes still on the screen, Sonya pulls my hand toward one of the rooms.

"No," I say, the spell broken at last. "*Esta bien.*" *It's all right.* I unfold her hand from my arm.

Now it's her turn. "*Qué?*" She says it sharply with a little bounce of her chin. What's up?

I open my wallet and take out the picture of my father in his dress whites. "Do you know him?"

She takes the picture in both hands and studies it. "*Su amigo?*"

"*Mi padre.*"

She nods a little too enthusiastically. "*Claro que sí.* I know him." She hands back the photo.

"You do? You know my father?"

"*Claro. Las conozco a todas.*" *Sure, I know all the fathers.*

It's just too strange for words. I put the picture back in my wallet and give her sixty dollars. She takes the money without hesitation and passes it the old woman, who locks it inside a gray metal box. Sonya tries again to take my hand and lead me to a room, but I catch her hand and nod toward the barroom. As we head back to the table, I figure Willy B and the women will get a big laugh out of this.

It starts as soon as Willy B sees us crossing the room. Loud enough for everyone to hear, he says, "Well, Sonya, did he bone ya? How was the little pud knocker? Fastest gun in the West, I think!" The women around him laugh, knowing well enough what he has said, whether or not they know what the words mean.

Sonya goes limp beside me, hanging onto my arm. She closes her eyes and shivers. "*Ay, mi coño! Hostia puta, Willy! Est un caballo!*" *Oh, my poor pussy! Holy shit, Willy! He's hung like a horse!* She leans against me with her head on my arm, so exhausted she needs another drink. I love this woman.

When we're back at the table, Willy B, not yet satisfied, turns to me. "Well? What'd I tell you?"

I put on my game face. "You said it, Willy B. I had my *chilé* diced, dried, fried, flambéd, and relleno'd."

He drops his chair forward onto all fours and backhands me in the chest. "That's what I been trying to tell you, '*migo*!" He spreads his arms wide. "You stick with me, kid, and we'll plow every inch of this acreage!"

There are many self-serving myths among the men who frequent Boys Town. As the night wears on, I hear them all. Boys Town, Willy B says, is run by the women themselves as a kind of collective, not by a network of pimps. "It's actually a feminist thing!" The only people who seem to believe this, though, are the customers. The women have no idea what I'm talking about, and one laughs outright, though she might be laughing at my bad Spanish.

He tells me Boys Town is run by the government, which is why it's "so clean and orderly." But there's nothing especially clean about the place, and it's about as orderly as a stockyard. It's more likely that "run by the government" refers to the *mordita* such places have to pay to keep the police off their backs. It's true that the *mordita* has been outlawed, but this is more true in press releases than in reality.

A college guy and his buddy sit down at the table next to us after being in the back room. "I really think she's sincere," says the one in the "Hook 'em, Horns" T-shirt.

The classic myth. That the woman you've just bought actually loves you, or at least considers you much more than a mere customer. Can you be wistful after spending time with a prostitute? We're all gullible romantics in Papagayo's.

"I thought she might be a minor, but she told me she's twenty-one."

And when you find that special woman, of course, she's not really a prostitute. She only does this on the side, a couple nights a week, a part-timer, no big deal.

"Actually, she's college educated and not at all whorey."

Actually, she has a Ph.D. Actually, she only does this with you if you can prove you belong to MENSA. Class with a capital "K."

"Heck," his friend says, "these women are so poor we're actually doing them a favor."

Hook-'em nods vigorously and says, "Hey, if we don't, somebody else will, and probably somebody a whole lot meaner and uglier and full of diseases."

Who knows? You just might find the woman of your dreams! And you just might be the big brave gringo who rescues them. Snap your fingers and you can have one of them for life. Worried about STDs? Don't! These women are regulated! (Not only that, but they'll do you without a condom if you ask nice.) And when a woman offers to do you for free, it's because you're such a good-looking *cabron*. Like the crack dealer so overcome with generosity that he can't resist giving you a free sample, it being your first time and all.

The same few assumptions are behind all these myths: that this is not really a bit of sordid flesh-peddling. It's human interaction, a reaching out. The exchange of money happens almost as an afterthought. It is, in short, anything but what it seems to be.

Willy B says, "Hell, most of the time they don't even charge me! I just give them money out of politeness."

He studies the women of Papagayo the way he'd study a herd of horses, recommending favorites like dependable mares. The kind shown by my father in his journal as he idealizes the female hitchhikers he'd pick up in his camper. A music major from Boston College, Barb and I passed several nights singing all the songs we knew. Spunky!

God save me from the desperate dreams of men.

Boys Town is, above all, a scary place, scary in every way. At any moment, you expect someone to relieve you of your intestines with a rusty knife. I think of all those old westerns where a couple of tough hombres always end up rolling on the floor, wrestling for a gun. And when the gun goes off, they stiffen for a moment before one collapses in an orgasm of dying, the victor rolling aside, his hand securely on his piece. It makes me wonder if all houses of prostitution are really no more than a way for men to have surrogate sex with each other. Like football.

We've been sitting around for what feels like hours. Now and then one or two men come in, but they don't even bother to sit down. They just point at a woman and head for the back room. Willy B's women have stopped trying to impress us. They're sitting here because he keeps buying drinks and because business is slow. Sonya gazes off into a dark corner of the barroom, rubbing idly at the dampness between her breasts. It occurs to me that Willy B has been coming here a long time, long enough to have met my father. I pull out the picture again.

"You ever see this guy around here?"

He paws the snapshot closer and holds it up. "Military," he muses. "I seen a lot of military types in this place, yes sir." He holds the picture closer to his eyes. "Not this one, though."

"He probably wouldn't have been wearing his uniform."

"Right you are. Incognito. Eyes only. Hush-hush. Deep cover. Keep it on the QT. Keep it on the down-low." He snaps a salute. "Semen first class Will B reporting for duty, sir!" He studies the picture again. "No, can't say as I ever laid eyes on this man." He spins the picture onto the table. "Girls?" he says. "Ever lay hams on this man?"

They look at the picture, but it means nothing to them. It's strange seeing a table full of whores leaning over my father's picture like this, his glowing dress whites so strangely formal compared to their worn negligees. More than anything else, it makes me realize he's dead. For a minute, the picture lying there among the sweating bottles and glasses might almost be his body laid out for a wake. Dad, what are we doing here?

A guy comes in wearing a red plaid hunting jacket and cap. He's obviously told his wife he's going hunting with the boys. That's the euphemism among certain Texas men who frequent these places. "Going hunting," they say. It explains the number of rifles stacked in the corner, the number of men in camo outfits having their thighs caressed. Never mind that the only game these hunters ever catch is bacterial in nature. Here sex is always in season.

The Great White Hunter steps blinking into the room, holding his bird gun by the muzzle, like a cane. He can't see. His eyes haven't adjusted yet to the darkness. To the swirling shadows, he says, "*Por favor?*," his "r's" as round and hard as marbles.

And that's all he has to say. In seconds—faster than swarming antibodies—three women fly to him, hands moving over him, tugging him by the belt toward the open doorway and the antique medical professional in the back room.

It's time for Sonya's break, so I follow her outside into the gathering darkness to a low cinderblock building behind the jail, thinking I can talk to her more easily there. Hard fluorescent light bounces off the blue-green walls.

Rough-hewn picnic tables are scattered around, with women sitting at each in two's and three's, all of them in faded and tattered underwear, like Fashion Week in hell.

Cooking heat pours from the large pass-through at one end of the room, making the air unbearably hot. Every face has a sheen of sweat. I don't breathe, I pant. The women at the tables talk and laugh. The old women in the kitchen work silently, stirring pots and making tortillas. Too old now to work a room of horny gringos, they cook for the younger women.

Sonya comes back from the pass-through with a bowl of menudo and sits at my table. My handful of Spanish is hardly enough to get the kind of story from her that I want. So why am I here? And does this place have anything to do with my father?

After she's had a little of the menudo, I ask, "Do you earn much money? *Dinero?*"

She stops eating and says, "For what you want?"

"Not for me," I say quickly. "I mean in general. *En general.*"

Understanding my anxiety more than my bad diction, she says, "Is OK. You too much worried."

All I can think to say is "*Por qué?*" *Why?*

She makes a face and, in slow English, says, "I don't know. That's you problem."

"Not that," I say and gesture broadly at the other women, at the unseen stream of men wandering the darkening streets of Boys Town. "*Por qué esto?*" *Why this?*

She smiles, shakes her head. As if speaking to a child, she says, "For the dolors."

I leave her to the menudo and step outside, feeling cheap of spirit, feeling just like the kind of person border people hate—the fly-ins who drop by for a bit of exotica and then leave as soon as possible, the people quick to see the excesses in other countries but blind to those of their own. How is this woman any different than the ones on the corner of 27th & Leavenworth in Omaha?

Outside, the sun has gone down, making it feel cool compared to the blast furnace inside. Men walk the dusty streets in shadowy two's and three's. The frail neon signs look a little stronger now, lighting up the dark. Many kinds of music and many hollow-voiced announcers echo off the broken stucco walls. "Come closer, mister! See!" It's still early in the evening, but already the little two-lane road outside the compound is lined with cars and semis with diesels throbbing. By midnight, the line will be a good quarter-mile long, the air choking with fumes, making the place seem even more hellish.

It's no mistake that Papagayo, one of the most gringo-friendly places in Boys Town, is closest to the gate and first on the circuit. The other two largest and best-kept places are the Maribu and Tamyko. They're laid out with Papagayo at one end and the Maribu at the other, like the anchors of a shopping mall. These places are meant to relax you, to soften you up for the horrors between.

But most of Boys Town is occupied by row after row of one-room shanties opening onto the street, each just big enough for a woman, a single mattress, a customer, and the occasional TV. I imagine all of them tuned to the same *telenovela*—Marimar in her filmy white dress facing the sea, waves crumbling at her feet.

When she sees me pass her room, the heavy woman climbs grunting out of bed and comes to the doorway. She leans in the open frame with all the allure she can muster, one knee raised, a sickly homage to Betty Grable. Framed by the yellow light from a bare bulb, she adjusts her ragged bustier, about as erotic as an old saddle. Twenty dollars is the asking price, but she'll take less.

"*No, gracias,*" I say.

"*Joto,*" she says—faggot—and turns back to *Marimar* on the flickering black-and-white.

The farther I walk into Boys Town, the edgier things become. The women get worse-looking, more aggressive, the decor more like a post-apocalyptic Vegas. In the shadows, there's a woman wearing bright blue eyeliner, red lipstick, and scorched yellow hair out to here. She's wearing hoop earrings as big around as the lids of mayonnaise jars. Her white pantsuit is covered with paisleys the size of hams. The hand she holds out to me is large, squared-off, and hairy. I shake my head and keep walking.

Dust whirls in the dirty street. Ahead of me, the rangy, chewed-up-and-spit-out dog gives me a cock-eyed glare, its mouth open, wet, and ready for anything. The dog darts between buildings as a car comes racing up behind me, tires tearing up gravel and dust as it skids to a stop a few feet in front of me. Before the car has quite stopped, a big angry guy in a flowered shirt jumps out and charges inside one of shabby rooms. Loud voices—first his, then hers. A loud slap. Silence. He makes me think of the guy in Guerrero, but it's not him. I can't help feeling he's somewhere nearby, though.

No matter how much ill will and imagination I conjure up, I cannot picture my father in these mean streets. Not my father, the fierce Christian, the enemy of all things unclean. Was Boys Town the kind of place where he belonged, these sweating, semen-stained streets? Was it God's work or the devil's that brought him here? Who was this man? I came here for answers, but all I'm getting is a deeper mystery.

Still, I make the circuit, the red-eyed dog leading me on, past one collapsing bar after another, many with spastic neon signs canted over the street at physics-defying angles. Ahead of me, a man jumps out of a doorway and yells, "Come see the donkey show!" I stay away from the bar fronts, walking faster now. The dust is finer than flour and deep. The red-eyed dog, my guide to hell, keeps checking over his shoulder to make sure I'm following. The bartender, I think, was right. They will kill me.

I pass "Dallas Cowboys" (where the women aren't women), past "The China Club" (where a few of the women are Asian) and "Tamyko" (where the women are younger and only the decor is Asian), then past a number of clubs thrown-together with old tin sheeting and signboards. The doors are open as if the sight of car seats for chairs and torn, crinkled lengths of aluminum foil tacked to the wall could entice anyone inside.

Finally I pass the place known as "Blow Row," an open-air smorgasbord of strung-out stragglers who'll do anything for spare change.

By the time I finish the circuit, I'm even more depressed. A different pair of cops are asleep in the chairs in front of the jail. I told Willy B I'd talk with him some more, but I think I've had enough of this place. The college guys are coming out of Papagayo's, the romance already gone out of their lives. They complain about the old woman's inspection of their privates. They're deeply offended at being handled by such a wizened crone. "It just ain't right, man!"

He's been shouting for a few minutes before I realize it's him.

"Buddy boy! Buddy boy!"

It's Willy B, who has headed off down the street after me, not realizing that I've circled the block and am behind him now.

He appeals to the dark swirl of empty street ahead of him: "Buddy boy, where you be?" He waves his white hat. His silver suit glows strangely in the phosphorescent light of the crippled neon.

"I found your dad, buddy boy! I only wanted to say! He's waiting for us, just like he said! I got us all fixed up!" He dances, jigging and hopping in a tight circle, kicking up dust and waving it away with his hat, singing:

"The very first step that I took in the dark
 I took this girl, Nancy, to be my sweetheart
 She smiled in my face and these words she did say
 Are you the young fellow called Ramble-away?"

When he finishes his song, he's facing back the way he came, startled to see me. He gives me a big bow, snatching the Stetson off his head and sweeping it so low it scrapes the dust. He starts walking toward me, slowly at first, but after a few steps, he starts to jog, then to all-out run, his feet plunging in the dust.

Behind me, a cab whirls in through the front gate, trailing a tall plume of dust that floats over me and down the street, toward Willy B. Another drunken wit climbs out of the cab, yelling, "Take me to the testicle festival!"

Before Willy B can reach me, before the college guys can get their arms and legs aimed in the same direction, I jump into the cab. But Willy B's right behind me.

He lunges for the open window of the cab, hands reaching inside, his sweaty face strobing with the flickering lights of Papagayo's sign.

"Your daddy's waitin' on us, boy!" He yanks at the front of my shirt as if he can drag the car and me back into the bar. "Come on!"

"*Puente numero uno*," I yell to the driver, barely able to pronounce the words. Bridge #1.

Willy B lets go but bangs on the hood, yelling, "Them whores don't love you! You think they do? Them whores is *whores!*" The taxi whines in reverse toward the gate, but Willy B won't let go. "Don't you get it, buddy boy? *I'm your daddy!*"

This time, the taxi's breakneck speed is everything I ever wanted. And as it whips into the street and streaks away, I sink back into the cracked black leather seat realizing that I'm a fool and a fake, and that I come from a country of fools and fakes. My father's son at last.

❧❧❧

This evening there was a parade in the village. Many of the participants were nearly nude and heavily painted, some black with tails and horns. Others were elaborately dressed and painted with wild fluorescent colors.

What more evidence of man's fallen nature do you need than the body and mind's tendency towards filth? I have scrubbed my own body raw in places, trying to make myself in all ways clean before my Lord. But to no good effect. Filth always returns, first in the form of perspiration, then as a mildly sour scent, and next as fine-grained particles of dirt lodged in the tiny creases of the skin, which no amount of rubbing can remove. All things fall away from the ideal, from the cleanliness and purity of God.

Today is my birthday anniversary.

❧❧❧

10

THE HEALING

Every father is part hero, part villain, part thrill-ride, part fun-house scare. My own has been all of those things, usually at the same time. Whatever he is, or was, I'm pretty sure I couldn't have figured it out staring down at his body in the mahogany box surrounded by his adoring family. But I'm feeling guilty about missing the funeral, so I'm driving through the night on the Mexico side, roughly parallel to the border but keeping to the back roads, through tiny villages like Don Martín, past small farms and dusty pastures. Many butt right up against the road, and more than once I'm startled by the luminous green eyes of a cow caught in my headlights as I swing through a turn.

I want room and time to think. The problem is I don't have a place in my mind for him. Or maybe I do, but the only place is one I wish were different. We always want our fathers to be something they're not, can never be. But they are who they are. Magician when we're young, hero when we're a little older, monster after that, and finally, if they live long enough, helpless child. Somewhere in there, if you're lucky, maybe friend. But some do things that freeze them at certain stages. My father got stuck at sideshow freak.

So here I am with these bags and bags of letters, notes, photos, and of course the *Mexico Log*. Not even his pallbearers carried a heavier load. And it's sick. Sick and ridiculous. Probably I'm the freak.

The dark two-lane curves through the countryside, up and down hills. No one else is on the road at this hour. The hard-edged stars look down. It's all very restful. Near Sabinas, I come around a bend to find my way blocked by a guy in a T-shirt and jeans. He's standing next to the flickering light of a smudge pot that's sending a thick coil of black smoke into the sky. With the muzzle of his automatic rifle, he waves me off the road toward a small tin shed. Thieves roam the back roads at night. I'm done, I think. End of the road.

But as I climb out of the car and he comes closer, I see the Federales Policia Nacional patch pinned to the front of his white T-shirt. Fear changes to worry. I know why I've been stopped. Too far in country without the proper papers. I follow him inside, where two other cops are seated at a small wooden table, playing cards. He motions to a chair at another small table and sits in the other chair, silently filling in a ream of forms before he speaks with me.

"Why you come Mexico?" the cop says in slow English.

"*Est la mas linda en todo!*" *It's the most beautiful of all.*

"You think so?" he says flatly, his tone contradicting me. "You no Zapatista?"

"*No! Soy maestro de vacacione!*" *No, I'm a teacher on vacation!*

So far my Spanish has served me well enough, though I must sound like a child the way I put sentences together ("*Me gusta Mexico!*"—"*Mexico tastes good!*"). He seems not to care, cranking a thick sheaf of paper and carbons into an old manual typewriter and beginning to peck out his report. Almost an hour passes. At least it feels like an hour. There's no sound in the shed but the slap of cards and the slow, deliberate punch of typewriter keys.

Finally I get it. "Is there a fine I can pay?" I ask.

"*Sí,*" the cop says, nodding gravely. And he pulls a calculator from the desk drawer and begins to tally it up. As if the calculator will make the bribe more legal. The *mordita.* As they say in Mexico, a bad thing never dies.

He tears the print-out off and says, "Seventy-five dollars." He says I can pay him and be on my way or take my chances with the magistrate. The other cops have stopped playing and are watching me. It occurs to me that seventy-five splits nicely three ways. But I quickly pay the man, sure that it's the quickest and easiest way to get back on the road. And besides, he's right. I don't have papers.

Once I've paid, the tension lifts, the men go back to their game, and my cop walks me to my car. But when he sees the big green garbage bags in the back seat, he points his gun at me again and says, "*Drogas?*" Drugs?

"No! No!" I reassure him. "*Mira! Mira!*" Look! Look! And I open all four doors and the trunk.

He approaches the back door and lays open the nearest bag with the muzzle of his gun. When he sees the papers, he asks, "*Que es eso?*"

"*Mi padre,*" I say.

And he nods as if this explains everything.

• • •

I make it back across the border, to Eagle Pass, without incident, and decide to stay on the north side for a while. But then I meet the angry family on the other side of the gas pump. His wife and two sweaty little kids are stuffed inside the car along with everything they own. The car's filled to the headliner with suitcases, blankets, pillows, lamps, boxes. She's holding the kids on her lap. Between them and the windshield is bale of blankets, towels, and pillows. A large crate is strapped to the top of the car, which is so heavy the car has no more than two or three inches of clearance.

He's a skinny white guy in a red muscle shirt and big black pants with zippered pockets all over. Clothes that seem to belong to a much bigger man. And a different man. He's got a dark brown pony tail and nearly no eyebrows. He's angry, he's pissed. His mouth is working so hard, it seems to be trying to eat him.

"I'm out of here, man! I've had enough of the border! Land of opportunity? What opportunity! Opportunity for crap! You can keep it! We're getting out! We're going to Arizona. That's where our destiny waits! We got it straight from the moon lady."

I think I must have heard him wrong, but then the man's wife leans across the driver's seat, the only empty space in the car. The two kids in her lap struggle not to be crushed. "Lunes," she says. "LOOOO-nessss. It's a Spanish name."

One of the kids on her lap squirms free and yells, "And Texas can kiss my rosy red heinie!"

• • •

It's crazy. I know this. But I can resist. As soon as the couple told me about the woman named Lunes, I knew she was a *curandera*, a witch, a healer. And as quick as that I knew I had to see her. This is what I've been looking for. This is what this whole trip is about. It has all led up to this. A healing.

Not much of the night is left. No point in renting a motel room. So I park in front of Santa's Beauty Salon, crank the seat back, and try to sleep. But I'm too restless. A healing. I'm not especially gullible, but I'm also not one to walk away from a chance. I go to the truckstop for coffee, sitting at the counter. The place is empty, as far as I can tell. Just the bored waitress, me, and the pie case turning on its creaky spindle.

She says, "You want to try the Fancy Catfish Platter?"

"What's fancy about it? The catfish or the platter?"

"I take that as a no." And she starts to walk away.

"Sorry," I say. "I'm just tired. Tired and stupid. Bring on the fancy catfish platter."

"I hear you, hon."

The food turns out to be surprisingly good—Gulf Coast catfish lightly coated in seasoned corn flour and fried in peanut oil. When she comes by to refill my coffee, I say, "This *is* fancy!"

"Like I said," she says.

Dawn, and a few customers, come and go. I decide to get started in my search for the *curandera*. But when I ask for the check, the waitress says, "The gentleman already paid."

"What do you mean? What gentleman?"

"He left a little bit ago, but he paid your bill."

I'm stunned. I stare around at the nearly empty café, the hard light falling on the counter and booths and scuffed linoleum floor. Just a stranger doing a good deed, I tell myself.

My father used to say that, because of the work he did on missiles, he was always under surveillance. A man followed him wherever he went. Sometimes the man paid for his meal. Over the years, my father got to thinking of him as a friend, though he never, as far as he knew, laid eyes on the man. But this, this is just some strange coincidence. It has to be. I mean, right? But then I think of the stranger in Guerrero Viejo. It's too weird. My father's death has my thinking all twisted. That's all. Now, more than ever, I know I need some kind of spiritual cleansing.

Part doctor, part faith healer, part therapist, *curanderas* are mysterious women who live in the shadows of Mexico. There are people who advertise themselves as *curanderas*, who run shops and give interviews, who maintain web sites, but they're not the real thing. The real thing is the woman living at the edges, just around the corner, out of sight.

At a decent hour I drive over the line, through Piedras Negras and out into the desert until I find the landfill the moon family told me about. I smell it before I see it, the air heavy with the dull scent of death, decay, and rot. Then I see the ragged wheel of turkey vultures in the distance. Soon the paved road ends, becoming a narrow dirt track of bumps, holes, and gulleys through the landfill. The smell now is so oppressive it's like a weight in the air. The track is lined with heaps of garbage. As I pass, vultures lift off on their huge leathery wings. In the distance, huge hills of garbage covered with scavenging vultures and here and there a person with a hemp bag.

When I come to a sickly green stream with a few boards thrown over it, I park and walk the rest of the way to the *colonia*, which is up ahead in a stand of mesquite trees. A maze of twenty or thirty huts made from cardboard, chicken wire, pallets, corrugated tin, plastic sheeting, aluminum foil, and whatever else was handy at the time. They lean together, depending on each other for support. Set apart from the others, the most incongruous of all—the shell of an ATM enclosure, its windows, door, and cash machine long gone.

I walk along the passageway feeling hugely out of place. Men and women on their way to work in town avert their eyes as they pass me. A boy of about five bolts out of a doorway, flings a handle of gravel at me, then ducks back inside. They're right. I don't belong here. But I can't help it. At last I stop in front of a largely cardboard hut, standing a little distance from the doorway, and wait. After a while, the woman inside looks out fearfully. She's wearing a man's work shirt and a pair of worn jeans.

"*Desculpe me, señora. Dónde est la curandera?*"

Without a word she leads me down the passageway, another, the mesquite trees casting spiny shadows from overhead. She stops in front of a substantial-looking hut made partly from pallets patched with flattened coffee cans and shreds of plastic. Before I can reach into my pocket to give her some money, the woman turns without a word and leaves.

I knock lightly on the makeshift frame of the doorway, but there's no answer. I step back from the opening, hoping to seem less threatening. It begins to rain, just lightly. From inside I hear a rustling. Then a heavy women with a round face, high cheekbones, and very brown skin comes to the doorway.

She looks up at the sky and says, "Where I come from we call this the *chippichippi* because it's just a little spit of a rain. But I guess I better let you in before you drown, right, gringo?" Her thick black hair frames her face. She's wearing a full black skirt and a white blouse, a *huipil*, covered with elaborate embroidery.

Her name is Lunes. She comes from a village close to the Guatemalan border. The little space inside the hut is criss-crossed with light from between the slats of the shipping pallet walls. She sits me down on the dirt floor in front of a small, sweet-smelling fire. As she settles across from me, she says, "You have to talk slow with me, gringo. English hurts my head." She throws out her arms. "*Híjole*, in my village we don't even speak Spanish!"

She acts as if it's the most ordinary thing in the world for strangers to wander into her house. And it probably is. There is no power or running water in the hut, of course, and no furniture. The floor is hardpacked clay. The fire is made of cypress branches, their ends pointed together on the ground in the center of the room. Maybe it's the firelight that makes the cracked brown skin of her face look so hard. Maybe it's the life. Her eyes are dark beads of light. As we talk, she tends the fire, sliding the cypress branches farther into the flames as their ends dissolve into ash. Some of the smoke finds its way out through the gaps between the mesquite branches that make up her roof. Even so, the room fills quickly with smoke that burns my eyes and lays raw the roof of my mouth.

"Where I come from, we don't like visitors much. They say once we killed a tourist for taking pictures without permission." Lunes dips her head back and forth, smiling. "Some stories are true, some stories are false, and some stories are somewhere in-between. You know?"

"Yes," I say. "*Sí.*"

"No you don't." She says it mildly, playfully. "But that's OK. You're not alone, *mi'ijo*. I come from a place where every cloth on your back and every turn of the air is a prayer. Hey, listen to me! I made a poem! That one's free but the next one's going to cost you." Her brown face breaks into an easy smile that takes me straight into her world.

She's a big woman in her thirties who seems comfortable with her weight. Something about the confidence in her gaze tells you not to get on her bad side. She rocks a little, resettling herself, straightening her skirt.

"Every once in a while I come up north to see the strange creatures they grow here." She looks me up and down with an exaggerated tilt of her head and laughs. "It's interesting!"

Between us the fire crackles and snaps. Outside the sun rises higher, people pass the doorway, but it all seems very far away.

Her village has no name, she says, but it's near San Juan Chamula. Her mother is a Mestizo, and her father a Tzotzil. They must have been—and remain—particularly liberated parents. When Lunes was ready for school, they brought her to the more cosmopolitan San Cristóbal, wanting her to have what few women of her generation were given, an education. After secondary school, she ran away from home to Mexico City, where she worked for two years before having the money to afford to begin a university education. Her hero, of course, is Sor Juana de la Cruz, the sixteenth-century woman who disguised herself as a man in order to get an education.

"When I think of where I came from and where I am—" Lunes says, "Jesus Christ, can you imagine that? I love it!"

When she notices her skirt has opened slightly, showing a touch of the white slip under it, she adjusts it, smiling. "You have to excuse me. I wore the wrong skirt today." She wags her index finger at me in the time-honored tradition of all Mexican mothers. "If you see any more, I'm going to have to charge you extra!"

She pulls a bunch of radishes from a pocket in her skirt and sets them on the ground next to her. "It's good to be sexy, but it's better to be smart. I know what you're thinking. 'Who is this crazy indian?' You don't want to hear these things. But forgive me, *mi'ijo*, it's the indian way to go around the bushes."

A figure appears in the doorway, blocking the light, the embers of the fire only enough to make a dull glow in the sudden darkness.

The man in the doorway says something to Lunes in Tzotzil, and she answers.

To my ear, Spanish has always sounded like water moving over stones. These words sound like a breeze picking its way through the mesquite thicket, the words catching on the twigs and branches, the guttural stops similar to the ones I've heard among the Lakota. The impression is of something rare being drawn up from a great depth, from a world I'll never know.

They speak for a few minutes, their words bubbling and catching in the flickering firelight.

When the man steps away from the doorway, the room seems to stay in darkness. I feel very far away from anything I know. Even time feels far away.

Lunes says, "He wants to know about the crazy gringos. The kind who don't seem to have jobs but who seem to have all the time in the world to visit places that have nothing to do with them. People who have all the money they want to spend. People who seem to hate children, or why else don't they ever bring them? Do you always leave them home crying for *mami y papi?* Is it true every gringo man has two wives? And what is it you want to see here? Don't you have your own village? All you do is go places and stare at people. What kind of gringo are you?"

I think for a moment of my father with his two wives and shake my head, saying, "I don't know."

She nods. "Ah, the I-don't-know kind, the most common gringo of all."

I take a breath, trying to explain, to tell her something about myself, but Lunes holds up her hand, saying, "Don't bother. There's only one thing I really want to know: what is it you gringos eat that makes you so big? Is it beans? And why haven't our people started eating it yet?" When she laughs, I can't help laughing with her.

"Look, *mi'ijo*, I know why you're here. You're here for a *limpia*, a cleansing. Before we do that, I'm going to have to tell you things. Things about *curandismo*. See, there is scientific medicine and there is religious medicine. You go to your scientific doctor and what does he say? 'Here, take this antidepressant and you'll be better.' And then, when you see what antidepressants cost—*híjole!*—you get even more depressed. Christ, that stuff's worse than marijuana! Now what about the religious doctor? He doesn't seem to be a doctor at all. More like a gossip. 'How is your family?' she says. 'Getting along with the wife? The kids? How do the neighbors feel about you?' It sounds like just gossip, but all this time the *curandera* is collecting information needed for the diagnosis. Then she takes your pulse. The scientific doctor takes your pulse, but all he's listening for is bump-bump-bump. The *curandera* talks to your blood, because blood talks, brother. You'd better believe it."

All those whippings so long ago were about spiritual cleansing, he said. He was making me fit for the Lord's company, he said. Only through suffering like Christ's could I ever hope to sit at His right hand, he said. "Where you going to be on the day when I and your mother and your sister and even your snot-nosed little brother are taken into His bosom, and you're left behind with the rest of the sinners? Huh? Where you going to be on that day? You ain't ready for the Rapture, boy." When beating didn't work, he tried other things.

Even now, years later, with my father fished up dead from the sea and planted in the ground, I feel the bony grip of that teaching. I am the unclean thing.

"Heal me," I say to Lunes. I can't help myself. I stare at her. "Tell me what my blood says."

She looks at me for a while with those shiny black eyes, trying to decide which of us is crazier. Then she says something to herself in Tzotzil and lays more cypress on the fire. She focuses her dark eyes on me, getting down to business.

"First I have to see your aura." She leans back and looks me up and down in the firelight, then shakes her head. "I got to tell you, I'm supposed to see a healthy red light around your genitals. Actually, all I'm seeing there is a kind of gray."

"That's not good," I say.

"You said it, *mi'ijo*." She stares at me a while longer. "Your blues and greens are OK, but your reds and yellows are a mess." She pauses, shakes her head again. "You need a lot of work, my friend."

She stands up and goes to the wall and comes back with three eggs. She kneels down next to me and brushes my stomach with one, moving it in widening circles. "How are you and your wife getting along?"

"I'm not married."

"Your girlfriend."

"No."

"Boyfriend?"

I shake my head.

"What about you and the neighbors?"

"I don't have any neighbors."

"You're a real Mr. Popular, aren't you? What about hate? Anybody hate you? Anybody put the *mal ojo* on you?"

My look must tell her that the list is too long.

"I got to tell you these things may be the problem." She touches the egg to my forehead, then to the top of my head, skims it over my chest, down each of my arms. She does this with the other two eggs and sets each one carefully on the ground next to the fire.

"Am I a three-egg omelet?" I ask. I'm nervous. I'm starting to feel both foolish and scared.

"Joke," she says, "but there's a lot of sickness in those eggs. They're hot with it. I'd let you touch them, but then the sickness would go right back into you."

She takes up a cypress branch and brushes its leaves over me top to bottom, back and forth across my face, up and down my arms. When she lays that aside, the man who was in the doorway reappears with a live hen, puts it into her hands, and goes away. Its red and gold feathers shine in the dark. Lunes holds the hen close to me, raises it above me, circles me with it. The hen seems unconcerned, ducking its head, its beak ticking back and forth, its dark eyes shining. Only when she presses its head to the ground does it make a gurgling protest.

She mimes breaking the hen's neck. "Usually the *curandera* does like this to connect with the power of Mother Earth. I don't think you're sick enough for that." She sets the hen down and it runs complaining out into the light. Then she takes my pulse, holding my wrist in her hand like something broken. Talking to my blood, I guess.

She drops my arm and cocks her head. "Your blood is saying, 'I feel like shit.' Can't you hear it?"

"No."

She holds the palm of her hand two inches from my stomach and then moves it in slow, widening circles. "That's because you're not listening."

I think of my father, the way he stood beside my bed night after night, moving his stiff palm back and forth over my body. Is there some poison inside that he was trying to expel? Can you see me, Dad? I'm getting well at last.

Lunes keeps circling her palm in the air around me. She says, "You're going to start feeling some heat and motion in your stomach. That's good. That's OK. That's the sickness leaving. And if you don't believe it, you'd better believe it, *mi'ijo.*"

She stands up and goes to the wall again, coming back with a Pepsi bottle filled with clear liquid. She pours a double shotglass full.

"P-o-x," she spells out, "but pronounced 'posh.' Mayan cane liquor. The point is not to get drunk, only to honor Father Sun and Mother Moon." She pours the glass so full it runs down over the sides and onto the ground. The glass goes back and forth between us as she talks.

"Used to be they used peyote. The *curandera* would tell you just how much to take. Only now that's illegal. *Pox* will do. Of course, used to be that *curanderas* weren't allowed in the churches at all. Too animistic. Now that's all behind us, except for the new breed, the *evangelistas*, the Seventh Day *Adventistas*, the *Mennonitistas*, the *blahblahistas*. They all want to save us poor Godless indians from ourselves. I tell them we got plenty of gods! It's you who only have the one and his son! I tell you if Jesus Christ could see what's going on today in His name, he'd have a coronary! When the poor guy comes back, they'll probably call him a Communist and kill him all over again!"

The *pox* tastes thick, sweet, and strong. I remember reading somewhere that too much causes permanent brain damage. I decide that a doubt like that might hinder the healing process. I make a mental note never to read another book.

When she's finished, Lunes gives me two red candles and two yellow ones, instructing me to take them into a church, where I will complete my *limpia*, my spiritual cleansing.

"Aren't you coming?" I say, unable to keep the disappointment out of my voice. She's already told me the *curanderas* accompany their clients into the church.

"I don't want to be a pain on your neck, but I get sick when I go into the church for the wrong reason." Healing a gringo, I'm to understand, is the wrong reason.

She says, "I'll bury these eggs. They're too full of sickness to eat."

"What about the hen?" I ask, paying her.

"Unless you want to give it to one of your enemies, I'll let my friend kill it, cook it, and feed it to the gringos. You guys eat bad luck and sickness like it's going out of style."

• • •

Following Lunes's instructions, I find the whitewashed adobe church at a nearby village. The walls are lined with glass cabinets containing icons of saints dressed in silk robes and other finery. Banners hang from the old beams overhead. The tiled floor is covered with a carpet of pine needles. There are no benches, no pews. At first all I can see are tourists shuffling slowly down one row of saints and up the other. Then, beyond the tourists, I see a number of families, each kneeling around a forest of candles standing on the floor, wax wands like mine rising straight from the floor as if by magic. Then I see a man soften the bottom of one candle with the flame from another. There is no sound but the shuffling of feet and the soft sound of prayer.

I find myself an out-of-the-way area on the floor, then, feeling watched, check to see if my shadow from Guerrero is watching me. I light my candles. My first attempt at standing a candle fails, the lit candle falling into pine needles. I quickly right it and pat out the flaming needles, ridiculously checking again to see if anyone is watching. I have them lit and standing now, alternating red, yellow, red, yellow, just as Lunes has instructed me.

My candles are among many hundreds, most of them white, some the size of a pencil, like mine, others as tall as a conductor's baton. I look for candles the size and color of mine, thinking I'll find a sympathetic soul, someone like me. Then I feel foolish. Before I can settle into a prayer of some kind, an unshaven man with cringing eyes holds out a kerchief-covered plate and asks for a donation for Santo Bartholomeo de las Casas. I give him some money, then fold my hands and bow my head in prayer. But before I can think of the words to say, a young boy appears at my side whispering "Peso? Peso? Peso?"

The way he says it makes it sound like a combination of "please" and "pssst." It's as if he has a secret to sell, one he'll share only with me. "Peso? Peso? Peso?" I give him a peso and try again to pray over the flickering flames of my healing candles.

"This place is *so* cool! Isn't this place cool?" He's a bearded American teenager in hiking shorts and Birkenstocks, and he's talking to me. "You been to Tepotzlan?" He gestures to the young woman beside him. "Me and Sarah been. That's a heavy-duty spiritual-type place, too, just like this. But trucks! They got trucks like you wouldn't believe. And every one of them went right by our hotel. Just when you thought it couldn't get any louder, it got louder. And you'd think, OK, this's as loud as anything could ever be, and then it went and got louder!"

It suddenly occurs to me that I've forgotten to get some *pox* for the ceremony. Lunes told me it would be hard to find, that I'd have to ask around. But then I see that everyone has forgotten their *pox*. Standing in front of each petitioner is a bottle of Coke or Pepsi, Fanta or orange soda. And as I see this and as I stare up from my knees at this boy with his downy chin hair and his granola-eating grin, rage begins to fill me up like a bathtub filling with blood. What made him think it was OK to interrupt a penitent, a man trying to heal himself of, of what? Nameless dread? Dis-ease? Hopelessness? Sin? Father Fear? And who do I think I am, trying to latch onto another culture's way of spiritual renewal? But how "other" can it be if Coke and Pepsi are the primary ingredients? I blow out my puny candles, gather them up, and carry them and my sick self, my unhealed self, back outside.

It's market day in the plaza in front of the church. *Rebozos*, plastic sandals, fruit and vegetables, tools. Men stand at small wooden tables chopping flank steak, dogs standing silently at a respectful distance. I buy a bottle of Manzanita Sol from a vendor in the market because it's my favorite Mexican soda—apple flavored—and because it's my protest to Coke and Pepsi creeping into the temple. Months later I will learn that the company is owned by Pepsi. But for now, I take a few swallows. I'll wait a while and go back into the church. This will be my *pox*.

A little girl in ragged clothes appears in front of me. "*Damé disfrutas!*" she says, shaking my pant leg. *Hand over the enjoyment!* And then, louder, "*Damé disfrutas!*"

I hand over the enjoyment and watch her march off swigging my soda. A cop walks by wearing a Raiders windbreaker. From a tinny loudspeaker, Elton John's voice singing "Rocket Man" comes sailing uncertainly, fluttering the plastic pennants that hang over the plaza. A man is making careful pyramids of fruit on the pavement nearby. I decide to buy some. Fruit can make you well. I start to kneel next to a pyramid of oranges, but before I can pick one, a dog steps in front of them, looks up at me, and lifts his leg, covering the oranges with a glistening shower of pee.

I'm afraid I will never be well. I'm afraid none of us will ever be well.

❦

I myself have lived among the cannibals in the jungles of South America. And though I don't approve of their practice, I do understand it and even respect it.

It is important to know that the cannibal culture is without disease, without hatred, without greed, and with none of the human failings so common in our own world. There is no separation between rich and poor. All live in a state of absolute equality. The concept of law means nothing to the cannibal because laws are unnecessary where crime is unheard of. Theirs is the perfect society. And as if underscoring their perfection, they go about naked, with nothing to hide.

Surely there are wars, you say. Yes, there are wars. Tribe fights against tribe. The people of the valley hate the people of the mountain, and vice-versa. Such is the condition of the world since the days of Cain and Abel. But as in life so are the cannibals perfect in battle, going to war in the vestments of nakedness, with nothing for a weapon but a pointed stick. Modern warriors could learn much from the cannibal's simple courage.

It is true that the cannibals partake of human flesh. But this is not a habit, not a preference, not a staple of their diet. It falls under the heading of ritual and symbolic acts. Prisoners taken in battle are brought back to the village, where they are fed well and given every latitude allowed by a six-foot length of hemp. In time the limbs are removed, roasted, and eaten, along with the internal organs, the head and heart being considered great delicacies. Parts of the victim are passed out to others, it being a gesture of utmost respect to pass the haunch of your enemy down the dinner table. And yet there is no enjoyment during this meal. They do it to symbolize the absorption of the enemy's power and spirit. Who are we to judge this act, where men are eaten every day in business, in politics, and even unto the American family? The steps of the Temple are crowded with the unrighteous.

I have lain with them at night in many a clearing, hip-to-hip, thigh-to-thigh, cupped together like spoons in a drawer. In this way, when one woke we all woke, and none of us ended up in that night's stew.

❦

11

ENTERING THE WILD

The Henderson men are embarrassed. They're bemused, bumfuzzled, and downright flummoxed. Here they've driven all those southern miles (which are longer than northern miles, longer and hotter) in their new RV, all the way to Big Bend, and now, at the end of their journey, they can't seem to hook up the RV's septic tank to the campground's waste pipe. *Dang* septic tank. Like my father, these men say *dang*. Big Jim Henderson, the husband, makes many attempts to screw the collars of various lengths of flexible hosing onto the park fixture, but nothing seems to fit. Papa Don't-Call-Me-Grandpa Henderson frets about wear and tear on the accordion folds of the hosing. In the meantime, turkey vultures wheel overhead in lazy cartoon circles, attracted, I suppose, by the faint scent of fecal matter, a scent that grows stronger by the minute.

The turkey vulture is a carrion bird in love with dry climates. Its six-foot wingspan makes it a dramatic sight turning in lazy spirals on warm thermals, like the hawk and eagle to which it's related. Lacking a voice box, it is one of the few silent birds, though it has been known to emit a hiss or groan, proving that misery always finds a voice. The turkey vulture, adapting to the desert, gets most of its water from the carrion it feeds on, and its powerful kidneys—like those of the kangaroo rat—make it possible for it to retain most of the water otherwise lost in the process of elimination. It thermoregulates by spreading its wings, which act as heat exchangers, and by defecating on its legs. It finds food by smell, one of the few species of bird with such an ability, a sense so keen that pipeline workers use the vulture to locate leaks in natural gas lines hundreds of miles away. Putrescine Diaminobutane, the odorant added to natural gas, has the smell of rotting flesh. Like the swallows returning to Capistrano, the turkey vulture returns to its summer feeding grounds on the vernal equinox. And through means not yet understood, it somehow communicates with other vultures many miles away when it finds carrion.

The curved beak and bald head makes it easy to dig between bones and tunnel into a body's dark, wet places. It eats, of course, anything. And yet, examination of vulture stool shows no trace of disease. Somehow, the vulture's system is able to process any food source, no matter how rotten, foul, or diseased, without causing harm to itself. The vulture's technical name, *Cathartes aura*, contains a variation on the Greek word *kathartes*, which means "purifying."

"Here, honey, bring that to Mama." Pearl Henderson gestures to her little two-and-a-half-year-old, but is quickly distracted by Big Jim's call for a pair of slip-joint pliers. Little Big Jim Jr. is dragging around three cans of Coke by their plastic collar, dragging them around in a circle like a toy truck, except that the bright red cans scrape and bounce across the hot macadam. He wears a pair of training pants and a red shirt too small for him. His short blond hair is so wet with sweat that it looks as if it's been carved onto a head of clay.

I've driven to Big Bend because my father spent time here in his camper, writing about the different varieties of cacti and desert-dwelling animals. But I'm also here because I can't shake the feeling that I'm being followed, that my every move is being observed, photographed, noted. So it doesn't hurt to be in a place where I'm the only moving thing in a trackless wasteland, except for the Hendersons, I guess.

Besides, I want to see what life is like in the toe of Texas. I've been to state parks before, and so I thought I knew what I was headed for. The difference between the state parks I know and Big Ben is the difference between the moon and a Moon Pie. In fact, that's what it most resembles to me, a lunar landscape. Not quite as drained of color but almost, even the green of the cactus seeming to vaporize into the shimmering heat. It's hot as in skillet hot, red-hot, hot damn hot. We're all way past sweaty, especially the Henderson men, at least the two older ones.

I've told them I'm a writer looking for insight into the camping life, especially at Big Bend, which is pretty much the truth, though I wouldn't mind being offered one of the bouncing Cokes before nothing short of a bomb squad can open it. But the Hendersons are suspicious and way too caught up in their wrestling match with the waste pipe.

"Mama? Mama?"

No one has any patience for Little Big Jim Jr. The goal is to get the line hooked up, climb inside the RV, pump up the air-conditioning, flip on the portable TV, and enjoy their camping trip like civilized human beings. I can poke fun, but after three nights on the hard ground in an Army-surplus tent, I would enjoy a little of that sybaritic life. Can I just lie on the floor a while? You can step over me, if you need to. Hell, you can step on me, for all I care, only just please let me lie under a cascade of that sweet frozen air. But I haven't wormed my way into the Henderson heart yet. And I've already been on the road so long that I probably look like a tabloid headline waiting to happen, especially after seventy-two mostly sleepless hours, where the mercury stayed above 90 even in the dead waste and middle of the night. I tried sleeping in the tent, on the picnic table, on the ground itself. I even jumped into my car and started up the air-conditioner for a few minutes, just to get some life back into me, like a diver coming up for a few swallows of air. And each morning I awoke from a half-doze, coated with a permanent gel of sweat and surliness. So no, I do not blame the Hendersons for not warming to me right away. And I have to say that their wrestling match with the waste problem is making the RV seem less and less like a haven and more and more like a port-o-johnny on wheels.

"Birdy? Birdy? Birdy!"

Little Big Jim Jr.'s bleak bleat makes us turn, expecting to see, at worst, a pinhole spray of Coke whizzing from a dented can. Not quite.

The turkey vultures have landed, three of them, with their big Dracula wings and their evil red eyes and their bald red heads and their scrotal-looking throats. Then it gets worse.

As we watch, one of them waddles across the macadam and hooks an empty ring of the soda collar in its beak. An outraged squawk from Little Big Jim Jr. Then the tug-of-war begins. The sweaty blond toddler against the Darth Vader of birds. And we just stand there, too stunned to do anything. Little Big Jim Jr. sets his fat little legs like a bull-dogger's, and with his pudgy, white-knuckled fists, holds tight to one empty ring. The vulture has snagged the opposite ring in its hooked beak. The Coke cans dangle brightly between them. It looks like a pretty even struggle until the vulture flaps those big coffin wings and back-pedals, pulling Little Big Jim Jr. toward him. Through it all, the Hendersons and I stand there like rubes at our first freak show.

"BIRDY!" Little Big Jim Jr. croaks. "B . . . I . . . R . . . D . . . Y!"

In reply, the vulture gives its wings a vicious snap that pulls him a step closer.

It's then that I leap into action, not really because I'm such a hero. I want one of those Cokes. I want to be lying on the tasteless orange shag of that camper. I run toward the birds, waving my arms and squawking. The other two skitter back a few feet, but Darth, the point bird, just keeps tugging until I'm nearly on him. Only then does he drop his end of the battle, causing Little Big Jim Jr. to plop down suddenly on his sodden training pants, his pale face collapsing with grief and fear and the plain injustice of it all. Before it turns away to flap-walk back to its friends, the vulture gives me a disgusted look. I wonder, though, if there's any other kind of look a vulture can give.

When I pick up Little Big Jim Jr. to carry him back to the fold, he screams and squirms as if *I'm* the threat. I deliver him into his mother's arms. I've saved her child. The least she can do is offer me a Coke, a little lie-down in the cool camper. No. Little Big Jim Jr. is crying harder now about the bad man and about the fall and about his mother taking the Cokes away and about the birdy, birdy, birdy.

"Well," I say, mustering up what I hope is a good impression of the modest desert hero, "I guess I've bothered you good people enough."

Oh no! Come in for a Coke and a little nap!

When they say nothing, I realize they're probably blaming me for every miserable moment of their vacation so far. I should have let the birdy fly off with Little Big Jim Jr. dangling from his offal-encrusted beak, an Addams family version of the stork.

• • •

With 801,000 acres of mountains and desert, Big Bend forms part of the U.S.-Mexico border in west Texas, following the Rio Grande for over 100 miles. On the map, it resembles nothing so much as a woman's foot delicately entering a nylon stocking. A place of limestone canyons, pale mesas, and a desert floor as hot as August in hell. A place larger than most European nations and only slightly more populated than the moon. And rock. Lots of rock. The Mescalero Apaches say that, after he made the earth, the Great Spirit dumped all his leftover building materials in one place, creating Big Bend. And in the 16th and 17th centuries, Spanish explorers looking for gold, silver, and—let's face it—anything they could lay hands on, called it the "Uninhabited Land." The Chisos ("Ghost") Mountains testify to this, standing tall and pale in the distance, omnipresent, haunting. You get the feeling, in Big Bend, that for all its lack of population, someone is always standing behind you. And someone—or some thing—is. A lot of good it did to come here.

Maybe it's the desert life watching from a millimeter of shadow. The more time you spend in the desert, the more you become aware of its teeming plant and animal life, some of it approaching the paranormal—desert amphibians like the spadefoot toad, the mosquito fish, and the kangaroo rat with its ability to metabolize water from the hydrogen in the seeds it eats and the air it breathes. Or think of more well-known desert dwellers—the flight-eschewing roadrunner, a chicken with an attitude and a fitness club membership; the jackrabbit, whose ears radiate heat away from its body (watch and you can see the waves shimmering off them); and the secretive coyote, outlaw of the desert. Or the turkey vulture itself, never very far from a prospective meal. And everything out here is a prospective meal.

Or maybe it's the Chisos Mountains themselves, standing quietly in the distance, watching like Orson Welles from the doorway in *The Third Man*, eager to share with you its little secret.

Or the desert itself. Some deserts—in Arizona, for instance—don't seem haunted at all. In fact, they're on their best behavior, just waiting for the right developer to come along. But the west Texas desert wants you dead. Whirl around and it hides. Not the desert but the imp of the desert.

Or maybe it's the guy who confronted you in Guerrero, or the one who paid for your breakfast in Eagle Pass. Watching through binoculars, satellites, sniper scopes.

Or maybe it's your dead father himself following you through his old haunts, biding his time, not yet ready to light into you or to lighten up on you. The dead hand of the past, etc. I think again of Keats:

This living hand, now warm and capable of earnest grasping would, if
it were in the icy silence of the tomb, so haunt thy days and chill thy
dreaming nights that thou wouldst wish thine own heart dry of blood
and thou be conscience-calmed.

What a wonderful word, "conscience-calmed." There are no calm consciences in the desert. You're either desperate as a lizard or you're dead.

And you, Dad? Are you up there in the mountains watching, those mountains like the shredded gray garments of the long-dead? Are you the desert's hot breath when it barely stirs? The empty hours baking in the sun?

• • •

I'm having lunch at the Chisos Mountain Lodge, headquarters for the park, the place you go when you miss the sound of human voices. It's also where you get your postcards and, if you've had enough of life as a sandfly, a motel room with air conditioning. I'm tucking into a roast beef sandwich to build up my strength for a hike with a park ranger. I'm nervous. If I'm being watched anywhere, it's here. But I can't help it. I'm too hungry. I can't help listening to the conversation at the next table. Hell, the truth is I live for eavesdropping.

The couple are dividing up the postcards they've bought.

"Aunt Flo," the wife says. "We forgot a card for Aunt Flo."

"*Now* you tell me," the husband says. Just then the waitress comes over and the man says, "*Quiero* burger plate."

"*Con queso?*" the waitress asks. *With cheese?*

The husband says, "Is it extra?"

"The burger plate's three ninety-five," the waitress says.

"All right! I'll have it with cheese!"

"Without, it's three thirty-five."

"Oh," the man says, "then I don't want no cheese. *Hablar?*" It's the wrong word, and he says it as if he's hacking up phlegm. "*No con queso!*"

The wife leans forward over the fan of postcards in her hand. "Isn't this place great?"

Her husband nods. "Yeah. Why stay down the road for sixty-five dollars when you can stay here for sixty-four?" Then he looks away. "Remember that plate of gizzards and livers in Bracketville? Only seven dollars with a side of gravy and fries. Now that was good eating!"

The woman said what she said in order to distract the man from his cheapness. But the man's teeth are so deep into the dollar that he turns even that into an occasion to tote up his savings. What I love, though, is that until the waitress told him the price of the hamburger without cheese, he thought he was getting a bargain. Is there some philosophical or psychological truth here? Something about relativity? Something to do with not being able to measure the value of a thing until you know the value of another thing?

My father covered all these nomad miles in his camper, and all along the way he kept his journal, which I dip into now and then. Most of it, though, has to do with the price of things. The price of oranges in Chihuahua compared to the price of oranges in Phoenix. A cup of coffee in Ruidoso, a cup of coffee in Marfa. Maybe it's too easy to dismiss someone as a cheapskate. Maybe they're only taking the measure of the world in the only way they know how. Maybe that's all any of us is doing. I mean, if quantifying is such a bad thing, what do I think I'm doing retracing routes traveled by my father? What can that tell me about this man? Who am I kidding?

I guess I think if I can stand on the precise spot where my father once stood, if I can find the exact coordinates, my feet angled in the same direction as his, my eyes aimed at the same vista, then maybe I can finally get him. Get behind his eyes, I mean. Behind the burning gaze. Behind the rock of his rage. But it's not working. My reasoning's wrong, my motives mangled. Maybe you can't ever truly know another person. Especially a father. Especially a father in uniform.

• • •

After lunch, I take a cold soda outside to a shady spot near a maintenance man taking a break. Oscar has just tried to take his break inside, but the guards and his female supervisor won't let him, and now he's squatting in the shade, watching her. She sits in the glass-walled room, watching television. Inside, it's dark and cool. He isn't a regular maintenance man; he's a *diablo*, a prison trustee on work release. Wherever they go, they go single-file, like ducklings. Oscar is the crew leader. The rest of his crew are nearby, sitting in the shade of the van that brought them, sitting under the gaze of two armed guards. Oscar sits away from them to show he's different and because he can. "Let the guards do their thing," he says. "Me, I can't stand the smell of canned meat." Prison inmates. Oscar is a slight but muscular man with a sinewy smile. Looking at his brown arm, I can't help thinking of beef jerky. He's watching the supervisor, can't get his mind off her. He's sitting on his heels like a farmer, rocking slightly, gazing steadily and malevolently at the woman watching television. Not once does he look at me.

"Know what she's doing in there? Just watching a movie. She'll sit there for two hours just watching a damn movie. I seen that *Godfather 1, 2, 3*. That's a good movie. Yeah. I seen that five times. I can see that again. How about that *Dorf on Golf*? That's funny. That little short guy? That's funny. I seen that. Big old woman sitting there. I can see her cheek marks on the sofa. *Sopranos*? That's some damn movie. *Pow Wow Highway*? Couple of indians driving, drinking, smoking weed? Funny movie. I seen *The Simpsons*. I seen *Beavis & Butthead*."

I can't figure out what he's doing. Is he toting up his qualifications for watching TV in that cool room, in the dark with a woman? Does he really think the guards should let him do that, trustee or not?

"That's what she's doing in there, just watching a movie. I ought to call in an emergency. I ought to. You see that *Goodfellas*? Now *that's* a kick-ass movie. Yeah. That guy's a vicious fucker. You remember that guy? That guy that shot him in the foot? Killed that kid? Yeah. That's a kick-ass movie. I could see that a couple of times. See *Raising Arizona*? That's a good movie."

"What's that?" I say, just to see if I can get him to look at me. "Like Cheech and Chong?"

Without breaking his gaze, he says, "Nah, nah. Different. It's good. You know a good damn movie is that Civil War movie, that twelve-hour-long Civil War movie. Twelve hours, you know, it's like on three tapes or something. Lasts as long as the *pinché* war. Not really. It's twelve hours but you don't know it's twelve hours. You don't think it's twelve hours."

I say, "Probably makes the time go by quicker. The time inside."

Now, at last, he looks at me, one corner of his mouth curling down. I'm out of line. I've reminded him of what he's trying to forget, if only for a little while.

To change the subject, I point out a wheel of vultures against the sky. "Yeah," he says, "there's always something dying out here." He stands up. "You see that Jackie Chan?" He slices at the air with the blades of his hands. "That's some damn movie." He looks at his men. "I got to get on over there and put those *chingas* back to work. I ought to call that emergency number, though. I really ought to. *Oralé, cabrones!*"

His men struggle to their feet and step out their cigarettes. They look like any other men being called to work, not especially liking it. Has to be better than time behind bars, though maybe that's relative, too. Like telling the paraplegic it could have been worse.

• • •

I join a band of diehard hikers adorned with bandoliers of water bottles and wearing T-shirts from other epic climbs and hikes. A few of them look like this, anyway. Most of us spend our days leashed to a desk, and it shows. One couple wears matching purple jogging suits that whisper with each swipe of their legs, the sound somehow making the air seem all the hotter. One guy keeps trying to make calls on his cell phone, cursing the desert when he can't get a signal. A robust-looking couple from Minnesota have brought their two little bare-legged kids with them, their delicate, spindly legs looking like lunch for mosquitoes or even the mountain lion someone claims to have spotted near the lodge. Our guide's name is Susan. She wears the regulation brown uniform of the ranger, complete with ranger hat, a flat-brimmed peaked affair that looks as though it would decapitate a saguaro if thrown just so.

We start out, Susan warning us to stay on the path, to keep close tabs on "our youngest hikers." As she tries to explain the various plant and animal life of the desert, one of the kids, the one with the face like a closed fist, keeps talking. Loud. "Yeah, yeah, yeah. Blah, blah, blah. I want to go home. I want to go home. I want to go home *now*."

Susan stops the lecture and politely asks, "Do you think I can talk now?" But before she can even get the request out, the boy says, "I know, I know." And before long he's back at it, complaining about the heat, complaining about wanna-go-home, complaining about the ranger who won't let him wear her hat.

He takes a big lunging step to punctuate each word. "I." Step. "Want." Step. "To." Step. "Go." Step. "Home." And it has nothing to do with the mountain lion and everything to do with *I want* and *now*. Within half a mile I'm hoping the mountain lion will do us all a favor and take the kid out.

Susan teaches us some home-truths about desert life, how a rattler will try to avoid you, only striking when it feels cornered. How the scorpion has survived for three-hundred-million years. How an arthropod called the vinegaroon, also known as the whip-scorpion, defends itself by secreting a vinegar-smelling acid from an anal gland. In Mexico the creature's considered a sign of good luck, since finding one in the house means finding no more cockroaches. Susan teaches us how there are more types of birds in Big Bend than in any other park in the country, over four hundred distinct species, including summer tanager, painted bunting, flycatcher, cardinal, sandpiper, killdeer. I can't help thinking of the bird couple of Matamoros, wishing I could share this with them, which is really, I think, a way of saying I wish I could share this—could share anything—with my father.

My favorite desert plant is the cactus known as the "century plant." It's the source of mescal (also tequila, mescal's more refined sibling), that mind-numbing concoction for which the mescalero Apaches are named, but that's not why I like it. The Apaches used the heart of the century plant for food, waiting until just before the plant was about to go into its cataclysmic growth spurt. Wait for it. Wait for it. Now! Cut out the heart, bake it, dry it, and reduce it to a paste. Live on that, but let some of it ferment to create mescal. Hey, it may not be *my* reason for liking the plant, but it's *a* reason.

So important was the century plant to the Apaches that Spanish conquerors, afraid to do battle with them, conquered them by destroying their hordes of food.

And yet, not even the century plant's historical importance is its most fascinating feature. Neither is its use as a hallucinogen.

What's most fascinating is its strange growth cycle, the way it will stand all but dormant for, according to legend, a hundred years (though it's actually more like thirty or fifty) and then, exactly like the speaker at the end of James Wright's wonderful poem "A Blessing," it breaks into blossom. It produces masses of flowers, thousands of them, attracting orioles, hummingbirds, insects, and ladderback woodpeckers, who literally set up housekeeping in the plant. At night, the flowers are pollinated by nectar-eating bats.

I don't know any other way to describe this sudden, self-consuming growth phase except to say that the century plant makes a party of itself, a suicidal one since all the wild effort of its growth results in its own death. Once the party's over, and after all the birds leave, wind rides down the shallow-rooted plant, and insects take up residence. In this last stage of the century plant's life, it resembles nothing so much as a crumbling casino bar in a forgotten corner of Boys Town.

Physically, it's Oliver Hardy to the tall wand of ocotillo's Stan Laurel. How and why does such a thing exist? It's said that you can tell when the growth phase is about to hit by the heat thrown from the plant's heart, heat so strong you can feel it. Hold your hand just here. Feel it radiating from the core? That's what I'm talking about. And once the growth phase has begun, the plant's been known to grow nine to fifteen inches in a day. It's the miser, hoarding money all its life, only to spend it, spray it, shotgun it all over town on the last day of his life. It's the terminal cancer patient who laughs at death by throwing herself one last party. It's the old-age pensioner who has saved and scraped all his life to afford that cruise to Cancún, only to be struck down by a heart attack after the last meal of the last leg of the voyage, a smile playing on her falling face, her last words "... worth it."

What is this plant thinking? Saving itself, saving itself, then *kaboom*! Maybe its wild growth is like the beautiful eyelashes of starving children— long, luxurious, a model's dream, but made that way, like their big bellies, by starvation itself—nature's cheap trick, the tackiest of ironies. The century plant goes from a Mao jacket and cap to a fat man in a loud Hawaiian shirt with plaid Bermudas and white penny loafers. I mean, who *is* this guy?

Want cheese with that?
Oh, yeah, baby, do I!
It costs . . .
Don't care!
Without cheese, it's . . .
Never mind the dime, darlin'! Bring it on! You hear me? I said bring it on!

My favorite desert animal is the javelina, a sociable beast who travels in small herds of eight or ten, always hungry, always on the move. They look like pigs, or more like wild boars, but don't tell them that. They may look like pigs, move like pigs, root like pigs, but they are not pigs. Pigs are Old World animals. Javelina are New World. Found in Central and South America mostly, they are what they are, not derivative of anything. Naturalists know them as "collared peccaries," named for the striking band of black around their necks, like the collar of a V-neck sweater. Originally a jungle dweller, the javelina doesn't like cold, preferring a nice, dry desert. They're picky eaters, never stooping to insects or lizards, lechugilla and prickly pear being their foods of choice and the source of ninety percent of their fluids. Lechugilla is a plant so fibrous that early explorers brought it home to use in the making of high-quality paper.

Pigs, of course, will eat anything that fits into their mouths, including their young, hence the deep insult javelina feel at being mistaken for them. I like javelinas because they're not predatory, because they're fairly ugly, they're smart, and because they're rarely seen. Call up some javelina pages on the internet and you'll find blurry images of something scooting behind a tumbleweed, of a field of tall grass with a reassuring caption: "Trust me—there's a javelina in there!" I like them because they don't pose for pictures and because they're relatively unknown outside their territory. At various times of my life, I've given up meat, but even in my most carnivorous phases, I'd never eat javelina, not even at the Luchenbach Chili Cook-Off. I once visited someone in San

Antonio who had a stuffed javelina as a hassock. And as he propped his big snakeskin boots on its back, it was all I could do to keep from pitching the guy out his own window. The javelina is a magic animal, and you just don't kill, eat, or decorate with a magic animal. Are we clear on that?

After the hike, back at the lodge, I've had enough of the majestic heights and scaly varmints of Big Bend. I've heard all I want about how it was once a fertile savannah and before that a swamp. How now only the garfish and turtles testify to this ancient history, when crocodiles swam here with prehistoric hippos. Now that we're back, all in a low-grade hypnotic state—whether from the grandeur of the place or from Susan's plummy voice or from simple dehydration—the little boy in his too-loud voice says, "Why does everything look so *dead?*"

Taped to the wall behind the counter in the gift shop:

FAVORITE TOURIST QUESTIONS
- *What did the Indians worship in kivas—their own made-up religion?*
- *Why did the Indians decide to live in Texas?*
- *Why did the Indians only build ruins?*
- *Did people live here, or only Indians?*

It's with these words that I return to my campsite at the all-but-deserted Rio Grande Village, twenty miles away, vultures whirling up from a carcass every few miles, the occasional rattler sunning itself on the hot pavement, at times requiring me to drive onto the shoulder to avoid flattening them. Hardly any sign of people. Cutbacks in funding have been so deep that the park can't even afford to keep a ranger down here these days. This means there's no one to collect fees. I take this as a bit of luck, then feel bad to be like Mr. Cheeseburger, to be like my father. *A pack of cigarettes in Laredo, a pack of cigarettes in Nuevo Laredo.*

• • •

I had pitched my tent on dry, cracked ground with here and there a fistful of struggling grass. But when I get back to the campsite, I find my tent clinging by one slender peg to the hard ground, the rest pulled out by wind, by kids, by someone upset that there's nothing inside worth stealing. Or it could have been the tent pegs themselves, slender wire curls that bend as you push them into the ground. Hardly my idea of a tent peg. There are a few other campsites scattered around, but I'm in no mood for new acquaintances. I restake the tent and lie down on the picnic table for a brief nap, hoping for a little air. I doze off, waking suddenly when I sense them.

There they are, the vultures, one on the lid of a garbage can, one on the low branch of a piñon pine, the third still circling above me. Are they the same ones from before? And overhead, more, circling, cross-sectioning my part of the park, signaling—no doubt—to faraway friends, nature's equivalent to a neon sign blinking *EAT . . . EAT.* I jump up and wave my arms, yelping, "Not dead yet! Not dead yet!" The birds on the ground flap off. The ones overhead, not yet convinced, continue their lazy spirals.

It occurs to me, watching them, that they're patrolling the park from the air in a way very similar to the way a hunting dog will quarter a field for pheasant, the way the Coast Guard runs a search pattern over the ocean when looking for a drowning victim. I used to live on the ocean in northern California, on the bluff right above the beach. An incredible place. The house shook with every breaking wave. And once in a while one of the commercial fisherman would fall overboard. In that part of the ocean, depending on the season, you die of hypothermia in about twenty minutes. Most of the fishermen couldn't swim. I'd see the Coast Guard helicopter flying patterns over the waves and know that another fisherman was down.

The realization comes to me like a blow. My father died this way. My father drowned, this man I hardly knew. He might as well have been one of the drowned fishermen. Is that the way they found my father's body, I wonder? The slow quartering of the ocean? They found him three miles from the spot where his sailboat was hung up on the jetty. Somehow the connection of my father's death, the Coast Guard searches for bodies, and the vultures regarding me as their next meal makes me feel altogether too close to my father. I want to understand him, but I don't want to feel his dead hand on my shoulder.

The whole idea of this trip has begun to seem like a colossal act of stupidity.

I'm not the only person, surely, whose mind clears when he hits the open road. There's something about leaving your life behind that frees you to consider all kinds of other ideas and possibilities, other lives. And there's the idea of borders. I could never quite find the one that existed between my father and me, and now that he's dead, I'm not sure I ever will. How do you get it through your head that your father has died, a man who'd been pretty much out of your life for over thirty years? How has his death changed anything? I mean, he was dead before he died. I should have gone to Key West. I should have stood over his dripping corpse. Then I'd know. Instead, I'm tracing this line between worlds—the U.S. and Mexico, my father and me. Somehow it seems that the careful tracing of this line, this wound between worlds, is the only way I might learn something about my father and what I feel about him.

My father's love was so conditional I'm not sure you can call it love. More like conditional regard. Ah, do I hear a flock of violins sawing out cheap sympathy? This is not about self-pity, I think, I hope. I'm just trying to understand the man. Things happened as they happened. I don't have an irrational desire to change what can't be changed. I just want to understand it. To understand, for instance, why I am a person so distrustful of happiness and stability. To understand why my first thought at good news is always to anticipate how the good thing will go bad. I wonder if it has something to do with my father, something to do with growing up poor. Or is it no more than an imbalance of ingredients in my neurological soup?

When something bad happens in a family, the bad thing becomes a possibility for others in the family. If Uncle Charlie commits suicide, surviving family members suddenly have one more item on the menu of life's delights. Until he takes his life, maybe no one else in the family considers that possibility. Suicide is a locked room in the mind's house. But then Uncle Charlie gives you the key, and suicide becomes a possibility.

The same thing is true for other family tragedies. One divorce in the family makes other divorces possible. Abuse, abuse. Abandonment, abandonment. Exile, exile. Sometimes I think most of my life's effort has been to shake free of patterns I inherited from my family. When my parents were divorced, in 1960, I didn't realize that was a possibility in life, that a parent could up and leave. And the pattern of ritual violence that preceded the divorce made it clear that my father was leaving because he was deeply dissatisfied with me in particular. It wasn't hard to conclude that I had destroyed the family. The result was a deep-seated dissatisfaction with the way things are, starting with myself. Very hard to be happy under those conditions. When the good thing happens, you don't feel you deserve it, and anyway, it's almost never good enough. And even when it is, don't get attached; before you know it, someone will take it all away. You end up feeling that there's an invisible barrier between you and happiness, between where you are and where you want to be. And that's the border I'm most interested in crossing. Ah me, look at this sorry sight. I've become what writer Stephanie Vaughn calls a middle-aged pathetnoid.

It's still early, even after I put the tent right, but I settle down for another sultry night. Too hot to read. Too hot for anything but trying to lie as still as possible. I have become skilled at detecting the merest thread of moving air and enjoying the hell out of it. I lie there feeling the muscles around my eyes grow tighter and tighter. I roll over on my stomach. Worse. I decide to record night sounds on my tape recorder. I hear birds. I hear the rumble of the bad plumbing in the campground's bathroom. I hear burros braying across the Rio Grande.

And then I hear something else. Footsteps but lighter. Many. Bodies moving through the brush, coming into my clearing. The guy from Guerrero has brought friends. This is it. They're through talking, threatening. They're coming closer, not at all careful of the noise they're making. I'm a dead man. The only weapon

I have is the tape recorder, which I leave running in case I have a chance to shout out a description of my killers before they gun me down.

The steps come closer. Any minute, I'm expecting, bullets will come tearing through the tent. Something strange about the footsteps, though, the way they seem to go side-to-side as they move forward, like someone dancing. And the way they seem to move so low to the ground. Commandos moving in for the kill. Don't ask me how I can tell. You see, when you're on the edge of death like this, all your senses heighten. I guess. And then I hear breathing—short ragged breaths, snorts, snuffling, the wet snap of jaws. And then they're at the tent. I smell the musk, the wildness. I retreat to the center of the tent, holding out my tape recorder, too afraid to speak, to move, to do anything. And I feel, seem to see, thick horned snouts prying up the edges of the tent, rooting underneath, the sides of the tent thrumming with each thrust. I curse the spindly wire pegs that came with the tent, picturing the whole thing rooted up and me dragged off into the desert rolled up inside like a Christmas tamale. It's only then, accepting the certainty of death, that I remember Susan's lecture on the flora and fauna of the desert. It's then that I realize my visitors are javelinas, a herd of them, sweeping through the campground, foraging. I know they can be nasty if cornered or surprised, so I keep still and let them look for whatever food they can find. I hear them crunching something hard, like the cold coals of an old campfire. It's not me they're looking for, it's whatever might be under my tent. I must have pitched it right in the middle of their hunting trail. I'm awake all night, long after they've gone, too scared to move, even to close my eyes. At one point, I poke my head out of the tent and see a skunk walking past, a moose in the distance. Impossible. I must be hallucinating. Maybe all of this, even my father's death, is no more than a bad dream.

But in the morning, I climb out of my tent to find that the broad path of the javelina herd divides right around my tent; that the few other campers are gone, having slipped off quietly in the night; and that, according to a surprised ranger I come upon, what I took last night for the rumble of bad plumbing was the sound of the prowling mountain lion. And I realize then that I have entered the wild.

❧❧

Today I placed my camper in secure storage; disabled its functional electric, water, and gas circuits; purchased $1,500 in travelers checks; and crossed the Mexican border in order to travel by bus to Chihuahua. I find my way to Immigration and use my passport to obtain a six-month Tourist Permit, not knowing for certain just where my travels will take me (a Tourist Permit is not required for travel along the border, but I'm going to let my spirit of adventure be my guide). I pass through Customs and find the bus station (Central de Autobuses) after inflicting my fumbling Spanish on several innocent locals. I purchase my ticket and begin the long, long journey to Chihuahua, with possible excursions south as my fancy, mistakes, and the whims of the drivers took me.

The bus is one of their best, an older Greyhound type, all seats reserved. However, it is quite beat up and the windshield glass, as well as several other windows, is cracked and pitted. The toilet has a busted bowl so the door is locked. These conditions obtain on many of the buses, but the locals are much worse than the expresses.

Heading along the highways and byways at break-neck speeds, we stop at some villages and all cities. Often I am the only gringo on the bus.

Contrary to popular opinion in the U.S., there are no live animals on the buses. However, raw meat, fresh produce, and many other items are common passengers. My bus has two drivers. The off-duty driver sleeps in the luggage compartment beneath the bus, which is rigged with a hammock for his comfort. I confess it looked more comfortable than my seat. Vendors serve the passengers at every stop except late at night. I find that the stops vary in length and, although the driver always tells us how long he plans to stay, I need to follow his lead because when he's ready to go, we go.

At one stop, I go inside the bus station for a walk and snacks. The station toilets charge 100 pesos and the door attendant hands me only enough tissue for three swipes. When I'm ready to return to the bus, I find the station exit barred by Police. They search my bag, charging me 100 pesos to do so but the fee includes a pleasant view of my bus heading into the glorious Mexican sunset.

Eventually, with the aid of another driver and another bus, I arrive at Chihuahua, a large inland city. I spent time here several years ago and didn't care for it then either. They brag on the purity of their drinking water. I lack the courage to make a test.

∽∾✒∽

12

AMOR PROHIBIDO

I pull into the dusty parking lot of the trading post at Lajitas, kill the engine, and sit there while the engine ticks and the car fills with heat and the dust cloud I churned up drifts out into the thin blue desert air. This trip is a mistake, a big mistake. I feel like the detective who gets it wrong, who talks to all kinds of people, gathers all kinds of evidence. At every gas station, diner, and *tienda*, he asks, "Have you seen him? Have you seen this man?" But in the end he finds he's been searching for the wrong one—for the dead man instead of the killer. Idiot. But I still keep at it, flashing the picture of my father.

As I climb out of the car, I hear loud voices, a fight inside the store.

Two men in the green uniforms of the Border Patrol. One of them backs a rugged-looking guy against a shelf full of canned vegetables. An illegal, I figure, though he's taller than most Mexicans. The guy's face is tanned and lined—weather-worn. He's got a big droopy fu manchu. The other agent stands at the counter staring at the clerk, fixing him where he stands, daring him with his eyes to make a move. When I come in, without looking, the agent points at me and then at the floor next to him. When I come to his side like an obedient dog, he says, "Stay calm, brother." Just then, his partner slams the other guy up against the shelves so hard that half a row of creamed corn falls to the floor.

A career with borders, but no boundaries, says the recruiting poster. Now I see what that means.

The partner grabs the rugged-looking man by his shirt-front and bounces him against the shelves. More cans dive to the floor. "*De dónde eres?*" *Where are you coming from?*

With a growl from the cracked desert of his face, the man holds out a crumpled sack and says, "I just come from seeing your wife. She says you forgot your lunch."

The agent knocks the bag out of his hand and gives the guy a quick, light slap on the cheek, an attention-getter, so light it's almost effete, a challenge to duel. But I can see that the life has gone out of the agent's game. The man has no accent, unless you count that trace of Chicago. And no Mexican would say such a thing to La Migra. The agent lets go of the guy's wadded shirtfront and wipes his hands on his own shirt like he's just touched a turd.

"Good day, gentlemen," he says with ear-popping politeness. And as soon as that, they're gone.

The rugged guy peels himself off the wall of shelves and comes to the counter, his eyes on the door. He reaches into a cooler next to the counter, pulls out a longneck, and points it at the clerk.

"I'm having me a beer, Ricky. Shit, I'm having me a *lot* of beers. And I'm not paying for a damn one of them. And son, if you got a problem with that, you got a problem with me."

The clerk, a guy in his twenties with black hair, holds his palms up, smiles, and shakes his head. "I'll just say the border boys took 'em." He fishes out two more longnecks and hands me one.

They talk tough, but I can see they're shaken up.

For the next couple of hours, we work hard to empty the case. I hear about every unjust detention—real and imaginary—that they have to tell. How one Mexican has to swim the river every day to get to his job on this side, then swim back every evening. "And all he's doing is trying to make a living!" Dietrich says. Dietrich is the tall one I took for a Mexican. Despite being as brown and twisted as a mesquite branch, it turns out he *is* from Chicago. His shirt is worn so thin, the purple paisleys are just a hazy memory. His jeans are so worn and molded to his body that they look as though he put them on once, twenty years ago, and has never taken them off.

"How'd you end up down here?" I ask him.

A shadow falls across his eyes. He leans in and whispers, "It ain't safe to say." The closer you get to the border—and the store pretty much sits right on it— the more marginal everything becomes, even and especially the people. Now Dietrich's working as a guide for hunters and amateur archaeologists. He's tracked all kinds of desert wildlife, including javelina. I tell him about my brush with the animal, but well before I finish, I can see from red-rimmed impassive eyes that he is not impressed. When I finish, his face clicks forward a half-inch. "That it? That your story? No killin'? No maimin'? No nekkid women?" I make a mental note to stop talking so much and start listening more.

Dietrich's a star. He's been in one movie, a western, as an extra. In nearby Terlingua, a ghost town now mostly catering to tourists but once used for many Hollywood westerns. "They hired me because they said they wanted the face of an authentic Mexican," Dietrich says with a raspy chuckle, his desert rebirth complete.

Ricky Eggles, the *bueno* guy working the counter, is good-looking, with a neatly trimmed moustache, a dark blue button-down shirt, and jeans so new it looks like it must hurt when he bends his knees.

He says, "This trading post is situated flat smack on the Commanche War Trail, the same trail Pancho Villa used to make his raids on Texas border towns." I'm inclined to believe him. Outside, in the sandy gully where I parked, I can imagine the hoof prints of a band of marauders sweeping down on us. This is an impression reinforced by the bullet holes in the front of the store and inside, all over the walls. They're very impressive, the bullet holes. "Pancho Villa's bullet holes," Ricky says. It's an old store and an old story. It could be true.

As if reading my mind, Dietrich kills another beer and says, "And it's the truth, whether it happened or not."

"Listen," I say, pulling the picture of my father out. "You ever see him around here?'

Dietrich takes the picture and studies it, then passes it to Ricky without saying anything.

Ricky looks at it and says, "This guy? Yeah, I see him all the time." He flips the picture of my father back to me.

"Are you sure?" I can't believe what he's telling me.

"Sure I'm sure. The Commander, right?"

I can't believe it. I mean, his journal describes his passing through Lajitas on his way south, but I didn't think I'd really find any trace of him.

Ricky's still talking. "For a while there I was seeing him every weekend I went down. Haven't seen him for a while now, though."

"Down where?"

"Chihuahua, man. My second home. Where I make my nooky-runs."

Like most things on the border, the store is and isn't what it seems. It *is* on the Commanche War Trail. Pancho Villa *did* use it as a crossing place. Are the bullet holes really his? Are they bullet holes at all, or something tricked up for tourists with a variable speed drill and a little ingenuity? Did Ricky really know my father? Or is he telling me the story I want to hear? The story that should be true, whether it is or not?

"You come with me to Chihuahua, we can probably find him."

Brave as he was in front of the border patrol, Dietrich won't come with us to Chihuahua. "There's places I can't show my face," he says. "One's Chicago. Another'n's Chihuahua." So Ricky and I make plans to meet tomorrow and drive to the bus station in Presidio. I'm bracing myself for several hours in the desert on a rickety bus full of livestock.

The actual bus is an air-conditioned double-decker with two attendants distributing magazines and selling tacos. The movie showing on several drop-down monitors is a dubbed version of *Judge Dredd*. Too strange.

I buy us a couple of tacos. Ricky shares his flask of bourbon. Every time he unscrews the cap, he lifts the flask and says, "To the Commander!"

My father, of course, is dead, dragged lifeless and water-logged onto the deck of a Coast Guard cutter. But the hope that Ricky can lead me to him is too rich to allow the truth to interfere. But once, for the toast, Ricky raises the flask and says, "To Commander Bond. James Bond."

I pull out the picture again. "You know him, right?"

"Know him? Of course! What do you take me for?"

This trip is about retracing my father's steps, tracking him to his lair. Key West is where he died, not where he lived. Sometimes he'd put his RV in storage and head to the interior of Mexico by bus. But Chihuahua? All I've found are a few passing references to the city in his log, nothing to suggest the place meant much of anything to him. And even if it did, what do I think I'll find there with so little to go on? Miles and miles of washed-out desert scroll past the window.

"You did know him, right?"

"Who?"

"The Commander."

"Oh, sure. Well, not really. He'd stop in the trading post now and then. Once he had a part for his RV shipped there. And once or twice I saw him in El Chi."

"Where?"

"El Chi. Chi-town. Chihuahua. Where-we-are-going. What's the matter—you hit the bourbon one too many times?" He raises the flask again. "To Commander Cody!"

The desert streams past the bus window. The air hangs in quavering sheets. We pass through cinder block villages, play tag with semis on the nearly empty highway, flipping past telephone poles and signs that read *Curva Peligrosa* (*Dangerous Curve*), *La Mordida es Corrupción* ("*Bribery is corruption*"), and other signs too sun-bleached to read. Playing on the bus TV now is an episode of the *telenovela Dos Mujeres, Un Camino* (*Two Women, One Road*), the soap opera Ricky prefers to call *Dos Mujeres, Una Camiseta* (*Two Women, One T-shirt*). Through the charming cobblestone streets of Coyame, where children pelt the bus with water balloons. In one village, we pass a man tending his plot of nopales. In another, a man burning what looks like a barrel of hair.

We know we've made it to Chihuahua, "The City of the Future," when, five hours after leaving, we pass a billboard in Spanish that reads, *If you love Chihuahua, kill someone from Mexico City*.

The bus lumbers into the station, which is filled with tough-looking Chihuahuans in rodeo shirts, Stetsons, and string ties. They make Dietrich look like a cigar store indian.

As we file down the aisle, Ricky Eggles looks over his shoulder and says, "By the way, down here I'm known as Rico. Rico Aguila. OK?"

"Rico Aguila," I repeat. Rick Eagle. "OK." I do not laugh. I do not tell him that the name and his neatly groomed moustache make him seem more like a porn star than the hombre he's hoping for.

The border is a place of transformation where you have to re-think your thinking and dig out the ground under your assumptions to see what they're resting on. Which is why I've agreed to be led into the heart of Mexico in order to find a man I know is dead. The poet William Stafford wrote, "You must revise your life." The border is the place where that can happen. Dietrich sheds his Chicago past. Ricky Eggles becomes Rico Aguila. And my father? What did he become down here? And me? What will I become by the end of this trip? Will I understand my father any better? And if I turn out to be no more than I am, what will that mean? Will it be a cause for pleasure or horror? The word "alien" is an anagram of the words "a line," in Spanish *la linea*, the boundary between realities. In the north, my father is dead and buried. In the south, maybe, he's sitting at a table wearing a *guayabera*, a shooter of tequila in front of him. I want to believe this is true, that I can sit across that table from him and look him in the eye. Maybe no more than that. Maybe that would be enough.

After installing ourselves in a boxy, aquamarine hotel that smells of mildew, Rico says, "First thing I like to do is get a haircut and a shoeshine."

And so we go to a barbershop on the *zocalo*, where we're both shorn in the Mexican style—short on the sides, longer on top, and absolutely no sideburns. Afterwards, Rico leads me out onto the square, where we climb onto ancient and elegant shoeshine stands. Without a word, the old man hands each of us *las noticias*, a newspaper, and a cigar, then gets to work on our shoes. Sitting there with the afternoon paper, a smoke, a fresh haircut, and my shoes being reborn after weeks of scuffling through deserts and ditches, I feel more civilized than at any other time in my life. I smoke. I look at the paper. I gaze placidly around the square at the women selling flowers, at kids eating tamarind-flavored popsicles from the *helado* cart, at young mothers pushing carriages, at teenaged boys standing in tight, guarded circles. The cigar—and maybe the square itself, with its nineteenth-century façades decaying like the frosting on an old wedding cake—makes me feel completely at home. After a few minutes, I even imagine my Spanish is good enough to read the paper. I'm starting to understand why my father might have settled in this place. Then I realize, of course, that he didn't, that he's dead.

Our first stop after the *zocalo* is a small dark basement bar tended by a pretty, young woman so shy she can barely look her customers in the face. The only other person the bar is an old man studying a small slip of paper, his brows knotted.

"*Qué tragedia! Qué lástima! Qué pena!*" he mutters. *What a tragedy! What a pity! What a shame!* He's clearly been there for a very long time. I'm a little impatient with his operatic misery, with Rick, with everything. I didn't come here to go bar crawling. But what did I come for?

"This feels like pure Mexico to me," I say to Rico. "Nothing border about it."

"Oh?" he says. "What about all the Americans in here?"

I look around. There's no one but us, the sorrowing drunk, and the bartender.

He gestures at the back bar, at the shelves lined with liquor bottles. "There's Mr. Johnny Walker, Mr. Jack Daniels. Oh, and there's Commander Jim Beam."

"*Qué tragedia mas tremenda!*" *What a tremendous tragedy,* the man at the end of the bar intones as the young woman brings Rico and me four bottles of Corona. The old man struggles to his feet looking at the small piece of paper in his hands, shaking his head. Slowly, a bit drunkenly, he moves around to our side of the bar. Rico gives me a tight, narrow look of warning.

When the old man reaches us, he holds out the slip of paper as if it weighs fifty pounds, his deeply wrinkled face filling with tears. "*Qué tragedia, señores! Qué injusta es la vida!*" *How unjust is life!* It's his bar bill.

Rico glances at it, nods solemnly, and says, "*Cada uno lleva su cruz.*" *Every heart has its burden.*

When the old man turns to me, I lower my head sadly. The old man shakes his head and says, "*Me quiero matar!*" *I want to kill myself!* He stands there for a long beat waiting for us to do the right thing, which we do not do. He sighs, sorrows back to his seat, shakes his head slowly, and says to the bartender, "*Una mas, por amor de Dios,*" which she serves him without hesitation, a double shot of Flor de Cana, clear cane liquor. A tragedy. But I have to say I love the irony that the only way to deal with the horror of a high bar bill is to have another drink. And I have to say that I love a country where the bartender in such circumstances pours without hesitation. It may be bad for business and worse for the old man's health, but it shows a good sound understanding of the human soul *in extremis.*

Rico is small and lean. He tips the brim of his Stetson back, showing a thick forelock of dark hair. He's twenty-three, twenty-four. He attended a community college "for about twenty damn minutes." Mostly he's happy working the counter at the trading post and making the occasional trip to Chihuahua.

The bartender is sweet and pretty with straight mahogany hair that turns under at the bottom.

Rico has been flirting with her, asking her if she has used up all the beauty in Mexico and why won't she share with other women? She smiles warily, appreciating the compliment and understanding its design. There's a kitchen so we order food, *pollo con molé*, the true test of a Mexican cook. And it's good, the essence of chocolate without the sense that you're sucking on a squeeze bottle of Hershey's syrup.

Rico has taken off his cowboy hat and fiddled with his food. He straightens suddenly, a look of mock horror on his face. "*Es pollo?*" he says, pointing at his plate. Is this chicken?

"*Sí.*"

"*No es gallo?*" Not rooster?

She examines the food, looking confused.

"*Entonces . . . ?*" Then . . . Rico points at something like a bent nail on his plate, beside the chicken breast. It's a cockfighting heel, the barbed gaff they attach to a fighting rooster's spur.

She smiles, getting the joke but not overly impressed, and snaps playfully at him with the bar rag before heading down the bar to refill the old man's glass.

Normally Rico wears the gaff in his hatband, one of the signs of his machismo, along with the six-inch quirt, a braided leather key chain, that hangs out of his pocket like the tiny tricked-out tail of a show horse. Which is how Rico sees himself. He's good-looking with delicate features and dark, inviting eyes. He's using them on the bartender, but it isn't clear she's going for it.

I show her the picture. "Have you seen him?"

She tilts her brown eyes up at me. Rico grabs the picture and looks at it as if he's never seen it before. He hands the picture to the bartender, who shakes her head. "*Claro que nó.*"

With great ceremony, the drunk from the end of the bar rises and walks down to us. He takes the picture in his hand, holds it at arm's length, brings it close to his out-of-focus face, then, shaking his head slowly, says, "*Qué lástima!*"

I'm ready to call it quits. I turn to Ricky. "I thought you said he came here."

"Sure, but you can't expect her to remember every gringo who comes in the door. It's only five o'clock, man. It's just the beginning of our night. This is just the first place. We'll find that old coot. Just stick with me."

We leave the pretty bartender and the sorrowing man, and soon we've been to so many bars it's hard to remember the names, the places, the people.

La Tenampa, La Cienaga, Albóndiga. The faces begin to merge, the smells, the bartops. We seem to be moving a few places down an endless bar rail, a few places farther. And nobody anywhere has ever seen my father.

Rico wants sex. It's what he comes to Chihuahua for. And with his dark hair, delicate good looks, and wounded eyes, he seems to me to be an easy catch, but none of the women we meet seems interested. It may be the tired line he gives them (again and again, "Why didn't you leave some beauty for the other women of Mexico?"). And before long he's so drunk his Spanish decays into "Why didn't you leave some beautiful women for me?" I begin to feel guilty, that his chances would be better without my tagging along. But he promised me my father. And the more dead-ends I find, the more eager I am to find him, to bring him back to life.

There's something strange about Rico's Spanish. Though his is much better than mine, at least grammatically, he seems always to have trouble making himself understood. Over and over, people keep turning to me for a translation, as if Rico is speaking English. I restate in my own stumblebum Spanish what Rico has said, and only then do they seem to understand. Very strange. And as the night wears on, very frustrating for Rico. For a while now he's been shooting me dark looks every time I translate his Spanish into my Spanish.

At times, though, Ricky is too well understood.

By ten o'clock, he must have flirted with fifty female bartenders and patrons, but with no luck at all. He decides to try prostitutes, and takes me to seedy bars in back alleys, places where large older women in cartoonish negligees try to sit on our laps.

"Are you sure this is the kind of place my father would come to?" But I know this is exactly the kind of place he'd come to.

"Your father? The Commander?"

"Yeah."

"The thing is," Rico goes on, as if he's not changing the subject, "I want them to want me. For me, you know? Not for money. A guy like me doesn't pay for sex, doesn't have to. But you know, now and then, you know . . . circumstances . . . you know . . ."

He dispenses with his pick-up lines. To the first woman who sits on his lap—so big in her lacy bustier that she looks like a Thanksgiving table—he says, "How much?"

"Fifty dollars American," she says, her mouth a bramble of brown teeth.

"For all night?" Rico says.

She may be a large woman, but she has incredible speed. She's on her feet and whaling on him before we know what's going on. She slaps him so hard she knocks him off his chair. No one else in the crowded bar pays any attention. Just part of the negotiation. Just Mexico.

Rico is red with embarrassment and with the prostitute's handprint. His eyes jump around, looking for an explanation. Out of courtesy, I focus on anything but Rico's stunned face—the stale lace of the prostitute's bustier, her picket of brown teeth, her terrifying smile. Does she think I'm turned on by such a display?

"The problem is," Rico says, turning to me, "we started too far down the food chain." At last he's found a place to put it in his head. He throws the woman a dark scowl. "These skanks aren't worth our time."

"Don't forget why we're here," I say, a little angry.

"I know why *I'm* here. *I'm* here to get laid. Do you know why *you're* here?"

We stand like that, staring at each other for a long second, but it's a good question. He leaves me to ponder it while he goes to the bar for another round.

When I was a kid, we lived in a series of tenements where we didn't have the price of a newspaper to cover the broken windows. Later, when things were a little better, we were still the poor people on the block, often the only white family in the neighborhood.

Now I think back on those days of one crappy tenement after another and of my father dividing his paycheck between two families. *La linea.* The line between reality and surreality is an open wound. I remember the constant cockroaches, the rats running across the floors at night, the afternoon we watched the police take away the neighbor lady under a sheet and her husband in handcuffs. When he saw my sister and me watching from the partly open door, he hissed, "Go back inside" as if we were the ones misbehaving, not him. *La linea.*

Rico's right. What do I think I'm doing? My father's dead. No one here, even if they remember him, will be able to tell me what I want to know, because even I don't know what I want to know. The key to his secret life, I guess. And it isn't here in these rundown places like El Grupo, with its aged whores and its down-and-out clientele hoping for a little sympathy screw, with its smells of sweat, sex, and stale beer, with its tabletops sticky with spilled beer and tequila, with prostitutes who must know they're a few light-years past their prime but will not undersell themselves, with a pale green gecko clinging to the wall, the vein in its scaly throat throbbing to *la musica romantica* from the decrepit jukebox.

I'm a person who can hold his own when it comes to drinking. But this cantina crawl is getting to me. The bars blur. The same prostitutes seem to appear in every one, the same one slapping Rico over and over. With my bad Spanish, I'm half-in and half-out of every conversation. Mostly I just show my father's picture, smile, and nod.

It would all be easier to deal with if it weren't for the circus-like atmosphere of these places. One after the other, mariachi bands come through, big-bellied guitars thrust in your face. They're followed by flower peddlers and by little boys seesawing accordions and by more mariachi bands and by toddlers selling trays of Chiclets and by older boys thrashing toy guitars and by more mariachi bands and by jewelry peddlers and makers of yarn crosses and by Indian women selling big-eyed dolls and by old women with nothing more to offer than the cracked cup of a hand.

In Sol y Luna, two men greet us with such enthusiasm that at first I think Rico must know them. He pumps their hands and sits us down at a table with them, diving into an animated conversation. When I ask him if he knows them, he says, "I do now." His eyes look hazy, unfocussed, vaguely angry. He smooths his moustache as though he's afraid it will come unglued.

Roberto has a sad, slack face with only a hint of chin. He looks at me from somewhere far behind his eyes. The kind of guy who's spent his life getting out of the way. Benny is small and round, with the malevolent eyes of a rat. He smells of pomade. He's loud, all hands and smiles. The waxed ends of his narrow moustache are like the blades of a stiletto. He's straight out of *The Wild Bunch, The Good, the Bad, and the Ugly*. He's all we-ain't-got-no-stinking-badges. A walking, talking movie cliché. Roberto tells us he and Benny work in a wire factory, but Benny stares at him grimly when he says that as if he's revealing a state secret. I don't like Benny. He's a man with a plan. His eyes are jittery, trying to see around the edges of every possibility. To them I am "Rubén," the closest Spanish equivalent they can come up with for my name.

When the waitress comes over, Benny yells, "*Vamos a chupar algunas chelas!*" *Time to suck suds.*

Roberto and Benny are a hard-drinking pair who never hesitate to order another round for the table whenever the waitress is within arm's reach. It's only later, when the bill is brought, that I realize they were ordering on our behalf. When the waitress comes, the gazes of our new friends scan every spot on the table except the small damp square where *la cuenta* lies. Everyone from *el gigante del norte* is rich, of course, and the truth is the bill doesn't come to much, so I gladly pay, but not without crying out, "*Qué tragedia! Qué lástima! Qué pena!*" Our new friends turn their faces full on me, nodding support as I bravely stack pesos on the waitress's open palm.

When she's gone and everyone's settling into a fresh round, I say, "Roberto, Benny, *mira.*" I show the picture. "*Lo conoces?*" *Do you know him?*

Roberto looks away nervously. Benny stares hard at the picture, then at me, with snake-eyes. Before I can ask anything more, another mariachi band erupts in brassy splendor, and to celebrate the settled bill, Rico orders a bottle of mescal, which we pass back and forth.

The first swallow makes me gag. It's the foulest stuff I've ever tried, like the taste of a rusty iron railing. And as I drink, I'm horrified at the sight of the ancient-looking worm doing back-flips toward my open mouth. But after the second pass, I'm greedy for my next gulp. I want mescal and more mescal, and give me that goddamn worm, too! On the next pass, when it grazes my teeth but evades my groping tongue, I'm truly disappointed. When Rico gets the worm, displaying it between his teeth before crunching through it to show he's muy macho, I'm so depressed it's as though Santa has skipped my house. Much later, on the bus home, he'll clutch his gut and say, "I don't feel so good" and "Maybe I shouldn't have eaten that worm." But now, tonight, it's a cause for celebration. More drinks! My immediate fondness for mescal is the first sign that I'm too far gone for my own good, for the good of humans everywhere.

The second sign that I'm way beyond drunk. A man comes through the bar lugging a box the size of a car battery, two metal rods attached by wires to the sides. Our Mexican friends nearly leap from their seats.

"Let's do the Mexican thing!" Benny yells, grabbing my bicep and petting it like a fat cat. "Let's do the Mexican thing!" He's half out of his chair and yelling in my face, the blades of his moustache twitching.

Roberto solemnly waves the man over and gives him a dollar, a dollar from my pile of change on the tabletop. Then he takes a rod in each hand and nods. The man with the box begins to crank a handle on the side. The box grinds, growls, whines. Roberto's face remains placid, but his hands begin to tremble. After a few more seconds, he closes his eyes, a tear oozing out the corner of each. He plants his closed fists on the tabletop and lowers his head as if in prayer. When the cranking stops and the whine drops to a growl, a grind, and then a few last ticks, Benny pries the rods out of his hand. Roberto smiles weakly at us. His face is pale, with creamy beads of sweat on his forehead. His left hand takes hold of the table's edge, as if to keep himself seated upright. I've seen these things in old movies about prisoners-of-war, about terrorists, and the hero never *asks* to be hooked up.

"I want to do the Mexican thing!" Benny yells, passing one of my dollars to the man and taking up the rods. The cranking starts, a scratchy grind at first and then a dry siren of gears on gears. His eyes snap shut, his mouth goes wide. When he screams, it's a combination shriek, laugh, and bark. I can see every tooth in his mouth. When the cranking stops, he throws the rods onto the table and drains the closest beer, mine.

Rico is next, the electrified rods sending his body into a paralysis so sudden that I imagine the worm frying in his gut. Later, in addition to his gut ache, he'll complain of a headache. When Rico throws down the rods, a dark look comes into his eyes, as if his hidden maniac is about to come out.

La linea. You're over the line when you find yourself doing something you'd never in your right mind try in the sane light of day. At the beginning of this little demonstration, I sat there in shock. How could these men willingly torture themselves? But by the time the rods come around to me, I can't wait to give them a try. Smooth metal rods the size and shape of a roll of nickels, still warm from the last rush of current and the desperate grip of men in pain. This is the second sign that I'm drunker than any human has a right to be.

He begins to crank. I think of John Wayne, of Gary Cooper, of—but Benny hugs my arm, puts his face close to mine, and yells, "Do the Mexican thing!" And all I can think about is the metallic whine of the crank and the electricity flowing into my body, a river rushing through my veins, my temples pounding, my heart hopping, and the fear that I'm about to bleed from the ears. When it's over—an hour later, it seems—the big fist around my heart lets go. I can taste the steamy flavor of my internal organs. I have done the Mexican thing.

That's all I can bear. When the new bill comes, I pay it and get up to leave before another round can be ordered. Benny leans back in his chair and says, "*Nosotros somos mas chingones, eh?*" *Ain't we some bad motherfuckers?*

"*Sí,*" I say. "*Viva los hijos de la Chingada!*" *Long live the sons of the fucked.*

Benny, laughing, raises his bottle of Corona. "*Hijos de la Chingada!*" And then he's up, beside me, petting my arm again, his voice low, his gaze supplicating. "You don't be going now, Rubén, sí?"

"*Sí. Hasta la proxima.*" *Until next time.*

His cheeks clench with consternation. He rubs my arm harder. He doesn't look at me when he whispers, "No, *guapo.* I thinking we do the Mexican thing."

I look around the bar for the man with the battery, but he's long gone. An old woman is moving from table to table selling flowers.

"No," he whispers sharply, pulling on my arm. "The *Mexican* thing!"

It's only then that I realize he's trying to pick me up. Rico has already headed out into the night. I want to be out there with him, but I don't want to offend. As I figure out what to do, I see Roberto's immensely sad face watching us from the table. I shake my head and point at Roberto with my chin. "*Los ojos de la Chingada.*" *The eyes of the fucked.* Before he can react, I pull free and leave the bar.

Outside Rico's walking crazy circles in the unlit cobbled street. There's no mistaking his mood. He's looking at me from way behind his eyes, clearly pissed.

"*Qué onda, ese?*" I say.

"Don't give me that shit," he says, stepping away.

"What?"

"You know! I ask myself how come I'm not getting any pussy? And my only answer is—you! How'm I supposed to get laid with you hanging around?"

"That's OK, Rick. I'm going back to the hotel now."

"See! That's what I mean! I told you! It's *Rico!*" He takes a few steps up the hilly street, then turns. It's hard to see his eyes under the brim of his Stetson. He rubs his forehead, tipping back the brim.

"OK, OK, I'm gone."

"Right. Do that. Go ahead."

"What the fuck do you want from me? I've had enough of bars and prostitutes for a lifetime."

"That's right. Leave me out here in this godforsaken shithole!"

"Hey, *you* brought *me* here! Did you ever even meet my father?"

"I seen him!"

"Where?"

"Around! I seen lots of guys like him!"

"I thought you were going to take me to him. I thought—"

But he's not listening. He's clearly turned a corner in his mind, and I don't want any part of it. I walk away, heading down the hill toward a better-lighted street and, I hope, a taxi.

After a moment, I hear footsteps following quickly. I turn expecting Rico, only to find Benny materializing from the darkness.

"*Guapo!*" he says in mock disappointment, his hands wide as he comes forward, his words wrung beyond their natural length. "Why you no do the Mexican thing with Benny?"

"No. *Ándale*, Benny."

Benny's hands drop to his sides, slapping his thighs. He frowns, turns, and heads into a dark alley. And right away I hear crying.

"Benny? Stop it, Benny."

When I follow him into the alley, I'm grabbed from behind, my arms pinned back. Someone much taller than Benny, who's nowhere to be seen.

The guy I'm facing steps forward and grabs my throat. He's wearing a blue flowered, short-sleeved shirt and chinos. His hair is cut close. Like the guy in Guerrero, but different. He squeezes my throat and says, "How they hanging, honey bunch?"

"What?"

"You heard me."

And the guy behind me, his voice a quiet breath in my ear, says, "He heard you."

I can't see Benny anywhere. I say, "I told Benny—"

"Forget Benny," says the man pinning my arms.

"But—"

"Let me explain it to you—shut up. Benny doesn't exist. What you want ain't here. Neither are you."

The man in front squeezes tighter now, and I can't talk. It feels as if he wants to yank my throat out. He leans close to me. His eyes are a blue you can see through. He says, "Here's today's lesson, Professor. You came here for the wrong reason. Go home." He squeezes tighter. I can't breathe. My eyes burn and blur.

"The wrong reason," the guy behind me whispers.

Together they shove me out into the cobbled street. I jump up, ready to run back into the alley. Crazy. But the blank wall of darkness at the mouth of the alley stops me. The street is empty. The alley stares back. At the foot of the cobbled street stands a cab, its engine idling, its back door open. I run for it.

Once in the cab, I say, "Did you see what happened? Did you see those guys?"

"*Los hombres mas chignon?*" His accent is thick, his voice gravelly.

"Yeah. The guys with the big balls. They—"

He puts the car in gear, pulls away, and says, "I have no idea who you're talking about, sir." His voice is suddenly hard, clear, and very American. He's one of them, wearing a baseball cap, his brown hair cut almost to the scalp, his right arm stiff against the wheel. In the smear of streetlight that wipes through the car, I see the tattoos running up and down his arm. An inky blue anchor. A banner with words. And, oddly, a mask of comedy. The kind used in the theater. I just don't get this.

The cab tears through the empty streets. I realize I can't remember the name of my hotel. It doesn't matter. In fifteen minutes, the cab jams to a stop in front of it. As soon as I climb out, it tears off.

By the time I get into the hotel room, it's three in the morning. Hot. I throw my few things back into the knapsack. I'm ready to go. I sit on the edge of the bed facing the window, willing the sun to rise, willing the clock toward our 9:30 departure. Why did I come here? My father's notes show no more than a brief, unpleasant visit to Chihuahua. Well, we have that in common.

I don't know what, if anything, to make of what's happened. I don't know for sure if anything *has* happened. I feel like someone's standing right behind me, moving when I move, always out of sight. What is the deal with those guys? Did he fake his death? Are they covering that up? No, my sister saw the body. Most of my family saw it. No, he's dead. So is this about something else? Or am I just losing my mind?

The swamper puts out a feeble stream of cool air that barely flutters the white ribbon tied to the grill. I lie back on the bed for a minute, falling into a stupor.

Days from now, back in Lajitas, I will find a dried out brick of documents I've overlooked. Carefully, I'll peel the stiff sheets apart. Some crumble into dust. But one of them, a small sheet with old gray stars of mold on it, is from a notepad imprinted with the letterhead "Hotel Chihuahua, Avenue Tecnologico 4702." The same hotel Ricky and I stayed in. And below that, in my father's squared-off printing, the words "*El refugio de la bestia hembra*" *The shelter of the female beast.*

꿍

On the desert highway back from Chihuahua, our bus had a flat on an inner dual and pulled off beside a roadside café. Gathering men and boys from the area, they attacked the problem. First, the jack didn't reach the axle so a search for flat stones ensued. Then, the jack didn't work because there was no oil in it. Motor oil was poured into its small hole from a five-gallon can resulting in a large puddle on the ground. Finally, the spare was mounted but two lug nuts didn't want to go back on so they were thrown away.

Back on the road, dodging large stones, cattle, pedestrians, burros, mules, horses, and sheep, the driver decided to try to make up some lost time so he drove even more rapidly and dangerously than before, passing on blind curves and hills. We rounded one twenty m.p.h. curve doing about forty. Unfortunately, no one had latched the luggage compartment doors. Everyone's boxes, baskets, packages, and my lonely suitcase were offloaded onto the highway. No problem. All the passengers went back and gathered their possessions. An Indian boy helped me with mine. The suitcase was still usable but was a comic sight.

The driver let me off at a village not on my map, in fact no more than a huddle of huts. I waited for the southbound bus, attended by a herd of curious goats. I could tell the next bus was coming when I saw the plume of smoke approaching from down the road. The goats made them stop for me. The drivers leaped out and began pouring cans of water into the radiator. Looking underneath, I saw a stream of oil running from the pan. They added oil, ran the goats off the road, and we headed south.

As I climbed back aboard, the driver said, "You must be a gringo."

"How did you know?" I asked.

He pointed at my sandals. "You wear socks."

Back in my seat, I took them off so as not to look conspicuous.

Later that night I woke up to find myself and my fellow passengers being tossed around the cabin of the bus. We'd hit a cow. I think it was a cow. There was a terrible crash in the left front, enough to skid the rear wheels to the right. Broken glass flew in every direction. The driver, bleeding from small lacerations on his face and hands, fought to regain control and bring the careening bus to a safe stop.

As we were getting out, he kept yelling, "A rock, a rock, I hit a rock." But the terrain here is very flat. There couldn't have been any falling stones. Besides, there was a very liberal splattering of a stinky brown substance and, having been a farm boy, I know what that is.

We were able to pry the steel away from the wheel with a long wrecking bar and remount one of the right headlamps to the left side—good enough to get to the next station where a crew worked on it for two hours. The driver kept telling everyone that he had hit a rock. I surmised that he was not permitted to hit a cow.

✎✎✎

13

BREAKDOWN

The next day I'm eager for the air-conditioned comfort of the bus. I've had enough of Chihuahua's nighttown, enough of Rick/Rico, enough of being jacked off my feet in dark alleys. Enough of the Mexican thing.

Except that what happened in that alley had nothing to do with Mexico and everything to do with my father. Those guys may have worn flowered shirts, but those short haircuts and tattoo-blackened arms made it clear they were military, a message they wanted me to get. And they knew me. "Professor," they called me. Another message. And in the twisted way of these things, they probably delivered their message in the place that has the least to do with my father, in case I decide to come back there filled with righteous anger.

Either that or I'm full of it, and they were only a couple of drunks out for a little trouble.

Then there's my father's shadow. He said his security clearance was so high that the government watched him day and night. Most of the time it made him feel safe, he said. But sometimes, in his words, "It gimme the heebie-jeebies."

As the bus gets underway, I can't help looking around to see if any of the other passengers looks suspicious, but except for Ricky's and mine, all the faces are brown. Several women with mesh shopping bags, a young woman bottle-feeding her baby, a guy with an oily carburetor wrapped in newspaper on his lap.

The driver calls out, "*musica!*" Music! I don't know why, but it's enough to reassure me. Nobody answers him, though. Nobody plays any music.

When Ricky showed up at my room this morning, his face was all banged up. "Don't ask," he said. And now he's just sitting in the seat next to mine with his head tipped back, his Stetson covering most of his face. I get the feeling he blames me for every awful thing that's ever happened.

"*Festa!*" *Party!* the driver calls, again for no discernible reason.

After we've been on the road a while, I realize no one's coming down the aisle with tacos. I wish I had eaten breakfast. It's a five-hour ride through the desert. What I took for—what do you call flight attendants on buses?—were probably just relatives of the previous driver out to make a little money. Then the movie begins, *Judge Dredd* again.

"*Colores radiantes!*" *Radiant colors!* the driver calls out.

I have mixed feelings about this trip. Mostly resentment for getting tricked into trailing along for Ricky's nooky-run. But those men. Oddly, getting mugged in the alley is the closest I've come to my father since this trip began, the closest I've come to uncovering his secret life. Some part of him is still out here in the desert, still alive. Those guys proved it. Why else would they bother with me? I look around the bus again, checking for watchers. The guy in the seat behind me gives me a hard look. I'm the only suspicious person on the bus.

"*Rojo!*" *Red!* the driver calls.

"Man," Ricky says meekly from under his hat, "I can't believe it, you know?"

"Believe what?" Here it comes.

"Thing of it is, I went back to that first bar. You know, to sweet-talk that bartender until I could get her to take me home with her? Come to find out, I been with her before, one of my other trips. And that's all good, you know. She doesn't give me a hard time about not remembering. So we do it, you know, and it's all good. And then her brother comes home and makes a big deal about what-are-you-doing-to-my-sister, you-have-wrecked-my-family's-honor, and all like that. He bounces me around the room a while. And before I can get up off the floor, he takes my wallet!"

"You're kidding."

He shakes his head. "He robbed me! Took everything I had, man." He tips his hat up and looks at me for the first time. His left cheekbone is a blue pad surrounded with angry red. The skin under his eye is a smudge of black. "Can you believe that shit?"

I shake my head.

"And the worst part? He's a cop. Can you fucking believe that shit?"

I'm still shaking my head. His friends, I'm thinking, spend a lot of time doing that. "You should get married, Ricky. Settle down. This running around is only going to get you in trouble."

He waves his hand like he's shooing a fly. "I got a girlfriend back in Lajitas. A college girl I met last summer. She come all the way back from Boston to be with me."

"You're kidding. So what was this whole trip about?"

Ricky shrugs.

He's a trouble-magnet, I'm thinking.

"Besides," he says, "I *was* married once. Nice Mexican girl. Married her the day after I met her."

"The day after you slept with her, you mean."

"'Met her,' 'slept with her'—what's the difference?"

I want to point out that maybe the failure to make such a distinction was part of the problem, but Ricky's suffered enough.

"*Ay, dios mio! 'Cosas tipicas!'*" *Oh, my God! Ordinary things!* The driver again. I try to see what he's doing, but he's alone up there, his head down. The bus tears up the road.

"We settled on a little *ranchita* south of the line. Plan was, I'd make money by taking tourists around the desert. Show them a few cactus plants, a couple of snakes. Then we'd serve them a meal back at the house. Didn't work out that way, though."

"*Celebracion!*" *Celebration!* Nobody's paying any attention to the driver. Am I the only one who finds this strange?

Ricky, still talking. "First day, my first group, everything's going fine. I have a knack for that shit. you know? Here's your prickly pear. Here's your coachwhip cactus. Don't step on that rattler. And all the while I'm working up their appetites. I'm all authentic-Mexican-cooking, authentic-Mexican-wife, and like that. Then we get home and everything turns to shit. And I mean literally."

"What do you mean?"

"I mean wads of used toilet paper blowing around the yard, flapping from my fucking prickly pear, stuck to my mother-humping coachwhip. A piece blew against this guy's chinos. That was the limit. Sort of killed the tourist business."

"I don't understand. I—"

"My wife was afraid to put toilet paper down the old *baño*. She was afraid the septic tank would fill up too fast."

"So you divorced her?"

"Hell, it was only one of those hello-goodbye marriages. And anyway, I never made the divorce legal. Who needs the hassle?"

"You're a piece of work, Ricky."

"I am," he says, tipping his head back and pulling the brim of his hat down over his face. "I am that."

"*Bandera!*" *Flag!* the driver cries, throwing a folded piece of newspaper in the air and waving his arms. I see now he's been playing a Mexican word puzzle while steering the bus with his knees. Through it all, the bus never fell below sixty or seventy miles an hour. All things, I think again, move from order to disorder.

. . .

True to the way things have gone this trip, about halfway through, *Judge Dredd* stutters to a halt. And a little while later, in the middle of the desert, the bus itself breaks down.

The driver shuts off the engine and gets out. A few of us follow. There's nothing out here but sand, cacti, the empty ribbon of asphalt, and the hot hand of the sun pressing down.

He cracks open the engine cowling. A cloud of steam pours hissing out. Slowly other passengers climb down from the bus. North of the border, the passengers would sit inside, complaining to each other bitterly. Here they take a lively interest in the problem, as if it's a curiosity the driver is kind enough to let them stop and see, another kind of puzzle, a historical marker. *And here is where we broke down and died.*

Hot water is spraying from a crack in one of the hoses and turning to steam when it hits the hot engine. We gather around the engine in admiration. *Qué tragedia!* Surely a bus like this comes equipped with spare hoses, a patch kit? No, not even a spare driver. Hot white sand in every direction. In the distance nothing but a quavering curtain of liquid air. It's well over 100 degrees, the sun a white hole in the sky. And yet standing next to me is the pleasant-faced young mother, the baby in her arms drinking the last of a bottle of water.

The driver has an idea. "No worries, my friends," he says producing an empty Coke can and carefully cutting it open with a pocket knife. I keep myself calm by thinking of the stories I've heard about wartime pilots repairing holes in the fuselage with flattened Coke cans. I think of lampshades made from cut Coke cans soldered together. Someone, I think, should do a study of the wondrous uses of the Coke can. How it can save sixty people from dying in the desert. By God, someone should give the inventor of the Coke can the Nobel Prize!

Ricky comes staggering down from the bus, his hat propped back on his head. He cheek is so wrecked it looks like somebody's shot him. He comes up next to me and watches silently as the driver curls the sheet of metal around the hose and secures it with a twist of baling wire. Climbing back inside the bus, the driver starts it up again, but as soon as he does, we yell for him to shut it down. All he's done is change the direction of the spray. He comes back to us shaking his head. Who could have guessed? He waves down a passing car, the only one I've seen for some time. The car stops immediately and picks him up.

"Wait!" I cry, running after him, my panic in full flow, though no one else seems worried, "What will we do?"

The driver waggles his thumb out the window as the car pulls away.

The sun beats down. The baby finishes the bottle of water and looks up startled to be sucking only air. The men stand around watching the lame engine as if it might suddenly heal itself. The steam slowly subsides. The hissing stops. There's nothing but the ticking of the engine and the shuffling of our feet. The women and children mostly stand in the scant shade of the bus. Ricky's sitting on the bumper next to the dead engine. He still looks stunned from last night's ordeal. Dear Lord, I have not lived the most upright of lives. I know this. I'm the first to admit it. But to die in the desert among strangers!

Then, as if by magic, one by one, the passengers are picked up by passing cars. At last an ancient pickup stops for Ricky and me. We climb into the back with a young goat that has pissed all over the truck bed. He seems to know that he's headed for the wrong side of a tortilla. We sit there in the goat pee, the three of us doomed in our separate ways, watching the Dead Horse Mountains slowly trail past in the distance.

After a while, the driver drops us in a small town, assuring us a bus will be along right away. And he's right. Only it's going to El Paso, not to Presidio. A couple of hundred miles out of our way. All I want is a clean bed, but we don't have much choice. We climb aboard the Greyhound and sit in bitter silence. The bus is too crowded for us to sit together. Or Ricky's trying to change his luck. At least this driver uses his hands to drive.

Drunk teenagers in the back of the bus play their music loud. The sound is so lugubrious and out of tune it's as if their batteries are dying, but something tells me it was recorded this way. One of the kids rolls an empty bottle up the aisle, where it clatters into my feet. In the seat next to mine, a Bible-wielding evangelist shouts, "Magnify me, oh Lord!" Babies wail. Children whine. In short, hell.

The kid climbs onto the bus at one our brief stops. Since the evangelist has stepped off to wrestle his angel, I take the opportunity to wave him to the now-empty seat next to mine. He smiles and sits down, clutching his bus ticket, referring to it frequently. A few minutes later, the evangelist stands in the aisle and scowls at us with the rage of the self-righteous. I ignore him. The young guy starts to get up, but I put my hand on his shoulder.

"You! Down!" the driver yells, forcing the evangelist to take a seat at the back among his drunken apostles, who wear so many piercings their faces seem to be held on with hooks.

Once the bus is moving again, I study the young guy from the corner of my eye. There's something odd about him, but I can't yet say what it is. He keeps studying his bus ticket, as if his destination might disarrange itself.

The bus bumbles through the dry white desert. It's a four-lane highway now, and we make good time, if heading two hundred miles in the wrong direction can be said to be making good time. I nod off.

When I wake up, I see that the young guy's ticket is as limp as an old cotton shirt. He stares at it for a while and then up at the road ahead as if he can actually see his destination. Slight but strong-looking, dressed in a clean T-shirt and fresh jeans, he might be all of sixteen. When he catches me staring, I just smile. He turns away, his gaze locked on the road.

The desert scrolls past. Heat curls up from the desert floor. The sun is a mean dog.

At last we get to the El Paso crossing. When the border patrol agent motions our bus over for inspection, I begin to realize what it is that's so different about the young guy. For one thing, his clothes are all new. His T-shirt, his jeans, his running shoes—all brand-new. And I realize that whatever his ticket says, the young guy's destination could be stated in one word: north.

When he sees that we're being pulled over, he shoots me a look, his face glazed with sweat. I can smell the fear. He jerks halfway out of his seat. His gaze whips to the back of the bus, but there's no back exit, only the chain-mail faces of the drunken teenagers and the evangelist's rolling eyes. Besides, the driver has already cranked open the door.

It's hot outside and the officer isn't happy. He wears khakis and moves methodically from passenger to passenger, asking citizenship, asking where we we're going, asking where we've come from. The young guy, his ticket crushed in his hand now, is a coiled spring, his right leg dancing, ready to push off. It's as though he's grabbed hold of a bare wire and can't let go.

I don't know why I do what I'm about to do, don't know whether it's a good thing or a bad thing. It seems like the right thing, which I guess excuses lots of bad behavior. But I know this: I've sat next to this guy long enough to feel the overwhelming desire he has for someplace far from the dead-end place where he grew up. The fact that he's dressed in new clothes makes me think his family has sent him. Otherwise, why bother? The clothes, which were meant to make him blend in, only make him stand out more—the red plaid western shirt, the cuffed jeans made of some gray-blue alien alloy, and the shoes with their hopeful logo on the side—Gala.

Hasn't everyone in this country been raised on stories of brave immigrants overcoming the odds? Grandpa Pat who stowed away in a crate of potatoes? Uncle Stash who came over in the hold of a cattle boat? And didn't those fellows have a much better time of it than this poor guy riding in a hot can of lunatic greyhound meat? If that doesn't explain it, maybe this: I do it because every small town is the same small town, every river the same river.

The young guy has raised himself nearly out of the seat. He looks as though he plans to scramble under the INS agent's arm as soon as he gets close enough. I put my hand on his shoulder and firmly pull him back. Our gazes lock and he slowly sits down, already caught, he thinks.

When the agent gets within a few rows, I begin to talk. Loud.

"And what the hell'd he expect?" I slap the young guy's arm playfully, ignoring the look of horror on his face. "First he gives us an eighteen-wheeler without enough rubber to cover the end of a pencil! I bet my CDL the piece of shit ain't seen the inside of a garage since God was in short pants."

Ricky has seen everything now. He's standing in the aisle, looking at me like I'm an idiot child.

By now the INS man is standing in front of us, his eyes sweeping our row from side to side. I'm talking so loud he has trouble hearing the woman across the aisle answer his questions.

"Then he says he wants us to make the Philly-El Paso run in a day-and-a-half! A day-and-a-fucking-half! Pardon my French, but can you believe that shit? Can you fucking believe that? And it's *our* fault when the shitbox ups and throws an axle?"

I'm thinking for sure the other passengers will screw things up—"Take him, officer!"—but they pay no attention. On the scale of their insanity, I don't even register.

The young guy goes limp. He must figure he's sitting next to a crazy man, that it's too late to get away, that nothing La Migra does can be worse than this. The INS man turns to us.

I make a playful grab at the young guy's thatch of black hair and shake it. His eyes go wide and circle frantically in their sockets. I laugh like a maniac. "And you, you goof! You were great! You're there, 'I s'pose it's *our* fault there's twelve-hundred crates of eggs getting fried, flambéd, and fandangoed on Texas asphalt? Well, the hell it is!'"

Then—oh I could have kissed him—the evangelist, stirred by the noise, comes ghosting up from the back, flashing a bright fan of are-you-saved brochures in the officer's face.

"Magnify me, oh Lord," he says, "even unto the jaws of my sin, even unto the porches of my iniquity!"

It's only late-morning, but it must have already been a long day for the INS agent. Dust lines the creases at the corners of his eyes. His khaki shirt is damp with sweat and rimy with salt under the arms. He's probably been in and out of the car too damned many times already today, maybe pulling a double-shift. No, he does not need this. He does not need this at all. He glances at us briefly, at the punctured youth in the back of the bus yelling "Arrest me, officer! Arrest me!" and then carefully backs up the aisle, followed closely by the evangelist.

Once we're through the crossing, it's the young guy who studies me from the corner of his eye. He sits there completely still, clutching his ticket like a dead flower.

When the bus pulls into a stall at the station, he jumps up and rushes for the door. I don't think it's his destination. Not the way he scrambles down the aisle. I think he's decided he can't take another run-in like that. I watch him slip out of the crowd and down the dark alley behind the terminal.

As I step down from the bus, he's standing at the end of the alley in the brightly lit street, looking back at me. I wave like a proper fool. He just stares at me and doesn't wave back. I'm a little hurt. I think I've done him a service. I want to be part of his future family's lore—the madman who saved him from La Migra. But he's not going for it. Maybe he's just waiting for his heart to beat slower. Maybe he has to rethink what he's been told about this country. Maybe he's already begun to suspect that I've only saved him for another misery, for some fresh hell up ahead.

Ricky steps down from the bus and says, "I thought *I* was the crazy one."

· · ·

I hate the thought of another long bus ride, but Ricky and I check the schedule, hoping for a quick departure for Lajitas. I'm eager to get back to my room and a good long sleep. While I study the schedule and map, an idea comes to me. A little crazy, I guess, but that's another line I've already crossed.

I toss the schedule on a nearby chair. "You owe me," I say to Ricky.

"What?"

"We're going to White Sands. It's only forty miles or so. I have something to do there that I'm not sure I can do alone. Come on."

Ricky isn't happy about it, but I tell him we'll take a cab, go in style, and he grudgingly agrees. While I head out to the cab stand, he runs "to get me a necessary for the road." And before we know it, we're on the road to White Sands. I'm grateful that Ricky isn't asking questions. Even more grateful when he introduces me to his new friend, "Señor Cuervo," his "necessary" for the road.

Once we're out of town, the desert stretches away whitely on all sides, hundreds of miles of sand, gypsum, and the occasional lava field, spotted here and there with cacti, ricegrass, and desert crazies, all of it bordered by a rumpled purple mountain range. In a little while, we're feeling pretty loose.

"Dunes!" Ricky says, looking out the window.

"Dunes!" I reply.

The driver throws us nervous glances. He's a big guy with a bald head. The bristly roll of fat on the back of his neck gives his neck a crease that looks like a wide, satisfied smile.

"Ufologists?" he asks. When we don't answer, he says, "You know, UFOs? I get a lot of those. Hell, I'm one of those. Shit, half the people I know are the spawn of aliens."

Ricky passes him the bottle and he takes a hit.

"UFOs," I say stupidly.

"Yeah. I'm not going to argue for their existence. That's a fact, man. They exist. No question, Earth is fucking Grand Central Station for interplanetary travelers. Hell, it's all over human history, from the Ica stones of prehistoric Peru to the Ampleforth Manuscript. Monks don't lie."

"You're a monk?" Ricky says.

"Not me. The Ampleforth Abbey monks. Ancient Rome. Cave paintings. Even Christopher Columbus saw one. So don't tell me they don't exist." He turns back to us, steering the car by guesswork. His eyes are pinched together. He has no eyebrows. "Thing is, I've been taken so many times I developed a stress disorder. Wears you down, man. And you think my insurance will pay for treatment? They will not. Oh, they'll pay for it if I put it down as work-related, but I won't lie. It's ASS, man, Alien Stress Syndrome. Electrodynamic reality really gets you down, you know?"

Ricky and I are both grateful when he turns back to the road. Ricky hands me the bottle and whispers, "Too much anal probing, I think."

"I heard that," the driver says, "and the fact is, you might be right."

The cab fills up with stories and conspiracies. The bottle goes around. More pale desert passes. In a little while, we cross a cattle guard and the driver drops his speed. We pass a yellow flashing light, another, and then make a sharp right, the purple mountains following us on the left. By the time we get to the Visitors' Checkpoint of the White Sands Missile Testing Range, we're so loaded we fall out of the cab.

When I pay the driver, he says, "Ask them to show you where they do the alien autopsies."

As we walk to the door, I turn to Ricky and say, "You smell bad!"

"*You* smell bad!" Ricky says to me. We fall together laughing.

A few visitors ahead of us are checked through fairly quickly. For some reason the humorless woman in green spends more time with us.

She looks from her computer monitor to the clipboard where she's attached our drivers' licenses. She says, "You boys sure you're in the right place?"

"Sure we're sure," I say. But everything feels floaty. I can't be sure of anything. And I suddenly realize I've forgotten to pick up the death certificate waiting for me at the El Paso post office.

She studies us for a long minute. She wears her dark blonde hair cut in tight curls close to her head. There's an alien gleam in her eye. "Gentlemen," she says, "in the interest of exercising good operational security, I'm afraid I have to deny your request for a visitors' pass. I'm required by base policy to provide you with this form for submitting an appeal. I wish you both good day." She hands back our licenses. I'm so drunk I'm not entirely sure which one is mine, so I stuff them both in my shirt pocket.

A family of four have stopped to stare at us. A wash-'n-wear couple with their bitter-faced teenaged girl and a little boy whose mouth hangs open, a crusty smear of red around it. No doubt. Alien.

I drop my voice into a confidential slur. "Sergeant—if I may call you that—if this is about the aliens, don't worry. We're not here about the aliens." When I hear myself talking, it's like I'm listening to someone else.

"Sir, be advised that our conversation is being videotaped for use in the event that legal proceedings—"

"—Because we don't care about the aliens, their autopsies, or anything like that."

"Proceedings!" Ricky says. The MP by the door takes an interest in us, moving slowly in our direction. "The only thing we're proceeding is to go into this place, for some damn reason that nobody has bothered to explain to me. What do you think, we're terrorists?"

The MP steps forward quickly now, a hand on the butt of his gun.

"Gentlemen," the sergeant says, "it's my determination that you're intoxicated. And since this is a secure facility, our policy is not to admit—"

Quietly and as soberly as possible, I say, "My father used to work here."

A nanosecond's pause and then, "Nevertheless, sir—"

I'm looking at the insignia on her uniform, a circled star against a field of smaller stars and the legend *Birthplace of America's Missile and Space Activity*. "I just want to see where he worked. Maybe talk to some people he knew."

I think I see a faint memory of sympathy in her eyes. "I'm sorry, sir. Under the circumstances, that's just not possible."

"He worked at the High Energy Laser Test Facility."

"I'm sorry, sir."

"I found it in his papers. There's a lapel badge, too. *White Sands Missile Range*, it says. Would you let me in if I had that?"

"I'm sorry, sir."

"What about if I had his death certificate? Which I can get."

"No."

"Is this about those guys in Chihuahua?"

And now her look goes hard. She's either part of it or she's had enough. "Excuse me?"

"Those guys who gave me a hard time?" I look out the window, pointing my chin at the barren desert beyond the fence. "My dad's in there. Sort of."

I'm pretty sure I've screwed up my chances for ever getting into White Sands. I'm depressed about that. I'd like to talk to the people he worked with, find out about him, how he spent his time away from the lab, what he did for fun in that godforsaken wasteland. Something. Anything.

I want to tell her all this, to make her understand, but all I can think to say is "He worked at the Electrostatic Discharge Facility, too, and with kinetic energy weapons. He called them 'God Rods.' Hypervelocity rod bundles. It's all there in his notes. Doesn't that count for something?"

Both Rick and the sergeant stare at me in silence. Then the MP comes forward.

The sergeant's voice, a whisper like a blade: "Sir, if you continue, you will be detained. Understand this: You do not want to be detained."

Ricky stands tall and says, "Don't make me get all extra-terrestrial on your ass!"

The MP is on us now, saying, "You're done. Leave. Leave now."

As we step outside the building, the MP at our back, the cab driver calls to us, standing next to his cab, waving his arms. "You're lucky I waited! I knew they wouldn't let you in!" He dances in a tight circle, pumping his right arm. "Attica! Attica! Fight the Power! Fight the Power! The conspiracy goes on forever, man!"

∽∾⌖∽∾

Dear Son,

I've never told anyone this. Why I'm telling you now is anybody's guess. I was but knee-high to nothing and living back on my folks' farm, where I'd play out back of the house now and then. My daddy'd plant corn right up to the edge of the yard, and I always liked wandering in there among the stalks that towered over me. Sometimes I found rabbits, and sometimes raccoons. But mostly what I liked was the soft green corn light. I don't know what else to call it. The way the light came around and through the leaves and the stalks as thick as your wrist. And the feeling that I was hidden, that nobody could find me. The world went away when I was in the corn.

One evening in late August I was out there just slipping through the rows with my chessy dog, a ceramic bank I liked to carry around. There wasn't any money in it, but I carried that thing everywhere. I was a scared sort of a kid, so my father threw a handful of old washers inside and told me to shake it whenever I was scared.

There I was just walking along between the rows, making up stories in my mind, when I began to feel this funny vibration. Sometimes a truck came by on the county road, and you could feel the ground vibrate, but this time it was the air that was vibrating. I began to shake the bank, the washers clanging against the ceramic insides. The vibration was crowding out every other sound. And soon I couldn't even hear the washers, though I was shaking it for all I was worth. All around me the air was getting bright as sunrise. And when I looked up, a great huge ball of light all fuzzy at the edges was slowly settling down on me. The stalks of corn leaned away as it settled to the ground, settled right over me, the air so bright it hurt my eyes and the vibration a steady throbbing in my head, my teeth. I couldn't move, couldn't cry out, couldn't do anything but shake my chessy dog.

And then it was gone, gone so suddenly it was almost as if it had never happened. But young as I was, I noticed the cicadas had stopped singing. In fact, everything was silent as the grave.

Back at the house, the lights were on, just like before. Nobody had noticed anything.

A breeze come up from somewhere, rattling the cornstalks, and I ran back to the house and straight to my bed, too afraid to say anything to anybody. I have always wondered what that was. A spaceship? A dream? Then why did my daddy bring me my chessy dog the next day, which he found in the field, and whip me good for trampling down the corn in a perfect circle, which I never did?

What did they want with me, these space men, if that's what they were? And did they get it? And will they come back some day? I have never seen that ball of light again, but I have been listening to that silence ever since.

Your father,
Commander R.C. Spencer

❧

14

DEAD RECKONING

I cut inland, north of the border, on Route 67, through west Texas, along the eastern edge of the Chinati Mountains. The road runs through a hard, flat, unforgiving plain of scrub brush and cacti no taller than a foot or two. It passes through the town of Shafter, an abandoned silver-mining town with a dusty "For Sale" sign hanging over the welcome sign. I'm following the route my father took on his way to Marfa, where people say mysterious lights appear out over the desert, a place where my father nearly got himself arrested.

The most personal and revealing letter my father ever wrote to me was about a supernatural experience he'd had as a child. A light descended on him in his parents' cornfield, just settled over him for a few minutes and then lifted away. He'd never felt the same after that night. I never answered his letter. I didn't know what to say, what he expected me to say. And I've felt guilty about that ever since. Until last night, when I found the carbon of his letter. Several carbons, actually. He'd written the same letter to nephews, nieces, cousins, to what looked like the whole family. Each of the twelve copies started with the same claim: *I've never told anyone this.* It was like him to lie. He probably thought he was making the recipients feel special. The letter to me wasn't so personal, so revealing, after all. I was just another name on a checklist.

But I still wish I had written him back, because I had had a similar experience as a boy. I was ten years old, walking home from a friend's house after dark. The streetlights were on, I remember. I dribbled a basketball, concentrating on not hitting the cracks in the sidewalk. I didn't want the ball to take an odd bounce into the street or under somebody's bushes. Halfway down the block, in the darkness between streetlamps, a bright light shone down on me. It was like a streetlight where there was no streetlight. I was too afraid to look up. I stood there frozen, my ball under my arm, the circle of light on the ground around me growing bigger and brighter as that single moment stretched into timelessness. I thought if I stood still enough no one could see me, but the light just came down closer and brighter until it seemed as though I was standing inside a ball of light so bright I couldn't see anything but its cold fire and the veins throbbing on the backs of my eyeballs.

And then it was gone, switched off like a table lamp, and the street was in darkness again. The streetlights cast weak cones of yellow, nothing like the light I had seen, the light that had been inside me. I've never drawn a conclusion about the light, never told myself it was God or aliens or a secret weapon. Some things in life just don't make sense. No explanation will do. But back when I first read it, my father's letter shook me. Here was another thing that held us together, a strange and inexplicable something we shared.

I think I never answered him, also, because I knew there was something more to his reason for writing to me, even before I knew he'd written to others. I think, for him, the letter was a kind of confession, a hint that there was something more behind his weirdness, something too hard for the ordinary people of the world to understand. It wasn't that he was crazy or evil, just that he was possessed by aliens.

I'm pretty sure I was taken at least once by people from another planet. Did they mess with me in some way? I can't honestly say. But sometimes I think the wiring inside me isn't the same as it is in others of my species.

What did this trip to Marfa mean to him? How did he feel about it—the man of science chasing little green men? I don't know. His log entries on Marfa are so matter-of-fact. He might as well have been solving for pi as hunting for Martians.

I don't know what I think I'll find there, beyond a tourist trap, but since he wrote about it in his Mexico Log, I decide I should check it out.

Every night, eight or nine miles east of Marfa, near the Chinati Mountains, people gather at dusk to watch what some call the "ghost lights" or "mystery lights" of Marfa. First sighted in 1883 by a rancher, the Marfa Lights have been variously explained as campfires, phosphorescent minerals, swamp gas, headlights, pranksters, static electricity, St. Elmo's Fire, and the lights of a super-secret military aircraft. But the story that's told most is that they're alien spaceships at play.

When I pull into the viewing area outside town a little before dusk, a few cars are already there, a scattering of people. No one talks much. Mostly men of various ages, but some women. There's a group of three young guys in matching black warm-up coats with gray piping. There's an old man with an expensive-looking telescope. A solemn-looking ranch couple sit in their pickup staring out at the desert, sharing a thermos of coffee. Others seem mostly embarrassed, acting as if they've only stopped for a roadside rest.

As the dark comes on, more cars pull in. Pretty soon there are twenty or so and a ragged line of people with binoculars, another telescope, cameras, and other equipment. And now they're talking, working each other up.

"Tonight's the night!"

"You got that right!"

What I wouldn't give for a GPS locator and a USGS map. What I have instead are a compass, a reliable timepiece, an event log, a selection of comestibles, and my trusty sextant.

I feel like a fool standing out here in the dark, gazing into the desert. All around me people are sharing stories about sightings, but I stand off to the side, looking up the distant mountains every few minutes.

"One time," a big guy in a bandanna says, "the light came right into the cab of my dually! The dang engine hasn't worked right since."

"Whatever you do," a quiet voice says, "you do *not* want them guys to get all up in you."

"You ever wonder," a skinny guy with a mullet says, "how it is these guys're so advanced and all they can fly clear across the universe, but when it comes to examining the human body, the best method they got is the good ole anal probe?"

"Roy!" the woman next to him whispers sharply.

"I mean—*hello!*—haven't they ever heard of the X-ray, the CAT scan, the MRI?"

The woman slaps him on the shoulder.

I calculate that if I can measure the precise angles between the moon and a few carefully selected stars, I can plot the position of the phenomenon. And then, with trusty compass in hand, and using dead reckoning, I believe I can track down the Martians. Or whatever they are. I have a few questions for them, if they are indeed extra-terrestrials and not a couple of teenagers with too much time on their hands.

Someone draws in a sharp breath, and then the whole group cries out. "Look!" and "There!"

In the distance, against the black backdrop of the mountainside, a fuzzy pinprick of light floating south to north, just sweeping along the side of the mountain. Through my binoculars, it seems to be one of a pair of lights traveling in tandem. Car headlights. But no one else comes to this conclusion. They're jumping up and down, slapping each other on the back.

"Dang!"

"You see that? You *see* that!?"

But soon the light blinks out, leaving nothing but the dark desert. Everyone quiets down. It's getting cold now. They stamp their feet and flap their arms. A few more cars pull in. People climb out, laughing, talking loudly.

"Gonna get us some little green guys!"

"Do not," a voice booms from the darkness, "contaminate the watch-zone with noise. And besides, everybody knows they're not green. They're gray."

The new people quiet down.

Then "There! There! Another one!"

A brighter light now, this one higher up against the mountains and seeming to travel down it. I can't tell if it's a headlight, even with the binoculars, but there's something strange. No highway engineer would lay a road straight down the side of a mountain. So this can't be a car, can it? The light seems to float smoothly down the face of the mountain. And now there's another light, this one more like the other, more like a pair of headlights. But they're dimmer, more distant. The other light glows and floats, dims slightly, and then makes a sudden turn to the south.

"You see that? You see that?" Nothing on this earth moves like that! Nothing!"

As that one fades, another light takes shape higher up the face of the mountain, drifting vaguely north and then up the mountainside. And now the other light is back, drifting up toward it. The crowd is speechless. The first light floats alongside the other for a little way and then dims as it veers off and dives quickly toward the floor of the desert. The crowd goes wild.

What I should have done was make a parallax study using a pair of cameras at different locations and coordinating the time of the exposures, maybe do a photometric study of the brightness of the lights, measure their luminosity function. But what I did, like a durn fool, was climb over the barbed wire and start walking toward the lights.

A half-mile beyond the fence, I can't hear the people back at the watch-zone calling after me anymore. The darkness is deep. I have to be careful to avoid the spiny reach of mesquite trees and the low-growing cacti. It's quiet, though I can hear a scrambling and scurrying every few minutes, noisy enough to make me worry about where I set my foot.

I'm a long way from the road now, but the mountains seem just as far as they did when I started out. The lights drift up and down the mountainside, then suddenly dart north or south. The mountains are some eight or nine miles from the road, and I may have walked two or three of those miles by now, but the lights seem no closer, no matter how far I walk. I keep going, my eyes on the lights.

I'd gotten maybe halfway there, watching the lights juggle themselves up and down the sky—yellow, red, blue, and back again. And I guess I was so focused on them and on what I'd say to the little green men that I didn't hear the van come tearing up beside me. Before I knew it, two fellows in blue fatigues grabbed me by the arms and threw me inside. They explained with a kind of menacing politeness that I was trespassing on private property.

"But the lights," I said.

"What lights? There are no lights."

"But—"

Then the other one, an older fellow with a snow-white flat-top, said, "What in blazes is that?"

"This?" I said, holding the instrument out for inspection. "This is my sextant."

"You got to be kidding me! What's a fellow swab jockey doing out in the middle of the desert? Lost your ship, did ya?"

It turned out he'd served as a snipe on the Forrest Sherman. Because of that, he and his partner let me off lightly, taking me back to the road as long as I agreed never again to try this stunt. Elsewise, they said, my next attempt would leave me with a painful memento, regardless of my rank.

"Aye-aye, sir," I said with a salute, consenting to be chauffeured back to the road. But I could still see the lights bobbing and weaving through the back window of the van.

I can't tell how far I've walked. The mountains are still an unreachable distance away. The lights, too, seem farther, more like headlights again. And then, as I watch their slow sweep, they disappear completely. I stop. I stand there for a few minutes waiting for them to come back. I wait a few minutes more. Nothing. Just the dark desert and the sharp stars overhead. I sink down to the ground in the moon shadow of a creosote bush and wait some more. Time passes. Nothing. I can see well enough to make out some of the plants around me now—apache plume, prickly pear—and I can hear some of the insects and animals begin to move again, thinking I've left. But the mystery is gone. No ball of light. No aliens. Not even a van-load of guards. Nothing but the black blade of the mountain.

❧☙

I spied my friend again today. I don't know for certain that it was my friend, having never gotten a good look at him, but I suspect it was. I was taking my midday meal in a small restaurant—a Salisbury steak with mixed vegetables and a baked potato, or as close to that as the cook could muster in Nogales, Mexico. I noticed my friend across the dining room, sitting with his back to me, the only other male sitting at a table by himself. I didn't really think anything of it, the restaurant being open and available to all. I remember he left a little before I did. When I tried to pay for my meal, the waiter said, "Oh no, sir. Your friend has paid for you." This is the third time in my life that my government "friend" has paid for my meal. I've never really laid eyes on him, have certainly never exchanged a word with him, at least not to my knowledge, and yet I feel I have come to know him as a kind of friend. I should keep a sharp eye out for him and sit down with him sometime for a conversation, except that then the game would be over, and I do enjoy the game, for the most part, though the feeling of being watched wears you out after a while. Makes me wish I were invisible.

But for now I will occasionally pay for a stranger's meal, on the off-chance that it might be him. For all I know, I'm buying meals for absolute strangers who can't believe their luck. Maybe that's all we are—absolute strangers sitting at tables in a restaurants, now and then paying for each others' meals. Or maybe the Lord is the stranger at the next table. And the Devil at the next one over. This one pays for somebody's meal. That one poisons it.

❧☙

15

MYSTERY WAYS

Ed Mulkey's head looks one size larger than it needs to be. The body narrow as a kid glove, the head as large and soft as a ripe melon. He brushes his wiry black hair straight back over the top of his head from a deeply scalloped hairline. The skin of his face is as rumpled as an old sack, with wiry red patches over both cheekbones. His large ears are partly hidden by thickets of gray. His earlobes are pendulous, from a lifetime of tugging them in consternation. He's doing that now as he thinks back to life with my father on board the USS Luce.

"Oh, I remember him good," he says, but his tone is doubtful, his memory swimming weakly against the current. I keep thinking it's a good thing to contact these men whose letters I find among my father's papers, to touch base with men who knew my father, who might let me in on some fact or feature that will unlock his secret. Mostly the trail is a dead-end, the man moved on, dead, transubstantiated. And when I find one of them, like Mulkey, I don't know what to say to them. I don't have the right questions to ask. The uncomfortable fact is that I don't know this man, any of these men. I don't even know the man I'm asking them about. The letter that brought me here is one that debates the virtues of several recipes for "Al'bam Fried Chicken," a letter Mulkey doesn't remember writing.

"That was an awful long time ago," he says. Then his eyes snap back into focus. His face brightens. "If this is about chicken, I know a place down the road that serves—"

"No," I said. "It's about my father. I just thought you might remember him."

We're sitting quietly in the front room of his Douglas, Arizona, house. It's late morning but the blinds are already drawn against the slicing sun. Mulkey is a widower, a recent one, from the look of it. Every surface of the room is decorated with lace doilies, making Mulkey, sitting awkwardly on the edge of the sofa with his big head and big hands, look out of place. Sad to think that slowly, over the next few months, the doilies will disappear—too much trouble and what will people think?—and then her death will be complete.

"I'll tell you this. I remember this. That ship was a floating paradise. Mostly we were a troop transport. A lot of Marines. In between we had the place to ourselves. I mean big? And nice. I want to tell you . . ." His eyes go wide and vacant as he tries to remember more, his voice fading. "I remember him good. I mean good. I mean my bunk was so close to his I could pret' near spit on him . . . not that I'd want to."

I take a sip of the blackberry soda he's given me. "What do you remember most about him?" I ask. "Anything special?"

After a pause, he says, "I remember he was tall. I do remember that. And I remember when the rest of us took liberty, he'd stay behind to work on the ship." Silence. He looks at me. "Is that enough?"

"Sure," I say. "Thanks for your time." As he shepherds me toward the door, I say, "I'm sorry for your loss."

"My what?"

"Your wife."

"Did you know her?"

"No, no," I say. "I only meant to say I'm sorry."

"She was something special," he says. "A real pistol."

Mulkey waves to me as I climb into my car. I wave back, thinking of all the irrelevant facts I know about my father. Since he kept every receipt, a thick deck of them, I know where he had his dry cleaning done, from Brownsville to San Diego, how many shirts, how much starch. I can tell you what he ate in a hundred diners, cafes, and bodegas all along the border. He kept the receipt for every cup of coffee he ever drank. At times he even kept a record of every bowel movements, complete with color, consistency, and approximate weight. I say again, who *was* this man?

I start up the car, but before I pull away from the curb, Mulkey's big head floats outside my window. When I lower it, he thrusts an index card into my hands. "I don't know about chicken," he says, "but my wife had a way with fried corn. Is that any he'p?" I read the card, the recipe printed in a frail, spidery hand.

Cut corn off ear
Toss corn and a little cayenne in pan
Fry up in butter 'til you just can't stand it

.

"Sure," I say, thinking the recipe is like a poem. "Thanks. This is great."

"I'll tell you what," Mulkey says. "I remember he was a good sailor. He was one heckuvah sailor. And I remember he was a man who loved the Lord. You can rest assured on that score."

• • •

I need a motel room for the night but find myself driving across the border into Agua Prieta. Just to look around, I tell myself. I park on a side street and walk to the corner, only to see a kid about ten-years-old come running at me with a bucket. He stops short, flinging the water all over me. I stand there gasping as water runs off my face, soaks through my shirt and pants. An old man comes up behind me.

"*El Bautista*," he explains. "*Dia de San Juan.*" The Day of St. John the Baptist. Buckets, water balloons, hoses, water pistols, puddles, whatever it takes—on that day everyone in Mexico gets drenched.

The old man walks to the edge of the sidewalk where he waits for a parade he says is coming soon. Others gather. Pretty soon the street is lined with people two or three rows deep. And in a few minutes we can hear the first sour notes of a trumpet a block or two away, and watch as a young band of *mariachis* stride by, followed by a gaggle of students, the boys in white *guayaberas*, the girls in starched dresses that stand out from all the petticoats. A battered brown pickup follows, dragging a wagon in which other kids dressed in *papier-mâché* helmets and breastplates confront other kids in loincloths, who pelt them with water balloons.

"*Cortés?*" the old man asks. Cortez, the Spanish conqueror.

"*Sí, y los indios.*" And the indians.

The old man nods.

We've been making polite comments for a time as the parade comes past. We admire the woman in shiny Lycra sitting on the back of an open car, the clowns on oversized tricycles squirting the crowd with big water guns. We nod sagely at the Ché Guevara float. When a pickup comes by with a large sculpture of a cow riding in back, we speculate about how it was made.

"*Luna de fibra*," I guess, hoping the words are something close to "fiberglass."

"*Qué?*"

But the biggest mystery comes with a line of low-riders inching down the street. It's too much for him, this old man peering out of the ancient architecture of his face.

"*Qué es esto?*" The cars come bouncing and lunging down the street, kneeling, tilting, leaping to their feet. An old DeSoto the color of brown sugar with wire rims and "Da Bomb" painted on the side, a gold-plated Camaro, a Gumby-green mini-truck, and a classic hot rod, red with yellow and orange flames.

My street Spanish is completely useless on this one. "They lower the suspension," I say in English, "and add hydraulic pumps and switches."

"*Qué?*" He's totally mystified. For many years he has been walking a mile to Beto's grocery store every day, where he counts and bags tortillas. It's as exciting and useful a life as he's ever wanted.

"To make the cars jump," I say, jumping a little myself to give him the idea. I can't get over the fact that the old maestro is asking me, the white boy, about the low-riders. How do I explain the low-rider ethic of spending every last penny on customizing kits and hydraulics, the unearthly grace of a car like that driving at eight-miles-an-hour down a busy boulevard, the sudden joy of one of these cars bouncing on its hydraulics at a stop sign, as if the dead metal itself can't resist the beat of Flaco Jiminez, Mercedes Sosa, y Los Tigres del Norte.

He just stares at me, assuming, I guess, that I don't understand his Spanish. "But why?" he asks, slowly, in English, giving the dumb gringo one more chance.

But I have no answer for this. In the face of this man's life, it's hard to defend such an expensive and pointless hobby. All hobbies, maybe. I'm glad I don't have to explain my trip to him, this trip that has begun to make so little sense to me.

The '64 Chevy Impala is so blue it's black, a real gangsta ride. It happens to pull over near where we're standing. "Pull over" isn't exactly right. The car's hydraulics are pumping so hard that the car jumps one tire onto the curb. The car throbs with the sound of Selena, the Tejano angel cut down in her prime, singing "Amor Prohibido." The air around the car shivers, each beat beyond sound, a fist in your chest. The old man covers his ears, shakes his head, and slowly walks away.

Abejundio Delgado, Abé for short, is a big man, pushing four hundred pounds, "morbidly obese," clinically speaking. He's so big he can barely fit behind the wheel of his car. Look at him. He's wedged in there like the victim of some cruel experiment, the disk of the steering wheel slicing into all that dough. When he pops the door, music jumps at you like something wild leaping from a cage. Getting out of the car is such a struggle for him that when he's finally standing beside it, I feel like applauding, as if I've just seen Houdini shuck off a straitjacket. The day is as hot as hell on toast, so hot my clothes are already dry from my impromptu baptism. Heat rises in wet waves off the pavement. Today, every gesture is an achievement, every thought comes soaked in sweat. Abé *is* Houdini. Getting out of that Impala is truly one of the great stage illusions of all time.

As he walks to the back of the car, where I'm standing, he starts speaking, shouting really. A moment passes before I realize he's speaking to me. "It's clear-coated and pin-striped, with McLean spokes, Gold ring Avalon rubber, and all original parts. The frame sits three inches from the pavement, and she's in turn-key condition." He's got a big worried face, his eyes, nose, and mouth clustered in the middle. He breathes heavily. Now what fresh hell will the world throw his way? He shouts, "If I was to sell her—which I will most definitely not—I'd get an easy fifteen-thousand. Guaran-damn-teed to impress *las chicas*."

Where the license plate should be is a chromed-chain frame around the words "Jesus Saves." He opens the trunk, propping it with a chipped plaster figurine of a matador in full regalia, one hand cocked proudly on a hip, his red cape falling in Rembrandt folds over his left forearm. It's the heroic posture contrasted with the mundane chore that makes me laugh, the trunk latch perched squarely on the proud matador's black winged cap.

And the music! Like flood water sweeping out and around us, washing us down the street along with the little kids carrying the banner for Our Lady of Guadalupe.

Inside the trunk are two speakers so large they extend from just inside the back bumper to just behind the front seats. They look more like twin coffins than speakers, coffins with thick hydraulic cables coiled around them. Fifteen-inch subwoofers, tweeters, mid-range speakers—the car is one huge stereo. And have I mentioned the music? How like a beast it is? The bass shakes the car, makes the metal buzz, melts plastic, cracks the windshield, makes passersby bleed from the ears.

Abé, it turns out, owns a business over in Douglas called "Juice, Tunes, and Booms." He installs stereo systems in cars and, it turns out, the occasional alarm system. I suddenly feel the need for security.

The next day he comes by my motel for my Taurus, promising to have it back in two or three hours. Three hours pass. Then five. I'm beginning to think my car has been stolen, except that he calls in with reports every once in a while. But in the end, the entire day passes. It's well into the evening now. At 8:00 P.M. he calls to tell me he'll be just a little while longer. He calls again just before midnight to tell me he's on his way.

I wait out in the darkened parking lot. I can't help feeling I'm waiting for some kind of criminal activity to transpire. Pretty soon I see headlights coming in my direction, a lot of headlights. And a deep-throated growl like an approaching storm front. In the lead, Abé drives my Taurus. He's followed by six cars that look as though they've come straight from the parade of low-riders. Abé parks in the middle of the lot. The other cars array themselves around mine like escort ships around an aircraft carrier. Lights come on in some of the other motel rooms. Curtains are pinched aside. The cars fill the tiny lot, and the drivers leave the engines running, exhaust, gray-blue and sweet-smelling, fills the air. The motel's manager comes outside, shakes his head, and goes back inside.

Before Abé does his escape act from my Taurus, his friends are already out of their cars and standing around me, a little back, though. Out of respect? Or fear of contamination? They're a mean-looking bunch of *cholos* with shaved heads, loose T-shirts or big plaid flannel shirts, and baggies on the point of falling off. No one talks to me. They only give me sidelong looks. They're waiting for Abé to extricate himself from the car.

At first, the women wait in the cars, but when they see this is going to take a little while, they climb out, too, and visit with each other. They lean against their boyfriends' cars, smoking and talking in quiet voices. They're mostly thin with lots of thick black eyeliner and wear their dark hair pulled back tight, except for one heavy-set woman whose hair has been tortured into a reddish-blond cloud.

While Abé struggles to get out of my car, one of the guys comes up to me. He's small but muscular, his pants hanging so low the crotch is at his knees. When he sidles up to me, he brushes at his nose, looks back and forth, then at my car. It's all an act, I guess, but a good one. I'm scared. Scared of him, scared I'll pee my pants.

He says, "*Que honda, ese?*"

Hoping my voice won't crack with fear, I say, "Just here to get my car back." And it's too late to take back my tone, which says, *I don't want any trouble.*

He catches my tone, spreads his open hands. "Just here to give it to you, man." He brushes his nose again and steps in close. "You know, you were right to buy this car. This a old man's car." He points at it disdainfully. "You might have some good shit in there"—he fixes me with his stare—"You *don't*. But even if you did, no self-respecting gang-banger would even take a look."

Abé has freed one of his legs, his foot feeling for pavement. My car rocks without the aid of hydraulics.

Now that this guy has broken the ice, one of the others calls out to me from his car. He's wearing baggy white chinos, a red muscle shirt, and an honest-to-God porkpie hat. "Hey, maestro, you want me to fix up your alarm like mine? Listen to this." He activates his alarm system, then trips it by waving his hand over the hood. There is the sound of metal sliding and snapping against itself. And then a cold hard voice: "You recognize that sound, motherfucker? That's my nine mill ready to cap your ass! Now get the fuck away from the car!" On the side of the car, rendered so beautifully in silver italics that it might be a company slogan, it reads, *No chinges con migo. Don't fuck with me.*

At last Abé is out of the car. "I see you met my *camaradas*," Abé says, a little winded from his escape. "Los Indios. I'm kind of their godfather. I used to be a banger back in the bad old days in L.A." He takes a ragged breath. "Now I'm a respectable businessman. I try to show them the better way. I let them work on the cars, give them a little money. Even if they don't want to work, they can hang out at my garage and drink sodas. They're good kids. That stuff about the murder a while back, that was mostly just an accident, a case of mistaken identity."

Abé explains the alarm system to me, the automatic door locks. He demonstrates everything, tripping the alarm, a *whoop* so loud I expect a SWAT team to draw down on us. But Abé is unmoved. I pay him, feeling as much guilt as if I were buying an eight-ball of cocaine. And then they saddle up to go. Car doors slam, engines ignite. The cars begin to pull away in a stately procession.

One car left. The driver starts to get in, thinks better of it, and sidles up to me. He's wearing black sweatpants and a white Adidas sweatshirt. He says his name is Coochie. For a minute, I think that's the nickname people like Xavier Cugat and Charo would give their kid.

"*Mí carnal* giving you that shit about he's the godfather? *Esta mas loco que la chingada*, man. That's whacked. We're *playing* him. Just so you know."

That's when I remember that the Spanish word for knife is *cuchillo*. He climbs back into his Duster. He flashes me what must be the gang sign for Los Indios—an "L" formed with the forefinger and thumb of his right hand, then slaps the Guadalupe gearshift into drive, leaving a long scream of black rubber on the pavement. When he's gone, the parking lot falls into a silence deeper than any midnight I have ever known.

• • •

My father was not normally an emotional man. In one of the letters I find, he describes his destroyer being hit by a shell during the Korean Conflict. "A piece of decking tore through my boot, slicing across the top of the left foot just above the toes. My first thought was that now both feet would match, since I'd cut the right in a similar fashion on a corn crib way back when I was a young 'un." Freakish.

My father was a religious man, a Pentecostal. His church didn't go in for saints and icons. No singing either. "Singing don't save," my father liked to say. His way was darker.

One hot Sunday in July, back in Indiana, without telling my mother, he took me to a brush arbor revival meeting. My father didn't take us on outings, least of all me by myself, so this was something special. I knew this and I made a point of being on my best behavior, sitting in the exact center of the passenger seat, sitting silently, my hands folded in my lap. I didn't want to do anything that would unleash the animal in him. But more than that, I wanted my father to be proud of me. I wanted this to be the first of many times he and I went out by ourselves. Maybe the bad times—the hard hand and voice—were over. Maybe tonight was the first step in showing me that I was worthy of his love.

It was a hot night full of locusts and spinning with stars. The heat was worse inside the arbor, even though the thing was little more than an arrangement of stout poles with a roof of pine boughs. Wooden folding chairs were set out in the dirt to hold the thirty or forty people who had come. We came in at the back and took seats somewhere toward the middle on the right side of the aisle. In front of the seating area was a cleared space with a wicker trunk sitting in the center.

"What's that?" I asked, pointing. They were the first words I'd spoken since getting into the car. It looked like an old steamer trunk, as if someone's grandma had left her luggage. Didn't she know the sermon was about to start?

"Don't point," he said. And then the old woman sitting in front of us turned around. I could see makeup caked in the cracks of her face.

"You, little man, is too young to handle, too young to be bathed in the blood. But I tell you what. You ain't too young to get right, boy. You hearin' me? Get right right now!"

"Yes ma'am," I said, not knowing what she was talking about but wanting to treat her with the respect my father said our elders deserved.

She turned her gaze to my father for a moment. "You raising him right?"

"Yes, ma'am. I'm raising him by the Good Book and the good belt."

She smiled. "I knowed that just looking at you." Then she brought her eyes back to me, her gaze narrowing, boring into me. "Choose Jesus, boy. You hear?"

"Yes ma'am." Insects whirled drunkenly in the air overhead. I liked Jesus. Jesus was all right with me.

To me the preacher looked ancient, though he was probably only about fifty, a heavy man who already had big shadows of sweat under his white sleeves, even before he began huffing and puffing for Jesus. He wore a skinny black tie and black pants slick with wear. His collar was buttoned so tight his face was red, or maybe it was the Jesus already coming into him. He started talking before everyone had taken a seat. "They's a seat up front," he said quietly to a latecomer. He was just a normal person like a teacher. "Horace, how's that corn comin'?" As more people came into the arbor, he talked about the weather and crops and how the people were so good to come out to hear him when he was nothing but a sinner himself, but a sinner who had heard the Word and got himself right with Jesus. All this he said in a quiet, conversational voice, farmers talking over a fence.

About the time everybody was seated and settled down, he began to pace slowly back and forth in the bare space before the chairs. He'd stop and stare off into the trees outside, then shake his head and pace again. He began to talk to himself, low at first, like he'd forgotten anyone else was there, like he had a problem he was trying to work out, like he was trying to remember something.

Then he stopped and turned to us. He had a strange smile, a widening of the mouth that had nothing of pleasure in it. His eyes were dead gray beams. If anything, the smile made him look as though he had smelled something bad. The stench of sin, I guess.

It didn't seem to bother him that someone's trunk was sitting right in the middle of things. In fact, as he talked, he walked around it, slapped at it, stroked it. The sweat stains on his white shirt deepened.

"It ain't the sinner God hates," he said. "It's the sin! But if you have not fessed up to your sinfulness, then, dear ones, you are nothing more than sin itself! *You* are sin! Walking, talking sin!" He loosened his tie and unbuttoned his collar, giving relief to his rubbery neck. He shook his head. "But lay your heavy heart at the feet of the Redeemer, and ye shall know peace everlasting, glory everlasting! Repent, remit, and relax into the ever-lovin' arms of Jesus Christ!"

And then he waded in among the chairs. Heads turned, a flash of surprise swept the crowd. The wooden chairs creaked. "Faust Funeral Home"—I swear—was stenciled on the backs.

As he moved among us, the preacher yelled, "A tree shall be known by the fruit it bears!" And then he turned and charged through the chairs to the other side of the arbor. A wing of his black hair fell into his eyes. He flopped it back with a jerk of his head. "Did you hear me, dear ones? Jesus said, 'I am the Vine; ye are the branches. You cannot bear fruit in yourself, but I throw My Ownself into the branch.' And what kind of a fruit did it bear?" He darted quickly to another part of the crowd. "'These signs shall follow them that believe.'" As he spoke, as he worked himself up, his shirt tail came dangerously close to working itself completely out of his pants, a whipping offense in my father's eyes. This made it hard to concentrate on what he was saying, even if I could understand it. I tucked my own shirt tail in deeper. Let the preacher get the whipping, I thought, fully expecting my father to take him over his knee. But he just sat there smiling, my father, his eyes following the preacher, who swept back and forth among the crowd.

"A tree shall be known by the fruit it bears!" By now we were all turning in our seats, trying to follow him with our eyes, trying to swing our knees out of the way so he could come charging by. The chairs ached under us as we swung back and forth, and some closed their eyes and raised their faces, holding out their palms, swaying lightly. And then he ran to the back, where it was hard to see him at all, and his voice came booming, "A tree shall be known by the fruit it bears! . . . And honey, I'm a fruit picker!"

There was a chorus of "Praise Jesus." Someone somewhere began to weep. He made his way back to the front, yanking on his tie like he was leading an old horse back to the stable. But the closer he got to the front of the crowd, the slower he walked. He shook his head, and the air seemed to go out of him by the second.

"I'd be lying if I didn't tell you my thoughts are heavy tonight," he said. "There's a heavy hand on my heart. And I just don't know what to do about it."

There was a shuffling in the crowd, a current of whispering. One lady meekly said, "Try Jesus," but the preacher didn't seem to hear her, lost in his thoughts. My father stiffened, his eyes on the preacher, who circled the wicker trunk, stopped in front of it, shook his head, and kept walking.

He stopped and looked at us like he had just noticed us, like we were old friends catching up. He said, "You know that feeling when there's something keeping your spirit down? Like you're being bug-squashed under a heavy boot? Truth is, that's what I'm feeling right now." He started pacing again.

A man's voice shot up from the crowd: "Jesus'll he'p you!" A couple others agreed that He would, but the preacher wasn't having any of it. He sighed heavily and slowly slapped his heart with a loose fist. He shook his head. "Ain't nothing for it," he said. "Time to face facts. This old preacher's gone bust."

A murmur of reassurance ran through the crowd. "No, no," people said. I turned to see a big old woman in a faded dress stand up clutching the back of the seat in front of her. She was trembling, shaking. She just stood there looking at the preacher, her eyes all wet with tears.

The preacher paid no attention to any of it. "I'm telling you, dear ones," he said slapping his heart again, "it's time to face facts: nothing'll grow in dirt this dead." His shoulders slumped and it looked like it was hard for him to hold up his head. "I'm done for, folks." He started walking up the aisle toward the back end of the arbor. As he walked he buttoned his shirt and straightened his tie. He was leaving us. "You want my honest advice, you'll go get yourself a decent preacher," he said, "one's still got some sap in him."

More people protested, quietly saying, "No, no." A man in overalls stood up and began to mutter words I couldn't understand, his hands flying out like frightened birds. When I looked up at my father, his eyes were still on the preacher, but he was shaking his head no, his movements measured, precise, strangely without emotion.

A young woman moved into the aisle in front of the preacher, blocking his way. She was shaking, hardly able to stand. Her knees began to buckle, but an older woman caught her and lifted her back up. The young woman's head rolled onto her shoulder, her eyes rolled back in her head. I was scared. I said, "Is she dying, Daddy?"

For the first time since we'd sat down, he looked at me. A long second passed, almost as if he were trying to remember who I was. Then he said, "The Lord's moving on her in mystery ways."

The preacher took the young woman by the chin and looked into her eyes. His voice was strained. "I can't he'p you, precious." He stepped around her and headed for the back of the tent, the clearing, the dark woods beyond. But some people from the back of the arbor stood up and locked arms to keep the preacher from leaving, then turned him back, toward the front of the arbor and the wicker trunk. The preacher's eyes were steamy with held-back tears.

"Don't you see, dear ones? I can't do it no more," he said. "I don't have it in me!" He slapped his chest again. Then he swept his arm out to include the crowd. "Maybe this tree has no more fruit? Maybe this field's been picked over?" The man in front was shouting out noises like coyote barks. The preacher looked around at us, trying to bring us into focus. "Now I ain't trying to get your mind going here, but maybe I'm not worthy to be your preacher! Maybe I've lost my fire!"

People had risen halfway to their feet now and were rattling their empty chairs, crying, "No, no!"

"If there was only somebody to he'p me," he said. "If there was only somebody to take this burden off'n me."

More faint cries. "Jesus. Jesus!"

He was edging back toward the front of the arbor now. "If I could just find somebody to do my work for me, why, dear ones, I'd be a happy man!"

"Jesus!" Louder now.

He was at the middle of the aisle now, and he bent over, leaning his head to the side. "What's that you say?"

"Jesus! Jesus!" the crowd hissed.

He held his cupped hand behind his ear. "Jesus?" he said matter-of-factly. "Is that what you're saying? You're saying there's a fellow name of Jesus who's willing to lend a hand to this old fruit picker?"

"Yes! Jesus!" It was the woman in front of us, the woman whose face was caked with makeup. She stood up when he was near and held her hands out, clutching at the air. "Jesus'll lend you a hand!"

But he walked right past her, still puzzling it out. "Because I would purely love to have somebody do my work for me out here on this hot night."

"Let Jesus! Jesus will he'p you!"

He was back in front of his congregation now. He looked around at us. He thought about the offer. He swept his hair back in place with one hand. He loosened his tie again, yanked it.

"No," he said, shaking his head. "I don't think so. No Jesus." He circled the trunk once and faced the crowd again. "Nope, no Jesus."

The chairs stopped creaking. No one spoke. Even the people waiting for the rapture opened their eyes a crack, afraid they'd stumbled into Satan's tent.

And then, louder, the preacher said slowly, "No. Jesus." And then louder still, his voice a raw blade, "Do you hear me, dear ones? I said, 'No Jesus!'"

The congregation began to stir. This was not what they had come for. Not at all what they had come for.

But the preacher seemed not to notice. He began to pace. "Now Jesus was sleeping on a coil of rope. And the wind was blowin', and the waves was goin'. To and fro the disciples ran. To and fro. 'Oh what are we gonna do!? Oh what shall we do!?' And the waves was goin', and the wind was blowin'. 'I know,' they said, 'let's wake up ole Jesus, the Son of God!' So they ran to Jesus. Do you hear me, dear ones? Are you listening? They ran to the Son of God, while the wind was blowin' and the waves was goin'! And you know what they did? They cried out to Jesus. They flapped they hands and pranced around." The preacher flapped his hands and pranced around, his knees pumping high. "They said, 'Jesus, you got to he'p us! Jesus, you got to he'p us!' And you know what ole Jesus did, dear ones? While the wind was blowin' and the waves was goin'? He stirred from his bed of rope, from his bed of sorrow, from his bed of pain. And he rubbed the sleep from his eyes, and he looked up at the disciples gathered all around, and he said, 'Do I have to he'p you guys with ever' little thang?'"

The space inside the tent was a caught breath.

His voice now was a high whine. "Do you see, my precious ones? Do you feel the dawn coming on? Sometimes you got to do for yourself. Sometimes you got to bear your own burden, shoulder your own cross. Sometimes you got to leave Jesus asleep on his coil of rope!" He'd worked his way behind the trunk now and, with a sudden jump, flung it open.

"Only one way to know," the preacher said, working himself up, slapping his heart hard now. "Only one way to tell." Slap. His words now riding the back of a droning incantation: "'And by these signs will ye believe. In my name you will cast out demons. You will speak in new tongues. If you pick up serpents, they will not hurt you. If you drink the deadly thing, you will not die. You will lay hands on the sick, and they shall recover.'" His words now a sharp shout: "So the Bible says! So the Bible says! So the Bible says!"

Even with the other woman's help, the woman in the aisle went down again, this time to the ground. She rolled around there, her back arched, digging at the dirt with her feet until her flat black shoes came off. And still she twisted and turned, her hands flying down between her legs and then up again, her neck sprung back, her eyes rolling.

The preacher pulled his tie clean off now and unbuttoned his shirt more, showing his swollen neck wet with sweat. "I ain't *playing* church with you now, dear ones. I ain't *schooling* you. I ain't giving you no psalm-singing Sunday sermon. I'm flat out *telling* you. Sometimes there ain't nothing for it but to grab the devil by the throat!"

He thrust his arm deep into the trunk and came up with a coiling handful of snakes, tails whipping, heads lashing.

I don't remember much of what he said after that. I couldn't take my eyes off the snakes. He held them in the air. He shook them. He clutched them to his chest, scrubbing himself all over with them.

The crowd cried out, "Yes! Oh yes!"

He talked about Jeremiah in the pit, about being stuck in the pit and trying to climb the sides of the pit, "but the sides are too slick and you'll never get out because the pit is sin and the pit is wickedness and you are trapped forever in the pit because you are an ungrateful sinner and they done digged a pit for thy soul and set snares for thy wicked feet!" And then, for a moment, his voice went all soft. "But precious, precious ones, you can't never stop trying to get your name in the Lamb's Book of Life!"

Then, with his free hand, he tore his shirt open and scrubbed his bare chest with the snakes. He reached into the box with his other hand, coming up with another handful of writhing, coiling death. He shook the snakes in the air and said, "'In My Name they shall cast out devils.' That's what He said." He pointed his coiling fists at the crowd. "Are you ready to do that, dear ones? Are you ready to do His work? Do *His* work. Don't let Him do *your* work. My God is a do-it-yourself kind of guy! Are you ready for Jesus Christ, the Son of God? Are you ready for Jesus Christ, the light everlasting? Are you ready? Are you ready? Are you ready?"

Hands were raised to the heavens. Tearful faces were raised to God. People fell to the ground, shaking and rolling and jabbering. The woman in front of us turned and, with tears in her eyes, said, "'They shall speak in tongues unknown.' He's open'n up now. You never see nothing bad out of that man. He's fame known."

My father gave her a stingy little nod.

Some of the snakes were thick and brown, like things oozed up from the bowels of the earth. Some were smaller, only the diameter of jump ropes, but they whipped and twisted, slick with evil.

Lots of people were up on their feet now, dancing, whirling, stomping, and calling out in wild, inconsolable jabber-songs. The woman who had been rolling on the ground was up now and moving toward the front, to a table off to the side, where she drank from a stoppered glass bottle. As soon as she did that, she staggered against one of the arbor poles, clutched it, scraped her face against the rough bark. Her eyes were closed but tears came pouring from under her lashes, and from her mouth came a mournful yodel.

A man from down our aisle stood up, his arms upraised and holding a long snake as big around as the inner tube on my Huffy. He must have brought it with him.

Until then, my father sat unmoved next to me, his head held high, the angle of his crew cut parallel with the earth. But now he jerked to his feet like a hooked trout and knocked chairs aside as he staggered toward the front of the tent. He leaned over the open basket and plunged his hand in deep, turning a dead-eyed gaze on me.

When his hand came out, he was holding a quick-coiling length of red fire. He took it in both hands, moving his grip to just below the head. The foot-long snake lashed itself around his wrist and then loose. When he raised the head to his face, the snake's jaws went wide, its tongue stabbing. And then my father took the whole head, the gaping jaws and flashing tongue, into his mouth. He held it like that, gazing at me with calm eyes. The snake went crazy, whipping itself against his face, a twisting, throbbing demon's tongue. My father didn't even blink.

I was scared unto very death. I'd been scared from the minute the woman in front of us told me I had to take a bath in blood. And even earlier, when I'd heard the locusts whine. And earlier still, when after supper my father had taken my hand and said, "It's time I taught you something about sin." And before that, more afraid than I had ever been on any of those nights when my father's belt lashed the sin out of me, the pain second to the fear, his big voice booming, "Jesus *Christ*, the Lord of Heaven! Jesus *Christ*, the Lord of Hosts!"

By now the crowd was a swaying, screaming mob. Women tore at their clothes. Men jumped like they'd tasted lightning. The preacher kept preaching, his voice lilting, then loud. And through it all, my father stood there with the snake in his mouth, telling me things with his eyes.

The preacher said, "Oh, dear ones, oh precious things, when he comes back, when he comes back, he ain't coming back as a little baby in a manger. No sir. When he comes back, precious, you're going to know about it. You are going to know about it. And you know what? He ain't coming back nailed upon the cross. No sir. And no, he ain't going to come back as the one who laid in the tomb. No, sir. Lord of lord and king of kings, he's coming back on a big white horse with a sword raised on high! Yes sir. He's coming back to do battle on the Fields of Armageddon in the Valley of Jehosophat. He's coming back to call down fire! And he will come charging with his sword held on high! Yes sir. And on that field the blood will run and on that field the blood will run as high as a horse's bridle on that day, on that day. Is this the day? Is today the day? Is this the day the Lord is coming back? Is this the day the Lord is coming back? Is this the day? And are you ready, dear ones? Are you? Are you ready? Lest ye be tested by fire, tested by serpents, tested by the deadly thing, you ain't ready! You ain't ready! You ain't ready!"

"Jesus knows," the preacher said. "Yes, Jesus knows. He knows the world. He knows this hard place. And he knows, he knows your heart is sore, sore from this hard place, from the world, and that's a hard place. But can you lift your heart? Won't you lift your heart? Won't you lift your heart to Jesus and say, I am here, Jesus Christ the Lord of Heaven. I am here, Jesus Christ the Lord of Hosts. I am here, Jesus Christ the Lord of Heaven. And of Earth. The Lord, I say, of this hard place. And Jesus won't you take and Jesus won't you take and Jesus won't you take and catch me into the Life Everlasting."

Just then it began to rain, first a shimmer blowing past like a curtain caught in a breeze, then big fat slapping drops that came pouring through the crossed branches overhead.

The preacher dropped the snakes back into the wicker basket and walked down the aisle. "Come on, dear ones," he said, waving us along with him. "Come unto the anointin'." When my father took the snake out of his mouth, it coiled around his fist. He had to shake it off into the basket. He came back to me slowly, his eyes on me and on me and on me.

We followed the preacher out into the rain, those of us who weren't still jerking like live things on a spit. He stepped out into the clearing and raised his arms, his face, so the rain could hit him square. He turned slowly, his face raised to the night sky.

There were tears in his voice. "When we believe in the Rapture . . . when we believe in the Rapture . . . when we believe in the Rapture . . . well done, my good and faithful servant . . . washed in the blood of the Lamb . . . well done."

A flash of lightning lit our upturned faces, and the rain fell like cold blades. And then the preacher saw the rest of us as if for the first time. Even though the rain was coming down hard now, his face relaxed into a benign smile. His whole body relaxed. He was wet all over now—we all were—but he didn't seem to notice. It was like the simple farmer had come back. He waved us toward him, his children, called us in, and we gathered close around him with the rain coming down so hard the spray bounced up off the ground as high as my knees. My father's big hand fell to the back of my neck, and he pushed me until I was right next to the preacher, right up against him. Everybody was crushing in on him, all the wet bodies. The preacher looked down at me and said, "That's right, son. Git on in here close, and git you some of this anointin' all over you!"

He gathered us close in and looked into each of our faces while the rain drummed down. When a streak of lightning splashed across the sky, chants and cries flew up into the stormy darkness, and I saw that my father was looking down at me, his eyes bright with the mystery.

◈

The Lord breaks before he makes. The Lord breaks before he makes.

◈

16

TWIN EAGLES DIESEL

Under an Arizona sky as bright and hard as a kitchen counter, I leave the two-lane for a dirt road that leads me through what's left of Twin Eagles, past the other end-of-the-road places—the Pink Elephant Bar, the Jolly Roger Restaurant—and into the potholed lot of Twin Eagles Diesel.

Twin Eagles Diesel is a dump, a one-pump truckstop made of corrugated tin on the outskirts of Twin Eagles, Arizona. I have nothing against truckstops. I was a driver for a while and liked the life. The changing landscape, time to think, the highway unspooling under your wheels, miles covered honestly, foot by foot. Righteous travel. Flying is magic. Your destination appears out of nowhere, a dream. Driving is work, penance, redemption. When you get somewhere driving, you've earned every inch. You see the land and the way you crossed it. I don't mean "the land." I mean the ground, the dirt rolling under your feet.

I've got a reason for stopping here, beyond the belief in small-town America, that once you're off the mainline, the people are nicer, the food is better, the wonders more wonderful.

The place does not look promising. Two rooms, one of them a dining area, the other filled with pegboard racks of sun-faded candy sacks, rows of shelves heavy with dusty quarts of oil, a stand stuffed with dog-eared roadmaps. At the back of this area is the men's room.

I have smelled some smells in my time. I once opened a freezer full of beef that had been sitting without power for a week. Another time the septic system backed up into my apartment. And I once helped gather corpses after a flood. So you'd think I'd be prepared for the Twin Eagles' men's room—the stench, the scum, the you-don't-want-to-know. Bolted to the wall is a sign

185

reading, "We haul our own water, so if it's yellow, let it mellow. If it's brown flush it down." Oh but Lord-God-Almighty it's *all* here mellowing, years' worth, a museum of excrement.

I compare the pain to my psyche and the pain in my bladder, deciding my bladder can wait. I leave, making sure the hellmouth is completely closed.

I thread my way back past the sad shelves of stale candy bars and bleached skin mags, past the indignant sign—"Smoking is permitted in this *entire* establishment," and into the dining area, a scattering of old Formica tables that seem to have been scavenged from a dozen kitchens. Two burly guys with three-day growths are the only customers. One of them, the bigger guy with the black ponytail, leans his head back to look at me, then raises his head to look back at his friend, saying, "He actually wants to *eat* here!"

And it's true. I do. Because—and this is the other reason I'm here—among my father's papers, I found a ten-year-old receipt for breakfast at Twin Eagles Diesel. I know, scraping the bottom of the barrel.

The waitress and cashier are the same person and the only employee, a rangy desert woman of indeterminate age the two guys call "Mom," the word wrung out of their mouths with a sour twist. As she passes them on the way to my table, they say, "Mom, where's them boys of yours?"

"Out hunting jackrabbits," she says flatly.

When she reaches my table, she just stands there staring at me from inside the frame of her gray-blonde hair, as if she's forgotten how to do her job.

"No menu?" I say.

The pupils of her gray eyes arc with slow disgust. "We got food, food, and food. What'll it be?"

"I'll have food!"

"Good choice."

I can see that someone once tried to widen the grim set of Mom's mouth. The scar extends straight out from the left side, like an extra pair of pursed lips. I picture the knife blade in her mouth, the short, sharp flick to the side. It hurts my face just to look at it. She's wearing jeans and a T-shirt with a cartoon of Custer lying on the ground and the caption "I've fallen and I can't get up!"

"That's funny," I say pointing. "Your shirt." She says nothing, does nothing, in reply.

I order a cheese omelet, hash browns, toast and coffee. Her expression doesn't change. When she takes her face away, it seems to linger, hanging in the air, the twin gray dots of her eyes indifferent as stars.

I'm still carrying the picture of my father in his dress whites, the picture I showed around at Boy's Town and everywhere else. I'd feel too foolish asking her if she recognizes him, a customer she had ten years ago. That's assuming she was even here then, and assuming she'd even bother to look at it, but something primordial about her makes me think she's always been here, and anyway, I can't help myself. I take the picture from my shirt pocket and lay it on the table in front of me, where she can't fail to see it. But what do I expect? That she'll go all loose in her boots? "Ooh, as I live and breathe, if it isn't Commander Bobby!"

Eventually she reappears with a platter of grease studded with vaguely organic matter. She snaps it down on the table in front of me, right on top of the picture. Serves me right.

The meal is beyond bad. The hash browns are like gravel, the eggs like burnt pieces of lace, the toast like a kitchen sponge soaked in battery acid. The only thing right about the breakfast is its price—$3.50—though it's a dollar more than my father paid for the same food ten years ago. I eat it, not wanting to cause embarrassment. And, I guess, because it was my father's meal. He sat here, maybe at this very table, served maybe by the same surly waitress, and forced down these same hateful forkfuls.

I don't know what I thought I'd find here, what evidence of my father, what lingering image, what sense of him. Standing in a spot in which he once stood, sitting in a chair in which he once sat. Driving the road he once drove. What's it worth? And the farther I drive, the more miles I put between myself and what's left of my father, the wet body pulled out of the ocean and hauled back to the homeland. Why didn't I identify the body instead of sending my sister? Why didn't I look into those dead eyes for whatever truth I could find there? Surely then I'd know something about him. Is this trip really about looking for something or am I just running away?

When I began this trip, I thought I was searching for my father, but maybe I'm looking for a way out, searching for another condition, the long journey out of the self. I have an extremely tenuous relationship with myself, the guest who won't—will never—have the good sense to go home.

What would have been the point of going to Key West to claim my father's body? He wasn't there, not in that wet slab of meat lying on the deck of that Coast Guard cutter. Not in that hole in the Indiana dirt. He isn't anywhere. He never was. He's as alive in the dead gaze of the Twin Eagles waitress as he is anywhere.

The two guys at the other table have finished their breakfasts, or at least they've stopped eating. They're leaning back, the front legs of their chairs off the floor. They've studded their leftovers with the bent blond pillars of cigarette butts, but somehow the food is no less appetizing than it already was. I'm out of here. One more failed attempt to connect with some shred of my father's life.

Up front sits a 50s-vintage cash register on a clouded, scar-topped glass case. As I pay the tab, I buy a pack of gum, something to cut the film of grease in my mouth. The stick I unwrap has all the flavor and texture of balsa wood.

I can't help it. As she hands me my change, I say, "I've eaten prison food better than this."

She slams the register shut and, without looking at me, heads back through the dining room toward the kitchen. "I'll bet you have," she says.

"Where you going?" I say to her retreating back, "Not finished slicing up road-kill for the dinner menu?"

She ignores me but the two guys have lowered the front legs of their chairs to the floor and are staring at me now.

I don't care. "What are you looking at?"

They say nothing. They stare. Ponytail grabs slowly at his sweaty face.

"Oh dear," I say. "I've violated the decorum of Twin Eagles Diesel."

The other guy, whose chin and jaw had been borrowed from the head of a much smaller man, says to his friend, "Not a satisfied customer."

"Indeed," Ponytail says.

Back outside, the sun has hitched itself a few rungs higher in the pale blue sky. Beyond my car, parked at the edge of the lot, heat curls up from the desert floor. The colors out there are so faded and thin you can see through them. Everywhere I look is sagebrush—gray, brown, and black. I miss the green and gold of Nebraska. In the distance, the mountains stand like unreal shadows of something else. In the sand just beyond the parking lot someone has spelled out a message with fist-sized rocks: "Jesus died for us.—Chas." I'm not surprised, Chas, not if his last supper was at Twin Eagles Diesel.

• • •

Four or five angry hours later and hundreds of self-righteous miles away, I realize I left the picture of my father on the table under the plate. Serves me right for making a scene. But the loss hits me hard. I didn't feel much of anything when I got the news that he'd died. But somehow losing his picture makes the loss more real. I have other pictures, one of him on a small boat facing aft in silhouette, hands on hips, another of him and some crewmates at a P.O. club in Guantanamo Bay. The patch on his left arm shows that he was a Petty Officer First Class at the time. He's got one hand on a glass of clear liquid. It has to be a 7-Up for the non-drinker. His pack of Pall Malls stands on end in front of him next to a dollar bill. This time he's looking straight at the camera, his gaze a little suspicious, maybe even hostile. But then none of the men at the table seems particularly happy. Whatever the picture's telling me is beyond my reach.

It's the missing picture, the most recent, that matters most. In it, my father is decked out with a chest full of stars, bars, and medals. He's all business in the picture, his face firm, his jaw set, his cap a hair off-angle, the ridiculous cap with its billow of white, its scrambled eggs across the black patent leather bill, its gold braid, its showy officer's crest. Ridiculous. Belongs on a circus clown. His gaze aims just to the right of the camera's lens, evading eye contact even in death. And now the picture's gone. I go so far as to call the place from a payphone, but no one answers. Of course. The waitress probably sailed it into the trash without a second thought, or just pushed it to the floor to be swept up at the end of the day. Not realizing, not at all, that the picture might mean something to somebody. Would it have been so hard to pin it to the bulletin board in case the owner came back for it? I want to tell her this picture matters, people matter. This was a man who lived and died, who gave much and took much, a man of faith, of too much faith, a man whose stories were about the daring exploits of others and about his own good fortune and goofiness, a man quick of mind, a many-minded man, a man of many lives, a man in love with the open sea, the sea that had been trying to kill him for decades, finally catching him with his back turned in the warm waters of the Keys, a man with a fixed idea, a plan, an idea of order and a way to impose it, a double man—one who lived by the law and one who lived by his passions, a man of stern good cheer, a man of sudden tears, a man who could commit ritualistic violence, a man at home with cannibals, a man whose idea of excess was sleeping until 6:30 A.M., whose idea of the upright life was marrying two women at the same time, a hero, a villain, a martyr, a madman, my father, trapped under a plate of bad food in Twin Eagles, Arizona. There can't be a worse way to go.

· · ·

"I know you don't want to talk to me." It's early evening in Long Island, but I don't think that's going to soften her mood any. The other woman. Not that. More than that. The other wife.

"Who *is* this? . . . Oh, it's you. I told you—"

"I know, I know, but I just want to—"

"I don't care what you want. Now goodbye."

"Did he beat you, too?"

Silence on the line.

I go on. "Every day? For a long time? And always 'for your own good'?" When she still doesn't say anything, I keep talking. "Or was it something else? Something different? With me it was the knife that scared me most. I hated him. I still hate him. I don't think there will ever be a time when I don't hate him. But I'm trying to understand him. That's why I'm calling. That's why I need you to tell me what you know."

Silence on the line.

"That's all. Just so I can understand."

And then, finally, she speaks, her words slow, all the anger dried to a scaly residue. "I can't help you."

"I know he hurt you, too." Silence. "Maybe in some other way."

A long tense silence, and then, "He disappeared is what he did. I loved him and he made a fool out of me."

"I know."

"No, you don't. He made me believe in a lie—that he *loved* me, that I was his *wife*, that *we* were his family. And then he left. Gone. Without a word."

"I know."

"No. You don't. You don't know." I can hear her pound her chest as she says, "He made me afraid of trusting anyone and anything ever again."

"I . . . I'm sorry."

A long silence and then, in a more collected voice, she says, "Nothing for you to be sorry about."

"Maybe not, but I'm sorry all the same." It occurs to me that she and I were both his victims at around the same time, that our fates were mixed up with each other.

She says, "What is it you think you can understand about him? It's nothing there. If he was gone before, he's really gone now."

"I want to know why he did what he did, why he was the man he was."

"Do you understand? It's nothing there."

"What do you remember?"

"Remember? It was over forty years ago. I remember he was a good-looking man in uniform. I remember he said his life was 'complicated.'" She gives out a short, sharp bark of laughter. "The understatement of the century!"

I was one of those complications. Were the beatings some half-symbolic, half-real effort to kill me, I wonder? To remove the complication? To simplify his life? His third wife said she was afraid for her life around him. That would seem to answer a question, except that it was my father himself who told me that, shaking his head. "Now why would she go and say a thing like that?"

"You must hate him," I say to her.

She exhales sharply. "I don't, no."

"You must. You have to." My rage wants company, angry little playmates with pointed teeth.

"No. To tell you the God's-honest truth, until you started calling, I didn't even think about him. Not anymore. Not much."

"How? How can that be so?"

"It was a long time ago, that's how. I'm past it. That's my advice. It was just something that happened. Move on. You want to understand something? There. Understand that."

I decide to play a hunch. "Did you ever get married again?"

The old chill comes back into her voice. "What the hell business is it of yours? And by the way, I need my skillet back."

"Your what? Your skillet?"

"He took it. A cast-iron skillet. I want it back."

• • •

Later that night, after killing part of a bottle of Beam, I work up the courage to call his brother, Carl. I don't pay attention to the time. I'm obviously waking him up.

His voice is soft. He's trying not to wake up his wife, sleeping next to him. "Oh, hi! It's so good to hear your voice! Hey, you missed a heckuva service! You would have had a really good time!" Really? "Hold on a 'sec." The ache of springs, a rustling, and then the quiet snap of a closing door. When he speaks again, his whisper bounces off the tiled wall of a bathroom.

But all Uncle Carl wants to talk about is my father's naval career, what a wonderful family man he was. Maybe he senses some criticism in my silence. He says, "As for some of the things he done," he says, "you know, to *you* or whatever, it's not my place to judge." Not anyone's place, he implies. Not even mine. "All I know is that a lot of his work was classified Top Secret. Maybe that had something to do with it." I love it. Child abuse for the sake of national security.

Still, maybe there's something to it. But a few months later, I'll receive the report from my Freedom of Information Act inquiry, and the most startling secret that turns up will be that he was an uncooperative patient for the Navy dentists. Top Secret work. Right. Does this mean that it's all a lie? Or that his secrets were so important they don't even show up in a search, not even as pages of blacked-out text? I don't know. I don't know anything. After all this time, my father is a bigger mystery than ever.

❧❧

Before beginning my travels, I packed a suitcase and a shoulder bag with clothing and other items which I thought I would need. I later discovered that I had taken too much clothing and not enough of other items. My updated list follows:

LIST OF NECESSITIES FOR MEXICO

Electric Appliances
Hot Plate
Water Pot
Soup Pot
Skillet
Plate
Bowl
Cup
Knife, Fork, Spoon
Can Opener
Crisco or Wesson Oil
Instant Coffee
Constant Comment Tea
Chamomile Tea
Vitamins and Minerals
Pepto-Bismol
Quinine Sulfate
Hydroclonozone Tablets
Undershirts, 4
Undershorts, 4
Socks, 5
Shirts: 2 Sport, 3 Knit
Pants: 2 Long, 3 Short
Swim Suit
Shoes: Walking, Sandals, Shower
Sweater
Books, 3 per Week
Notebook
Writing Paper
Envelopes
Pens, 2

Electric Razor
Safety Razor
Shaving Cream
After Shave Lotion
Tooth Brush
Tooth Paste
Mouth Wash
Bath Towel
Wash Cloth
Nail Clippers
Pocket Knife
Wrist Watch
Alarm Clock
Sun Glasses
Binoculars or Telescope
Camera, Film, Flashbulbs
Suntan Lotion
Toilet Tissue, 1 Roll
Paper Towel, 1 Roll
Drain Stopper, 3" Flat Rubber
Candle and Match Book
Playing Cards
Cribbage Board and Dice
Small Chess Set
U.S. Dollars, small bills
American Express Traveler's Checks,
    $100 Units
Mexican Pesos from Mexican Bank
VISA Card
English/Spanish Dictionary
Berlitz's Spanish for Travelers

17

SHIPMATES

I'm driving through washed-out desert, through walls of shimmering heat. The map says I'm somewhere just over the California line, but it feels like a western suburb of Hell.

I keep thinking about luck. I can't help thinking of my father's. Finding work that doesn't feel like work is a form of luck, isn't it? He enjoyed his life in the Navy. Even in retirement, he found great pleasure in dropping in on old shipmates and stopping in at naval bases around the country to lend a hand with various engineering projects. Maybe Robert Frost was right, that home is "the place where, when you have to go there, / They have to take you in." And maybe that's all my father was looking for, in marriage after marriage— his true home. In the end, it was the Navy, the only home he could endure, that could endure him, that always took him in.

I realize suddenly that it's the age of the internet. After I check into a room at La Florita, a motel in the middle of nowhere, I go through my father's service record and make a list of his ships and the years he served on them: USS Chilton (APA-38) 1949–55, Beach Jumper Unit Two 1955–56, USS Laning (APD-55) 1956–67, USS Rizzi (DE-537) 1957–58, USS Cromwell (DE-1014) 1958–59, USS Luce (DLG-7) 1964–66, and USS Eaton (DD-510) 1966–68. After that his positions were all on land, at the Pentagon, the White Sands Missile Range, the Naval Postgraduate School, and other places not in the official record, like the jungles of Latin America.

There's a small, battered table in front of the room's only window. I set up my computer and fire up the web browser to search for references to the ships. Almost immediately, I find several sites honoring the men who served on them. On each one I go to the members listing and find the names of men who served at the same time my father served. Most listings include e-mail addresses. I love the internet! By evening I've fired off a dozen or more messages to his former shipmates, feeling a little like my brother on that train so long ago. *Oh, Daddy! Oh my daddy!* And now I wait.

I can't get over the fact that my father was married to two women at once. What was he thinking? I guess I can understand someone who's been separated from a woman for a long time and then decides to remarry not bothering with the legality of divorce. But this man maintained two households, was husband and father to two families at once. The guy with the orderly mind, the a-place-for-everything-and-everything-in-its-place guy, the live-and-die-by-the-rules guy.

I remember the story he used to tell about his days on the swift boats in 'Nam, how once they stayed too long upriver, the tide going out before they could accomplish their mission, the river sliding out from under them like a tablecloth being whipped from under the good china. They were hung up on the mud, the engines useless. As the shock of their problem hit, the Officer-in-Charge went below and laid in his bunk. My father took over, somehow getting the boat out of the mud and back into navigable water. He told me that story several times, and every time he told it he told about the follow-up, how he looked up the officer after the war and asked him why he had given up his command like that. "The man just shrugged," he'd say.

How I'd like to sit you down now, Dad, and ask the same question. How could you? What was going through your mind?

Maybe he fell in love with the other woman, and unable to sleep with a woman he didn't intend to marry, proposed to her. And maybe before he could divorce my mother, the other woman became pregnant. Maybe he thought marrying her would be, not the right thing to do, but the next-to-right thing to do. Maybe he thought he could sort it all out later. But before he could do that, the river disappeared right out from under him and he was left stuck in the mud, his engines useless, enemy mortar rounds coming closer and closer. If someone were to tell me my father had killed someone in cold blood, I could believe it. But that he would break such a fundamental rule of civilized society? *This* man? Impossible. And yet.

La Florita is on the edge of town. Nothing much between me and the desert. All the while I work and wait, I watch the arena across the road, where a youth rodeo has been going on, first the wide-eyed little mutton-busters, then the lithe fourteen-year-old barrel racers. Now it's time for the older kids, the tough-looking guys, smaller versions of their fathers, I'm guessing, hat brims locked down tight, wads of chew or chewing gum lumping their cheeks. Forget the kids, they seem to be saying. We're the show.

I watch over the screen of my laptop. Between contestants, I hit the "Retrieve Mail" button. Nothing. And so I watch as, one by one, the young cowboys fall off their horses and bulls, miss their steers, get tangled up in their own ropes. Over and over, the announcer groans with sympathy. Not one of them has a successful run. I'm feeling a lot like them until I get my first reply, just as the rodeo is breaking up.

Ted Ruloff, who served on the Chilton, didn't know my father but expresses sympathy on his passing. I'm disappointed, though I don't know what more I expected. Years and years have passed. What are the chances that any of these men knew him?

Another hour passes. The last cars have left the rodeo lot across the highway. I hit "Retrieve Mail" again. Nothing. I hate the internet.

Another hour passes. I should sleep, check the e-mail in the morning, but I can't help it. I have to wait, to see the messages as they come in, if they come in. It's like I'm waiting for election returns. Darkness falls fast out on the desert. The sound of traffic on the two-lane seems to change, the sound of each engine deepens and swells in the darkness. Another e-mail shows up.

Gerald G. McGlinn, from the Luce, probably knew him, he says, "but not very well. I would suspect that his GQ station was in the WEPS control center which was part of CIC (Combat Info Center) & within about 30 feet of mine, or on the bridge at the Weapons Console. In either case I would probably have interfaced with him from time to time."

I hear the sound of my father's voice in his, even in an e-mail, the love of the technical. Here's a man who probably talked to my father every day. But knowing this—even if I could decode the terminology—what do I know? Not much. He's given me the shape of a memory but not its substance.

I'm asking for the impossible, I guess, but I sit at the computer anyway, watching the night ripen outside my window, watching the traffic on the highway slowly dwindle until only an occasional car comes by.

Who was my father? Mr. Law-and-Order or Mr. Bigamy? Mr. Aw-Shucks or Mr. Wrath-of-God? How I wish one of the stops on this trip were to his camper in some shabby desert town. I'd drive through the gate in the low pink cinderblock wall, past the fringe of dusty willows. I'd bang on his tinny door, and there he'd be, the long face, the dark eyes, the thinning hair, a deep dimple socketing each cheek. *I'm so glad you've come,* he'd say. *There are so many things I need to explain.* And we'd sit on either side of the fold-down table, him refilling our coffee cups from the ever-present gallon thermos at his feet. And we'd talk and talk until the river came pouring back under us again, and the engines of our little boat would gun to life.

A ship is a small city. Impossible that two crewmen might know each other, I guess. That's what David Nowell, of the Eaton, implies in his message.

"As with most things on a ship, you have a tendency to be involved with only the people in your Division. For the most part. I do have a vague recollection of a 'Mr. Spencer' as the OOD (Officer of the Deck) during some of my watches in CIC as a CIC underway watch supervisor, & again as one of the OODs on the quarterdeck watch when we were in port." Again, knowing this, what do I know? Nothing.

Another shipmate from the Eaton, one who signs himself T. Rex, is not much more help: "I was enlisted and I was in a different division. I may have been on the same watch on the bridge or quarterdeck with him but I do remember the name. I couldn't say much more about him, I never had the opportunity to work with him directly. I do know that a Lieutenant Ferguson replaced him."

Another writes, "It's been almost forty years since I left the USS RIZZI and although his name sounds familiar, I cannot place what he looked like. Was he an actual Officer, or was he an enlisted man? If he was an Officer I may have delivered Radio messages to him from time to time. (I was a Radioman.) If not, then I am sure our paths crossed at some time or another."

My brother and sister were too young to remember him. His former wives won't talk about him. The rest of his relatives remember him as a joker, a generous man, a war hero, a family man. And now I realize that not even the men who served with him knew him. What hope do I have of recovering him, of doing with his life what the Coast Guard did with his body, hauling him up from oblivion?

The last message of the night comes in just before midnight. Another shipmate writes, "I knew who he was but didn't know him personally . . . I only was in the Laning for about a year and then went to a school I had requested and on to another ship . . . I am sorry for your loss as you said your late father. . . ."

I stay up for a couple more hours, staring out at the desert, but no other messages come through.

I fall asleep thinking of his signature, the way it evolved into other shapes and names, and of the birth certificate for "Cornelius Robert Spencer," and of the marriage license in the name of "Bob Cornelius." I decide I'll never know this man.

In the morning one more e-mail is waiting for me. Jack Targer served with my father in Virginia. And, miraculously, he lives a few hours west of here, near Nogales. "Sure I remember him," he writes. "We were in the Beach Jumpers together. I could tell you more about it, but then I'd have to kill you."

How can I resist? I load up the car and head west.

• • •

"A little medicinal alcohol," Jack Targer says pouring our coffee mugs half-full of bourbon. He taps the rim of his mug against mine and says, "Confusion to our enemies." He's a small man in his seventies with a full head of silvery-gray hair. His curly white sideburns stand out like quotation marks.

We're sitting on his glassed-in back porch. Outside, the bright, bleached desert stretches for as far as I can see. The desert's inside, too. Targer is painting imaginary desertscapes on old hubcaps. He says he works on several at once, painting desert floors on each first, then going back to fill in the cacti on each, then the coyotes. He sells the hubcaps in the tourist shops, claiming they're painted by Indians or Mexicans or whatever the trade requires. After telling me he's "sorry as shit" to hear about my father's death, he settles into his drink and goes back to his painting while he talks to me for the next couple of hours, telling me what he remembers about his time with my father. He sits on an old piano stool in front of an easel with two half-painted hubcaps propped in the tray. His stiff brush dabbing at the metal hubcaps almost has the effect of a brushed cymbal underscoring his words.

"It was the Navy where we learned to lie. In the Beach Jumpers at Little Creek Amphibious Base."

"The Beach Jumpers?" It sounds like the title of a forgotten Gidget movie.

"Hm-hmm," he says, humming around the brush handle he's clamped between his teeth while he retrieves a hubcap from the floor. "A Navy SEAL unit that engaged in 'special warfare.'" He paints the air with imaginary quotation marks. "'Tactical cover and deception.' The kind of activities that today would be called PSYOPS—that's 'Psychological Operations.' Our activities were so secret that we trained on a separate part of the base and wore no ship/unit shoulder patches on our uniforms. No one, not even our wives, knew exactly what we did."

The perfect duty, I think, for a man like my father.

"Some of what we did was simple, like dropping leaflets and broadcasting propaganda over loudspeakers, but we also did more sophisticated things, like deceiving the enemy with false amphibious landings, fouling radar and radio signals. Spook stuff, you know, James Bond stuff. Our goal was to harass the enemy in any way possible, drawing attention away from the true assault."

The bourbon burns nicely all the way down. "You were spies," I say. "You're saying my father was a spy."

He stops painting and gazes up at the ceiling, a dollop of brown paint threatening to slide back down the handle of his brush.

"Not exactly spies," he says, but he's clearly taken with the notion. "More like marauders . . . stalkers . . . pirates. Or maybe tricksters." He points at the hubcap he's working on. "Like our coyote friend here. We'd do crazy stuff like drag a blimp behind a small boat to enlarge our radar image, purposely drawing fire from the enemy. We'd attach half-pound charges of TNT to small buoys and set them off to simulate the gunfire of a large invasion force. You had to be tough to be a Beach Jumper, you know?"

I'm thinking of my bedroom in our Indiana house, where I had the top bunk, my brother the bottom. I was in training, my father always said, and so I had to sleep in the nude. "Pajamas are for girls and sissies," he told me. So were sheets and pillowcases. I slept on the bare mattress with an uncovered pillow and a ratty blanket so thin I could see through it. How else could I hope to qualify for the service?

I slept on my back because, my father said, it was healthier and because sleeping on your stomach was for babies and non-qualified pukes, who didn't care if they got knifed or not. For some reason I couldn't asleep well on my back, slipping instead into a night-long half-sleep that left me groggy all day. Some nights, I'd roll onto my stomach, grateful for the sudden plunge into deep sleep, but I learned one night to stop that when my father, charging into the room, flipped me onto my back and held the cold blade of his diver's knife to my neck.

"Congratulations, boy! You're dead. You just killed yourself."

I learned to sleep on my back and to get by on half-sleep.

After some weeks of this, I woke up one night more frightened than usual, but something told me to keep my eyes closed. I couldn't hear anything, but I could sense a presence, an area of warmth, a displacement of air beside my head. He was standing next to my bunk, very close.

After a time, I opened my left eye just enough to see through my lashes. The blade of the diver's knife was less than an inch above my eyes. I stopped breathing, thinking. I could smell the steel, the leather-wrapped hilt, the seawater that had dried between the cracks. He held the blade very still and studied me. His white T-shirt glowed in the dark. In the bunk below, the thin ripple of my brother's breath went on undisturbed.

That night, and for many nights to come, my father stood beside me for a long time. He'd hold the blade over my eyes, my nose, my throat. PSYOPS. Special warfare. And I was the enemy.

One night, long after I'd stopped pretending to sleep, he gave me a whispered lecture as he held the blade across my open eyes, so close everything was a blur.

"You need to know that pain and fear are only choices we make. Choose fear, feel fear. Choose pain, feel pain."

He lifted the blade away from my eyes.

"I'm asking you to choose something else. I call it 'Jesus.' Maybe one day you will, too. Remains to be seen. Until that day, call it fire."

He touched the blade to the skin above my left eyebrow. I held my breath. He held his breath. We waited, as if for a natural and necessary process to unfold. The blade came away wet. Something like a tear slid down the side of my forehead.

By morning, the blood was dry, an inch-wide red ridge over my brow. It looked like no more than a bad scratch.

After breakfast, with my father sitting right there, my mother turned me to her and raised my chin, making the cut sting freshly.

"What's this? What did you do?" She was asking me, not him.

"I don't know," I said. "Nothing, I guess."

The truth is, I was proud. Proud I had been able to lie there and take it. I had been blooded. Never mind that I was the prey. I was proud of being brought into the fraternity of blood. I wanted more. I wanted scars. I wanted to be a man. *When can you cut me again, Dad? I want it. Please.* I couldn't wait to lie under the knife again. I wanted whatever it took to win my father's love, my place in the world.

In the many nights that followed, he'd cut me on the neck, the shoulders, the chest. And always the light touch that barely broke the skin. He'd lower the blade by tiny increments until it touched, then let my skin take the weight of the razor-thin blade.

Through it all, every time, I held myself as still as possible, knowing that, if I moved, I'd hurt myself badly. That's how he would see it—that I had hurt myself. So I lay there, night after night, while he marked me with cuts as thin as hairs, whisper cuts, filaments of fire that would be almost gone by morning. Sometimes the cut didn't even draw blood, raising only a tiny ridge of pale skin. In the morning, in front of the bathroom mirror, I'd brush it with my thumb and watch the wound blossom. This was knife dancing.

And always he did it with such delicacy, as if he were studying me, as if my blood might tell him some secret. He stared at the lines of blood the way a psychic stares at Tarot cards.

Over time I learned to hypnotize myself as the blade's bright edge lightly touched my skin. I kept still as the blade made its shallow cut. Now here, now there. Just enough to sting, to leave a thin red thread. And all the while, his quiet whisper in my ear: "In the name of Christ Jesus, I rebuke thee. In the blood of the Lamb, I rebuke thee. In the name of Christ Jesus, I rebuke thee. In the blood of the Lamb, I rebuke thee. . . ."

I take another hit of bourbon and try to clear my head.

"How tough was he?" Jack says, as if I've asked. He paints a flat-bottomed raft of clouds. "You ask how tough? Plenty. Look at it this way. It was the job of the Underwater Demolition Team to clear landing zones and beaches. When they were finished, they'd plant a sign on the beach"—he drew an imaginary line in the air with his brush—"'Welcome, Marines!' Meaning that they were there first, you understand, and that the Marines weren't such hot shit as they thought. Well, us Beach Jumpers were there *before* the UDTs, and if we did our job right, not a blessed one of God's creatures ever knew we were there."

He propped four finished hubcaps on the narrow window ledge to dry, then picked four more from a pile of fifty or more stacked next to the door. They were already covered with a base coat of beige. He propped two of them on his easel and painted a dark brown horizon line on each, then smudged below the line to make the desert look more natural. They were really terrible paintings. His cacti looked like tuning forks, his coyotes like can openers.

"Our boats were trash mostly," he went on, "reconditioned World War II PT boats, AVRs, PTFs so crappy-ass we called them 'nasty class' boats, or experimental jobs like the Osprey with engines so touchy they sometimes blew up in our faces."

"But what about my father," I said.

He gave me a quick, disapproving look. I was rushing his story. "We were in Unit 2," he said. "Had some fun on the Mekong Delta in a PCF. That's "Patrol Craft Fast." A swift boat. About 63-foot, armed with a twin 50-calibre gun in the forward tub, a single in the stern, 5-inch rocket launchers, sonar, radar, loran, and electronic countermeasures we referred to as 'the black box.' The rest of the crew called us 'science majors.' That was your dad and me."

Just this morning I found his official record for this period of his life. Listed under "Primary Duty," it says, "Technician," a suitably vague reference for someone involved with high-tech countermeasures.

"We had us a world of fun," Jack went on while he dabbed away at the next pair of hubcaps. "What we'd do was wait in the South China Sea for the tide to fill the dry river beds of the delta, then scoot upriver to take out a gun emplacement, insert a VN marine, deliver supplies, pop an egg here and there. And then, before the ebb tide left us high and dry, slip on back to blue water. From poop to soup, slick as snot. I probably shouldn't be telling you all this, but what the hell. Your dad's dead, right? Our mission was to support Operation Sea Dragon, the maritime equivalent of Operation Rolling Thunder, the cruiser-destroyer patrols that took out shore batteries and the like."

"Sea Dragon?"

"That's right."

Another piece of the mystery falls into place. "'Sea Dragon' was the name of his sailboat, the one he died on."

Without telling me much of anything about my father himself, Jack has filled in some gaps. My father started his Navy career as a Gunner's Mate and ended it working on laser-guided weaponry. Among his papers I find an "Officer Preference and Personal Information Card." His self-assessment gives a good idea of how he spent his life:

My first choice duty preference is as a Weapons Systems Engineer at the Naval Ship Weapons Systems Engineering Station (USNSWSES) at Port Hueneme, CA. I have technical knowledge of Surface Weapons Systems including conventional and missile systems, and surveillance, detection, evaluation, identification, designation, acquisition, command and control, fire control, gun, missile launching and guidance subsystems, telemetry, and target damage assessment equipment. I have the education, training, experience, and ability to design and test as well as to maintain and employ. I desire to be used in a job for which I am most qualified and capable in order to best serve the U.S. Navy and my country.

Jack goes on: "Our overall objective was simple—to screw things up, to misdirect the enemy, to mess with their minds. The motto of our unit was 'Keep 'm Guessing!'"

My father was good at that. His time in the Beach Jumpers was just the beginning of a life-long effort to scare the bejesus out of any and all comers.

At the end of our talk, Jack walks me to the back door, shaking his head. "Can't believe the old coot is dead," he says. "It's tough to lose your dad all on a sudden like that. Wait a minute." He hustles back inside the house and comes out again a few minutes later to press an embroidered shoulder patch into my hand.

"I had some of these made up a few years ago. It's not official or anything, but it's just like the ones some of us wore. Something to remember the good old days by."

It was a cloth patch embroidered with a stylized mask of comedy over a red "1" and the words "Beach Jumper Unit USN."

I can't believe it. I look up at Jack and back at the patch. I stand, hardly able to speak. It's the same mask I saw tattooed on the arm of the cab driver in Chihuahua, the one who raced me back to my hotel after his buddies yanked me around in that dark alley.

He gives my shoulder a shake and says, "Good luck to you, son. May your smokestacks always point up. And remember these words to live by: if they're on the river at night, kill them."

≈≈≈≈

The cannibals, though constantly warring with neighboring tribes, are great ones for gardening, which they do, as they do most things, in near nudity. It is not uncommon for a husband to beat a wife or child when necessary, and not uncommon also for a man to have more than one wife, polygamy being a way of increasing the population and of demonstrating achievement. I did not have the opportunity to take a meal with the cannibals, though they had at least one prisoner being fattened for the feast, a fellow from a neighboring tribe. They'd given him the run of the village, it seemed to me, going so far as to assign him a wife, yet for some reason he didn't try to escape. Perhaps he didn't realize he was on the menu? Who are we to call this practice barbaric? Is tucking in to your neighbor's haunch bone really any different from taking the wine and wafer? If so, it is merely a matter of degree.

Among the cannibals, the preferred cooking method is to quarter the individual, then barbecue him, saving prizes like the fingers, the penis, and the heart's grease-sack for honored guests. Human flesh tastes best when cooked, I'm told.

❧

18

WORST OF LUCK FOR A BOY IN THE FUTURE

Bats seem to follow me. I have all the same movie-inspired fear of bats that creeps out everyone else. But I'm talking about actual bats. I remember years ago waiting in a long hallway for a dance studio to open up for play rehearsal, a bat strafing me over and over. Too scared to run, I just sat there on the floor quivering, ducking. Years later, in the living room of my future wife's parents, I looked aside from my book to see a bat squeeze itself out a crack in the built-in bookshelf and then go flapping around the room like a rubber knife. A little while after that, I found a dead bat in broad daylight plastered to the cinder block foundation of the farmhouse where I was living. I peeled it off the wall, the devil's ivy.

So when I look up from my father's papers, spread out on the bed next to mine in my room at the Motherload Motel somewhere in the California desert, the bat flapping around in anxious loops is old news to me. Once I would have swung a broom at it, cursed, prayed. Now I open the door. Let it find its own way out. But as I open the door, another bat, larger than the first one, comes flying directly out of the darkness and at me. It's big. The tuft of brown hair on the chin of its baby face makes it all the more frightening. I slam the door in its downy face.

Tomorrow I meet with another guy who served with my father at the Naval Amphibious Base in Little Creek, Virginia, back in his beach jumper days. I go over the papers that have led me here. Copies of my father's letters to the guy, though no copies of his replies. In the letters, my father is chatty, telling him about the sailing course he teaches and about the Chinese Junk he hopes to own someday. He sends him Bible passages for consolation over the death of the man's son. He signs off every letter "Your Sea-Daddy." They clearly know each other well. When I called to ask for a visit, he agreed right off. He hadn't heard about my father's death, and I could tell it set him back some, though he didn't say much. I'm eager to meet the man.

But all that's tomorrow. I'm too tired to do anything about the bat. I need to sleep. I climb into bed while the bat sweeps frantically overhead, quartering the air like a cutter looking for the lost.

• • •

Next morning, I find his small ranch house without any trouble. It's on a busy highway, the last lot not to be converted to a fast food restaurant. It's a pink stucco nightmare with barred front windows and a huge radio antennae standing on the roof. I knock for several minutes without much luck. Then, when I'm about to leave, the door opens slightly, and a small child's face appears in the dark slice of air.

"Grampy says go out back!" The door slams shut. I go out back.

He's sitting in a lawn chair drinking a screwdriver and watching a bulldozer level a few hundred acres behind his small yard. Several other big yellow earth-movers are strewn across the landscape, along with stacks and piles of I-beams, big round bales of pink insulation, and a lonely huddle of saplings, their roots balled in burlap.

He rises as I walk toward him with my hand out to shake. I say my name and shake his hand. He replies, "Randall Colley, Radarman, Second Class." It's like we're taking part in an interrogation.

He motions me to the empty lawn chair next to his. The left and right sides of his yard abut on parking lots for a pancake house and a busy taco stand. With the bulldozer, the highway traffic, and the cars in the parking lots, the noise is deafening, and I quickly become profoundly depressed. How can anyone live here?

Colley has the brown leathery skin of someone who's spent many years in the desert, his smile no more than a grimace, his every look a sidelong glance. He sips his drink slowly, stingily. His still-black hair is cropped short. He's in good shape for a man who must be in his seventies.

"Big job," I say looking toward the construction site.

He nods. "Discount store coming in, buying up every blessed acre in sight. I'm the last one to go. I'm holding out for more money. They need my place." He holds out a clenched fist. "I got their nuts in the cracker." He takes another stingy sip of his screwdriver. "Money in the friggin' bank." He smiles, raises his glass, and says, "Who knew retirement would be this grand?"

"I'm happy for you," I say.

"You should be," he says, looking back at the house. "Place's always been a shithole, but it's finally a gold-plated shithole." He takes another drink, then looks at me for a long moment. "You know, I didn't know your dad."

I'm stunned. On the phone he said he remembered him. On the phone he said I should come out to he house. Now this. "Excuse me?" I say, a little too loudly.

He gazes out at the construction site. "Did not know the man."

"But when I called, you said—"

"I said I'd see you. That's all." He's still looking out at the torn up acreage.

"But he wrote to you. I have the letters."

"I wouldn't know about that. I can't tell you about that."

"But you trained with him at Little Creek."

He sighs, takes another sip, and watches the bulldozer make another pass at a mound of earth. "Lots of fellows were at Little Creek."

"But you're the one he wrote to. I called you. You said to come. You said you knew him."

"I told you about that. I don't know about that." He still won't look at me.

We sit there silently for a while watching the heavy equipment, listening to the diesels grind up the peace. I'm even more deeply depressed now than when I arrived. I don't get it. All those letters. It crosses my mind that he may be lying, but why? I try a different tack.

"Good memories of your years in the Navy?"

He nods, still not looking at me. "The best." He raises his glass in a silent toast.

"What do you remember most?"

"I remember the boats were for shit. 'Beach Jumper Boats,' they called them, BJBs, but we always just called them 'Blow Job Boats.' Least that's what I called them. I remember they had us in them quonset huts. Tin cans is what they were."

"What about 'Nam?"

His mouth twitches slightly before he answers. "Did my time like the next fellow."

We sit there like that for a while, me watching his face, him watching the construction, giving nothing away. It's hot and loud in the backyard, but the silence that hangs between us is as loud as the earth-movers. The engine of the bulldozer in front of us roars and a bright blue plume of smoke shoots up from its exhaust pipe. Colley's gaze goes soft as he remembers something. "We used to go through gallons of Brasso polishing the brightwork . . . I remember I had the sit-up record before Vince Piscitelli took it way—1,327 in fifty-six minutes."

"You look like you could win it back."

He looks down at his torso as if it's something apart from him. "Might have one day, but them days're lost in the bilges."

"See any action in 'Nam?"

He gives out a bored sigh. He's tired of me, tired of my questions, tired of everything. "I was Ass Oink for a while. Called in 105's, 155's, and four-point deuce rounds on troop movements. Is that what you want to hear?"

"I want to hear about my father."

"I told you about that." He drains his glass. "Son," he says, standing and holding out his hand, "it's been an experience, but I have to hit the head."

No more than ten minutes have passed since I arrived. I stand up slowly and take his hand. Even when he looks directly at me, his eyes seem far away.

I say, "You're not going to tell me anything?"

"Nothing to tell. Like I said." His face is a stone.

"He sent you Bible quotes when your son died. What was his name? Michael?"

Without a pause, he says, "I told you. I wouldn't know about that." Nothing flickers through his eyes, and now I know he's lying.

He leads me to the corner of the house, to the driveway, and holds out his hand again. "Good day to you, sir."

I don't take his hand. Instead, I just look at him. "He was your sea-daddy."

Colley finally focuses on me for a long beat, then says, "You got to understand."

"Understand what? Did they get to you? Those guys with the buzz-cuts? Did they tell you not to talk to me?"

He looks at me hard. "You need to think before you speak. You know? And then you need to not speak."

"No, I don't know. I don't get it. I—"

He holds his open palm up to stop me. "Don't speak." Then he lowers the hand and holds it out again, and this time I take it.

"All right," I say, giving up, turning away.

He reaches out and lays his hand on my back, halfway between a pat and a push. I feel like turning and punching him in the face. Why did he even bother inviting me out? What have I learned? What has he gained?

I head back along the side of the house to my car, parked at the mouth of the driveway. He watches me from the backyard. When I'm standing in my open car door, about to climb inside, I can't help myself. I say, "Is my dad really dead?"

His gaze traces a broad arc through the high, hot sky. When he levels it at me, it's as though he's aiming a gun. "You know, son, they don't call it 'special' warfare for nothing. OK?" Before I can say anything else, he does a smart turn and then he's gone.

• • •

Back in my room, the bat is a black sack hanging from one of the tracks of the drop ceiling. It's fidgety, exhausted, can't get a purchase on the track. As I watch, it curls upward and pushes through a hole in the ceiling tile. I hear it take off, the tick of its wingtips touching the inside of the ceiling panels, the drywall, as it flies back and forth through the foot-thick layer of darkness.

I can't leave it like that. I pop the ceiling panel and set it aside, giving the bat a larger exit, not sure what I'll do when it comes back into the room.

My father, it occurs to me, is like this bat. Here and not. Not there but there. He's dead and gone, but knock down a few ceiling panels, and there he is, the man himself. I know all about paranoia and delusion. But listen—can't you hear the flicker of his wings?

When the Coast Guard called to tell me they'd found my father's body, the first thing I asked them to do was to send a photo. I wanted proof that he was dead, though I was too scared to go to Key West and identify the body for myself.

I still haven't looked at it. I slip the stiff white envelope out of the side-pouch of my suitcase, then slip the 5×7 out of the envelope.

He looks like an old man who has fallen asleep in his chair, his head lolling to one side, his eyes closed, his mouth open. But there's something too complete about his relaxed look, the nap from which you never come back. His cheeks glisten. He's still wet, pulled like a marlin fresh from the sea, though you'd never know it by his hair, which was always so short it looked the same wet or dry.

• • •

When I was growing up, it was easier to say my father had died than that my parents were divorced. Death people understand, except the way I told it.

"He made us all so ashamed," I'd say, my eyes lowered to my untouched lemonade, my words strung on a quiet thread. It was a well-practiced lie, so shiny I could see my face in it.

"My father died the way he lived—as a fool. He was a Navy pilot who didn't know how to land." I'd shake my head. "I guess you could say landings were his downfall." And here I'd look up slowly, lifting my eyes to the new neighbor's gaze. I hated myself for this. But most of all I hated you, Dad, for putting me through this, over and over.

"One day his commanding officer sent him out on a training mission. The plan was for him to practice landing on the carrier. 'Until you get it right, sailor,' he said. I guess Dad wasn't much of a pilot." I studied my empty hands. "Don't get me wrong. The captain wasn't a mean man. He was a hard man, but not a mean man."

The neighbor's mouth would be a little open by now, eyes peering wetly, face canted like a curious dog's.

"The sea was calm as he made his approach. He swung the jet in from the east and began his descent. The carrier was no bigger than a bar of soap bobbing in a bathtub. Close. Closer. Did I tell you how calm the sea was? As flat as the bottom of a skillet. His jet dropped like a rock. At the last moment, an unseen swell rose up. It was like the sea stood up to meet him, lifting seventy-thousand tons of steel in greeting. There was a flat slap as he hit the deck."

I'd slap my hands together. I liked the flinch. I always went for the flinch.

"His tires exploded like toy balloons. His jet skittered off the runway, one wing dragging across the tarmac, a big arcing shower of sparks streaming from it. And then the jet cartwheeled over the side in flames."

I'd brush off the knees of my chinos. "That was the end of him."

Why I made him a pilot, I'll never know, except that I knew he loved sailing and maybe this was a way of intensifying the insult.

The more I told the story, the more details I dreamed up. How the hot steel hissed as it hit the water. The muffled explosions as the plane sank, the flashing flames. And finally, how nothing was left but the calm sea and his body sinking slowly through bright water.

And now, after years of telling the lie, my rough magic has finally worked. I've killed my father. Or have I?

• • •

My father was a family legend, a war hero, a violent and demanding man who made our house into a battlefield. Only when he shipped out was there any peace. And now that he's dead, I've learned that half the time he didn't ship out at all but went on to terrorize some other wife and child on Long Island.

I couldn't wait for his leaves to end, for him to go back to the sea or the Black Lagoon or wherever the hell he had come from. Night after night, after his visits to my bedside, after he'd cut me—just a little, just enough—I'd lie awake waiting for the blood to dry and wondering why he hated me. The reasons came to me in dreams: I was the child of gypsies, spawn of the devil, a walking virus, my mother's dirty trick. In the end, I realized he was only sick. He had the illness all fathers have—a son.

Didn't you know? Doesn't any father ever know? You were the sun, moon, and stars to me. You were the air I breathed and the blood pumping through my veins. You were the sky over my head and the ground under my feet. The weather in your eye meant everything to me. You dope. You jerk.

My father's marriage to his third wife had not worked out, despite some twenty-five years of trying. His travels began as the consequence of a trial separation that later turned into a full-scale divorce. He was trying to avoid, I think, the feeling of failure, the long lonely nights in an unfurnished efficiency going over every bad decision he'd ever made. On the road, he could live and think and feel in the here and now. On the road, he wasn't a three-time loser but a man separated from his family by his spirit of adventure, by the lure of the open road. He may have thought that somewhere along the way he'd lost the thread of his life, and he meant to find it again. I guess I was one of those threads.

Maybe, after all the years of lying, I owe it to him to tell the story of his death. To tell it straight. Along with the death certificate, my sister sent me newspaper accounts of the accident and the full Coast Guard report.

By all the accounts, it was an ordinary night. The weather was clear. Visibility was fair. He was sailing with a woman named Alison, his fianceé, who lived in Naples, Florida. The boat had left the city docks at Naples on January 3, 1991, a little after noon, heading for Key West, ninety miles away. Except for the rough waves and the brisk temperature, it must have seemed like any other trip in my father's new home.

The Northwest Channel is the most common route to the shallows of the Keys. It's the best marked, the best lit, even though some sailors say it can be treacherous. By the time they reached the channel, late that night, conditions had become treacherous. A cold front had moved in. The sea had become rough, with two- to six-foot waves. The wind blew at a stiff 15–25 mph. The air temperature was 59 degrees, the water 69. Near midnight, at 24.38.10 north and 81.53.12 west, six miles off Key West, my father made his last mistake as a sailor, the last mistake of his life.

As they entered the channel from the Gulf, the Sea Dragon suffered what the Coast Guard calls a "collision w/fixed object," in this case a submerged granite jetty. They know the time of the incident because the last word they had from the Sea Dragon was a mayday at 11:43 P.M. saying the boat had struck the east jetty of the Northwest Channel and was taking on water. The Coast Guard launched a search and, at 12:30 A.M., found a mast sticking out of the water about 150 yards southwest of the north light. At 3:40 A.M. they found my father's body, about a mile from the accident site, wearing a life jacket, 50 yards south of marker "9" in the channel. Later that morning, at 8:37 A.M., a Coast Guard helicopter found Alison, two miles away, also wearing a life jacket,

¼ mile northwest of channel marker "12." At 10:00 A.M. a Special Response Team dove on the sunken sailboat, recovering items and papers that helped them identify the bodies.

The hull was holed on the starboard forward quarter. The keel, skeg, and rudder were severely damaged. And though the hole was 1'×1½'—enough to cause the boat to sink rapidly—the collision couldn't have been severe enough to throw them into the water. My father's mayday said the boat had struck the jetty "with two people on board."

The rocks on the east jetty were partially submerged. That and the rough sea must have contributed to the accident. Patrick J. Langley, who made out the Coast Guard report, goes on to say,

> With the information I was able to obtain, it is impossible to come up with the real reason for Mr. Spencer to strike the jetty. In talking with F.M.P. officers who are familiar with the channel, they advised it is tricky to use due to all the different lights in the area. Without using a chart it would be dangerous. Whether Mr. Spencer miscalculated where he was, or was inattentive in his operation, is unknown.

Local sailors claim the safety of the channel depends on conditions, remembering an experienced captain and crew who took on the rocks during the Naples to Key West sailing race. They, too, ran aground on the jetty but were rescued. My father must have assumed the channel was easier than it was, or he must have misread his charts.

How could my father, so meticulous in all things, ever miscalculate or become inattentive, especially when it came to sailing and the sea, a man with thirty-three years of active duty in the Navy, a teacher of sailing whose former students—women, always and only women—went on to win races? The thought is so contrary to what I know about the man—and the accident so unlikely—that at first I thought there must have been foul play. How could a lifelong sailor hang his boat up on, of all things, a jetty, the standard architecture of every inlet? It was the accident of a novice, not that of a veteran sailor.

Among his papers, I find certificates documenting the several sailing courses he completed through the Naval Post Graduate School in Monterey. "I sail whenever I can," he once wrote to me, "and am still helping teach the basic sailing course as a training skipper." He read books, attended lectures, and worked tirelessly on a variety of sailboats to learn all he could about sailing techniques, racing, wind, and currents. He wrote a sailing manual that he used as a textbook in the classes he taught. His dream was to sail a Junk from China to the U.S. Does this sound like a man who would do the nautical equivalent of parking a car with one wheel up on the curb? No, I tell you, not my dad.

But as I go through more and more of his papers, I keep finding bills for having his boat towed off this or that rock, bills for hull repairs. My father, I discover sadly, *was* inattentive and prone to miscalculation. My childhood story of his death was more accurate than I knew.

But to be fair, my father was a man who liked to take chances. He was not afraid of failure, except, I think, when it came to families. He saw great risk and actual failure as signs that you were pushing the envelope, that you were reaching down for everything you had. "I have noticed," he once wrote to me, "that when men are challenged, they are at their highest morale, and few back down." My father served in Korea, Vietnam, and in several other conflicts, and in countries around the world. He told a lot of war stories. I tend to believe them because he was never the hero of those stories. They were always about the heroism or the mystifying behavior of others. And often the lesson was the same: "No matter how hopeless the situation appears, it is only hopeless for the guy who gives up." I've gone back and forth about my father. I hate him in ways beyond words, but I'm also proud of him, and it's for lessons like this one. You don't give up. You never give up.

Did he give up? Is that why he and his fiancée died? I think I know how they ended up in the water. Once the boat started to sink, they must have decided they'd be safer away from the wreck. Even then, you'd think they'd stay with the mast, a vivid marker for the rescuers, who found it within half-an-hour of the mayday. But for some reason they didn't or couldn't. Maybe the waves were too rough. Maybe they just grew too weak to hold on. The autopsies indicate a scattering of contusions, one on top of her head and a few around her knees, a deep abrasion on the back of his left ear and several small contusions on his fingers, inner thighs, and calves. It may be that these injuries were caused by the waves knocking them against the mast as they tried to hold on. I imagine them floating in the dark water, the waves and the coldness working at them, driving all the body heat out, making every breath shorter than the last. One of them must have lost consciousness first. Which one? Did the fact that she was found farther away indicate that, when my father died, she tried to swim to safety? Or that she died first and proved to be a lighter burden for the current? They were only two miles from shore, for God's sake, two miles from Margaritaville. Even on my worst day I could swim—have swum—that far. Why wouldn't you, Dad? Why did you stay there in the cold water, waiting? You broke the two biggest rules of your life—never give up and never depend on anyone. Not even your loved ones will save you. Like the sailor in that Viet Cong pit, like Jeremiah in the pit, you have to climb out on your own, kill the enemy and break for home, all on your own. What made you wait? What made you think strangers would save you? For both my father and his fiancée, the cause of death is listed as "salt water drowning with asphyxia secondary to exposure to cold."

It's strange to read my father's autopsy, an account of his drawing and quartering, to read the itemized list of every organ and detail, right down to the anchor tattoo on his left forearm and the "mask tattoo" on his right shoulder. But I have to admit it's something he would have liked, he who spent so much of his life listing, measuring, and documenting.

At 60, my father was in better physical shape than I have ever been, a fact he proved once by jumping one-handed over a fence. A fact proved more dramatically by the details of his autopsy. Even dead, he's healthier than I am.

The word the medical examiner keeps using is "unremarkable," which is, in this context, a good thing. The viscera of the neck, the thyroid gland, the pleural surfaces, the pericardial sac, the major vessels, the larynx, trachea, and bronchi, the adrenal glands, kidneys, bladder, lymph nodes—all unremarkable. The lumen of the gall bladder showed several small black irregular stones, and the prostate gland was slightly enlarged and nodular, but these things were otherwise normal.

The skull was intact with no internal bleeding. The cranial fossae were intact, and the sella turcica normal. The pituitary gland is described as "grossly normal." The gyri and culci were of normal width. Cranial blood vessels show no significant evidence of arteriosclerosis or congenital anomalies. Sectioning of the brain revealed no abnormalities.

The lungs, like his fiancée's, showed severe diffuse edema. The longer they were in the cold water, the less efficiently their hearts were able to pump, the excess blood backing up into the heart, the lungs, the other organs. But even this was normal, to be expected, unremarkable.

How can this be? How can the mystery of my father be reduced to these weights and measures? Was my father no more than a "well-developed, well-nourished but slender Caucasian male weighing approximately 180 pounds, measuring 75 inches, representing the stated age of 60 years." This and no more? A man whose heart was described as symmetrical and weighing exactly 390 grams?

I have never seen my father so relaxed as he looks in the Coast Guard picture. Like a man lying down after a long day of back-breaking labor. His face is not twisted with pain. He's a man resting, a man exhausted, a man kicked back in his recliner, slack-jawed, grizzled, snoring. His brows are raised, though his eyes are closed. Maybe the Coast Guard closed them, but they still couldn't remove the stunned look from his face, the open-mouthed awe.

The only evidence that he's dead, the only remarkable thing, is the white foamy fluid in his mouth, a ghost caught by the camera, a cloud, a mist. At first I think it's some kind of fluid discharge, then that it's a kind of seaweed, but it's too diaphanous for either of these things. Then I think "ghost." I think "soul rising." Prayer is sometimes described as the soul's breath. Is that what I'm seeing?

Mouth vapors correspond to the soul. The ancient Hebrews believed that, at death, the body returns to earth and the soul, the breath of life God breathed into Adam, returns to God. In all Semitic dialects, the word for "soul" derives from a root that means "breathe." In Akkadian-Assyrian, *napasu* means "be wide" or "breathe" and *napistu* means "life" or "soul"; in Hebrew *naphash* means "take breath" while *nephesh* means "soul," "life," or "person"; in Arabic *tannaffus* means "to fetch a deep breath" and *nafs* means "breath of life," "soul," or "self." Consider Greek, where the word *pneuma* refers both to "air" and to "spirit." Or the Latin word *spiritus*, from which is derived both "spirit" and "inspiration" ("to breathe in").

Is this what I'm seeing? A picture of my father's soul rising? Or stopped at mid-rise, locked in the body, redemption forever beyond his reach? And then I think that any second the head in the photo will right itself, the mouth will close, swallowing back its essence, and the hard, bright eyes will open. *Just what do you think you're looking at, mister?*

I feel the sun before I see it, an insinuation of desert light, cold, pale. It's been another long night without sleep. As the first sun edges into the room, I wake to the damp wreckage of my father's life.

The bat hasn't come back into the room, but I can't hear it either. Maybe it found another way out. But when I get up to go to the bathroom, I find it. The bat is lying on the throw rug, a small pouch of brown-black fur. Is it dead? I can't tell. With the edge of the autopsy report, I flip the body as gently as I can. It rolls open like a velvet glove and lies on the floor, the ragged V of its body spread wide as if in flight. With the edge of the report, I lift one wing.

The bat is still alive. It flexes its wings but, too weak to fly, has only enough strength to roll its head toward me and bare its teeth. The photo of my dead father is back in its envelope with its stiff piece of cardboard. I use it to roll the bat onto the autopsy report and pin it there. The bat's head, inches from the belly of my thumb, swings slowly from side to side, its jaws searching for its tormentor. I'm afraid it will find the strength to stretch out and sink its teeth into my thumb. I hold it tightly in place with the stiffened envelope. The bat squirms and clicks. I carry it outside into the parking lot and launch it into the early morning sky.

And then it's gone. But every time the wind rattles the windows, and every time the house shifts under the changing rays of the sun, I'll know it's him looking for a way back into my life, back into my dreams.

∽◦◦◦∽

Mexico is a poor and hungry country. It is remarkable to me that there isn't more crime than there is. I have seen hunger in my time on this earth, and I have seen the violence that can be the result of hunger.

I was in Casablanca in 1952, before the great Moroccan Revolution, during a significant uprising of the people of that city. The uprising was due to the extreme hunger of these people. They had found food, which would never reach their agonized stomachs unless they resorted to violence. This food was on a pier where it had been off-loaded from a ship.

Standing relaxed among the scattered crates of food were twenty-five of the famed Ghurka soldiers—seven-foot-tall, three-hundred-pound giants dedicated to violence. The Ghurkas' only weapons were huge police clubs the size of baseball bats.

I strode among the Ghurkas and the crates of food in the warm sunlight while enjoying the tepid Moroccan breeze blowing in from the desert. I was unaware of the impending danger. I was daydreaming of the coming month during which I was planning a visit with family and friends.

I suddenly realized that the possibility of that visit was being threatened as the Ghurka giants began to come erect and fidget with their clubs. I looked toward the head of the pier. Assembling there was a horde of desolate people. Torn and tattered clothing hung from the wracked bodies of these children of destitution. Large beady eyes stared greedily from their gaunt faces. I felt a rush of sympathy for these fellow humans who were forced to live like animals. My sympathy was tinged with regret because I was unable to help them climb from the depths of their misery. Even so, I experienced nausea from the very sight and smell of their bodies. Their utter depravity sickened me.

Slowly, all my previous emotions receded into oblivion, only to be replaced by one of fear for my own safety.

The Moroccans were going to attack. Something like electricity ran through my body as I watched the angry horde shuffle forward on two-hundred pairs of bare, callused feet. Their mumbling voices sounded like the roar of a large engine in the distance. This roar became louder and louder, almost overpowering the sound of my heart beating in my chest.

The Moroccans came closer and closer, gaining speed with every step. Finally, they were running at full charge, screaming and yelling as they came. I looked to my right and left and saw the Ghurkas standing ready with their backs to the food crates and their clubs extended toward the oncoming attack.

Upon observing this scene, my first impulse was to run. This was not my fight. But there was no place to run to. The only avenue of escape was directly through the attacking mass. Furthermore, I couldn't select sides in this fight because, to all Moroccans, I was their enemy. I dashed quickly to the side of the nearest Ghurka. In a flash, my trusty diver's knife came to hand.

Before I could turn to meet the onslaught, the Ghurka swung his club, and a piercing scream rent the air as a Moroccan's elbow was smashed to splintered pulp. A body dropped at my feet and still another as the Ghurka's club traced a pattern of death in the afternoon sunlight. My sympathy for the Moroccans was overcome by fear for my own safety. My knife flashed as I dodged the flying stones.

Slowly but surely, the Moroccans were being overcome. The Ghurkas' clubs beat down the Moroccans' courage, which was born of desperation. The attack slowly subsided, leaving only the courageous few to continue the battle, but these few were quickly felled by the tireless Ghurkas.

The Moroccans who could still move under their own power quickly retired from the field, leaving the bloody, broken hulks of their comrades to the relentless Moroccan flies. There was a terrible stench of human blood and sweat in the still, hot air. I turned to the nearest packing box, bent over, and released the contents of my stomach.

Later, I turned again to the hot afternoon sunlight and breathed the desert air deep into my lungs. I contemplated the scene of massacre before me as the victorious Ghurkas strode among the fallen, counting the dead and dying. I then lifted my face to the heavens and thanked God for the toughening my father gave me as a boy.

Robert C. Spencer
Theme for Freshman English
Purdue University, 1960

19

IT'S WISE TO GO WHIZZER

Night. I'm sitting on a Tijuana hilltop, my back to the ocean. On my right, in the distance, is the glowing bowl of the *Plaza Monumental* bullring. On my left, the chain-link border. And beyond, San Diego's little Oceanside Park. Yelling distance.

My trip is over. I've failed. I'm drinking *pox*, the holy hallucinogen and mind-bending home brew that Lunes, the *curandera*, prescribed for me. If I couldn't accomplish my spiritual cleansing on the floor of that church, maybe I can do it here on this dark hilltop. The *pox* is strong stuff. One sip, I remember, alters brain chemistry forever. Like child abuse. I raise my bottle to the dark. Here's to you, Dad. I drink to his victory over me, then take a long burning swallow.

You win, Pop. I can't crack your code. Your secrets are safe. *Pox.* Like the English word for disease. If the disease of the father is the son, I guess the disease of the son is the father.

The moment this easy thought comes to me, cheers erupt from the bullring as if they're for him, my father. I can't see the killing ground, but I can see the fans in the top row of bleachers, hats thrown into the air, arms pumping.

Eventually my bottle of *pox* gets lighter and the cheering fades, though the disk of light, like a Hollywood spaceship, continues to shine well past the last *Olé*.

Even in the dark, I can see the border's corrugated tin wall come slicing toward me from the East, a dark blade dipping into every arroyo, shooting across the desert floor, diving into canyons and dry washes, skimming over creosote flats, and finally, transformed into a chain link fence, crossing to my left between my hilltop and the oceanfront park on the San Diego side, then dropping down the sandy beach to plunge into the Pacific.

End of the line, end of my trip, time to put the bucket down. What have I proved? What has been the point of this trip? I feel profoundly depressed. Maybe it's the *pox*. Maybe it's the final and complete realization that my father has gone to ground.

After 1,800 miles and most of a bottle of *pox*, I realize this trip was never about you, Dad. Not about you at all. It's about me, about the rest of my life. I've come so far to find you, memories of you, to see you plain, to get out from under the rock of you. Something I couldn't do standing next to your flag-draped body with the weeping family all around. *All I can say is, no matter what he done or what you think he done, he's always going to be my hero.* Uncle Carl, his brother, in another phone call I made earlier today. I was right not to go to the funeral.

Oh, Dad. From here, from this hilltop—you know what?—you're just a sorry-looking old man wandering the back roads of his life. I've had you in my head too long. It's time you left.

Despite the glowing disk of the bullring, it's dark here on the hilltop. To my left, the ground drops away toward the fence. In daylight, it's braided with the footprints of *huaraches*, all of them pointed north. At night it's a different story. The shadows are deep, the night is a tight blue hand. But the sand is alive with sound—a quick scurrying, short stabbing steps, a brittle rattle. And the wind. You can hear it plucking at the branches of mesquite, ironwood, palo verde, and juniper. And from farther off you think you can hear it raking through the arms of saguaro, bending the wands of ocotillo. But your thoughts are broken by the sudden coiling in the sand next to your boot, and by something stretching toward your ear. Inches away. Closer. Closer. Now as close as the breath of a cactus needle.

Eventually, the bullring lights go out, plunging into total darkness so quickly and completely that it feels like sudden death. For a long minute, I can see nothing. Even the desert falls silent. After a time my eyes adjust and I can see the hard line of the fence again. Then a shadow appears, takes a human shape, comes closer, a woman, her face growing more distinct as she passes on her way north, saying in Spanish, "All that ground"—she aims her gaze at El Norte—"as far as you can see belongs to us, to the people of Mexico. Truly."

"*Claro que sí,*" I say. *Of course. Absolutely.* But my accent gives me away.

A sharp light comes into her eyes as her northward gaze cuts back to me. I'm not who she thought I was. "I know," I say in English. "I'm not who *I* thought I was, either." She fades back into the darkness.

I sit there for a long time, taking a pull now and then from my bottle of *pox*. It's the end of my long journey. *De dónde eres?* The Border Patrol's constant question is, finally, philosophical, theological. *Where have you come from?*

Tienes tus papeles? Do you have your papers? Proving you are who you say you are. Proving you have a place in the world, that you aren't a stranger in a strange land.

It's a cliché to blame your parents for your lousy life. I know this. And in fact my life isn't lousy. I'm a reasonably happy, productive person. I've got money in the bank and a car that won't quit. I've got friends. But there are moments, islands of discontent, a certain emptiness that asserts itself now and then, and I trace the source back to the violence and insanity of my father.

Until I was eight my only memories of my father were as a visitor to our family. I knew he was my father but didn't know what that actually meant. He was the tall smiling sailor who came home on leave, ducking through whatever tenement door we lived behind, sitting down long enough to tell us to mind our mother, a man who never remembered our birthdays, never wrote to us from overseas, a man to whom we were no more real than distant relations.

So when my mother announced that the family was going to live together at last in Indiana, it was a big deal. She told us we had to be on our best behavior. The message was clear. We could assume nothing. We had to make him want us in his life. We had to prove ourselves worthy of his love, his name. We had to earn our place in his world. The groundwork for rejection had been laid. Then the craziness began, the beatings. And that message, too, was clear.

A father's primary duty to his son is to stand by his side, to make a space for him in the world, sometimes even to treat him like an honored guest. These were things my father was never able to do. He wasn't wired that way. Maybe he never felt welcome in his own world. I think of him as the little kid dragging his "chessy" dog bank with him wherever he went, shaking it when he was scared. Maybe he was always, all his life, scared and only found ways to mask that fear—violence, bigamy, divorce, the open road, the regulated life. My father's theology was based on the principle of not belonging, on being shut out of heaven, condemned to walk the earth in mortal sin. There is no place for you. You do not belong, not here, not anywhere, and least of all by my side. You're not my son. You do not exist to me. It's a lesson he drove home with every snap of the strap.

Then the divorce. It meant an end to my torment but it also meant an end to any hope for our family's survival as a family. At least the beatings were an obscure effort, twisted as it was, to make me a better person, to give our family a fighting chance. By leaving, he was giving up on me, on us. Like any kid, I thought the divorce was all my fault, but in this case, my father made it seem true. After the divorce, there were days when I longed to be beaten, to feel his hands on me. It would mean that my father hadn't given up on me, that he still had hope. No matter how hopeless the situation appears, it's only hopeless for the guy who gives up. Isn't that right, Dad? Isn't that what you always said?

Well, you gave up. The years passed in silence, making me feel the sting of your lesson, as if there truly were no place on earth for me.

Maybe I haven't learned anything from this trip, but at least I've discovered something I couldn't have learned by staring into your boxed face. During the year of torment, he was married to another woman, had another family. This must have torn him apart, though I never really saw it at the time. What I saw was that he let it tear me apart, in the time-honored tradition of fathers everywhere. He tried to beat me out of his life. He tried to pass all that embarrassment, shame, frustration, and rage onto me, incising it into my back, letting me believe for thirty years that I had failed him and the family, that I was the only wrong thing in his right world. Most sons wonder if they ever mean anything to their fathers. Victims of abuse wonder if they ever mean anything at all. To anyone, anywhere. But even that puts too hopeful a spin on it. Victims of abuse know they mean nothing, that they count for nothing, that nothing will come of them.

The fact that haunts my life: a single act of violence changes the victim's brain chemistry forever. It lays the groundwork for a certain measure of paranoia. To the victim, even well after the days of rage, the world is a place of danger, and everyone else, even—maybe especially—a loved one, is a potential threat. After all, if your father can turn on you like that, can lay into you with belt, board, strop, stick, switch, with his two hard hands and with his diver's knife, why do you think a stranger will treat you any better? His beatings instilled in me the belief that nothing is certain, nothing lasts, no amount of love can't be undone with a raised fist, the flash of a belt, or the turn of a cold eye.

You get a little shaky living that life, you know? Can't get your bearings. Up and down don't matter. Time and again the ground rolls out from under you. On your moral compass, North trades places with South, East is obscure, West disappears into the haze. Nothing is where you left it. There's no room for you on the bus, no seat in the class, no space anywhere for you, not even in your own mind.

Some twenty yards in front of me, a line of shadows scuffles slowly over the hilltop and down the blue dark toward the fence. By this stage of the journey, their water has run out, and they've dropped whatever belongings they thought they'd need. They carry only a phone number, if they're lucky, the only *papeles* that matter. I feel like a fool lugging my black plastic bags of damp documents clear across the country, as if a piece of paper held the answer to anything. I think of all the pages I've so carefully dried and filed. *Mis papeles.* All I've done is create a catalogue of mysteries.

Across the line, on the northern side, a jacklight flares up, sweeping the fence, impaling two men and a woman who've just climbed over. They freeze, raising their hands slowly. On this side, the line of shadows stops and drops, becomes the desert, the dark. The Border Patrol has what seems like an endless supply of pale green Ford Broncos, ground sensors, infrared cameras, night-vision goggles, 50,000-watt searchlights. But the shadows fight back with vast amounts of patience. The wave rises and the wave falls. The wave rises again.

The jacklight comes lancing down the hill toward the fence, and even though the shadows are on the Mexican side, a whispered cry goes up: "*Viene la Migra!*" And the tight group of shadows scatters, "goes quail," to use Border Patrol slang. I think of Sister Caroline's words back at La Posada: "These people, they come here hoping for a better life. What they find is a jail."

More *pox*. Too much *pox*. Too much and not enough. The Bronco has gathered up the three and driven away. The heavy curtain of dark air swings in the breeze. I feel disconnected, as if I might float away. In the dark my hands look like desert creatures. I can feel my head opening up, my brain turning in its sleep.

A figure sits down in the darkness nearby, too far away to make out the face. Waiting, I guess, for things to calm down before he makes his run.

When I speak, the words blur. "*Vas al otro lado?*" *Going to the other side?* "*Allá?*" There? I point the way. The Bronco and its jacklight are gone, for now. The fence is a wedge of deeper darkness at the bottom of the hill. From here it looks as though you could step over it. A cool wind moves just a few inches above the ground, as real as an animal. It noses under the cuff of my pants, a wet tongue on my leg. At first he sat facing the border, but now the figure seems to be facing me, though I haven't seen him move. I can't see his face. He's just out of sight, inside the darkness, a piece of the darkness. It's my *pox* he's after, I think, my drink, my disease. He's just trying to think of a polite way to ask. Even begging for a drink requires a certain measure of *cortesía*.

But from the dark, in the flat twang of my father, the shadow says, "It's wise to go Whizzer!" The buzz of the last word hangs in the darkness, fades to a razor whisper. The desert is silent. The world. A hollow ache in the pit of my stomach.

I must be hallucinating. It's the drink, the disease. But the figure's there, a darkness against the darkness. All at once everything makes sense. I should have known. This business of dying was just another lie. Back in Indiana, the twenty-one-gun salute was fired and the flag was folded over an empty hole in the ground. It was all just a trick to draw me out into the open, to get me back under his hands.

I take another hit of *pox*, trying to hide my fear. I say, "You should have died for real."

The figure takes a long, hollow breath. "Sonny boy, this is 'bout as real as she gets." He leans closer, his face coming into hazy gray focus, but only for a moment, the glassy eyes, the foamy white mist in his mouth. And then he leans back into darkness. "*Al otro lado.* The other side. That's the ticket."

Another jacklight crucifies two men north of the fence. The Bronco bounces down the hill to get them. One man lights up a cigarette while he waits. The other drops to the ground with a shudder I can feel all the way to here.

I want to get up and run away, but I can't. Once my phone line got crossed with another and I found myself talking with a total stranger, each of us thinking we knew the other, our words making just enough sense to keep us talking. This man, this illegal, he just does a good imitation of down-home English. And yet.

But hell, why miss the opportunity? And what if? So I say, "You took advantage. Talk about borders and boundaries. Talk about the other side. You crossed the line. You crossed it a long time ago."

"What line is that, sonny?" He sounds so like my father. Even the silhouette of his head is the same. I feel cold air moving through the inside of my head.

"The line you cut into me. All those little cuts." It *is* my father. It is.

A strange music comes into his voice. "Come here and let your daddy kiss it and make it all better."

"You took advantage," I say again. "You crossed the line."

"You see—may I say?—that's been your mistake your whole living life. I crossed a line? What line?" The voice rising now. "I'm your father. I own you. Nothing ever changes that. Ergo, there is no line. *Comprendez?*"

I scramble backward a few feet, but he's closer than before, his breath in my face. I turn aside. "I don't want you here. I don't want you in my life, my head. Go away."

"*Qué vida, esé? What life is that? En otros palabras,* there is no *away.* In other words, I'm here for the duration, young 'un."

I hold the bottle in front of my face, pinch my eyes shut, crying, saying— hoping it's true, "You're just some kind of, of hallucination . . ."

"Believe what you want," he says, his hands—his shadow hands—floating out at his sides, the palms turning up, the arms lifting, calling down the Holy Ghost. "You will anyway. You always have."

". . . some kind of chemical event in my brain."

He claps his hands. "*Claro que sí!* Now you're talking! That's all a father ever is or hopes to be!"

I sit up straight and stare into the bright coals of his eyes. "I don't just believe what I want. I believe the truth."

A dry scraping laugh. "Yeah, right. What truth? Whose truth? All you want is a way to tell your sad tale about a poor little boy who was made to suffer at the hands of his bad ole daddy."

"That's the truth."

"It may be the how, but what about the why? You never could picture the big picture."

"Then tell me something that will make sense of you."

"You want sense?" He leans forward, turning the shadowy planes of his face at me, his voice narrow and hard. "You just don't get it, do you, boy. Let me put it to you like this. Sense is an imaginary line. Stand on the one side and your life is peaches in syrup. Stand on t'other and it's devil-take-the-hindmost. Folks want to believe in that line the way they want to believe in Santy Claus. But remember I told you there ain't no line." He touches his fingertips to his chest. "There's always only me. Not you, not your mama, not your mangy dog, only little ole me. On that day, years from now—or maybe tomorrow—when they shovel dirt into your upturned face—surprise!—it'll be me looking down at you with the shovel in my hands."

He leans back now, lifting the shadow of his face to the night sky, and then down again to me. I can't move. My hands are like dead things. "Is that any help? Does that shed any light at all? Is that what you're looking for, bunky? By the way, *tienes mis papeles?" Do you have my papers?*

This can't be happening. I feel the hard ground against my ankle bones, the slick sides of the bottle. Below, I see the darkening thickets, the ugly ravines, and in the distance to my right the dark monolith of the bullring. And at my back I hear, feel, the surge and shimmer of the ocean. All this, I know, is real. But he can't be real. Not him.

"What papers?" I ask.

"Those sorry sacks of bilge you're dragging 'round. They're mine and I want them."

"No, they're mine now."

"Yours? They ain't nothing yours, you knothead. Ain't I made myself clear enough on that particular point? How many times I got to say it? Everything you are is me. Everything you have is mine. They ain't no you."

I take another hit of *pox* to build up my courage. "Why don't you crawl back into whatever slimy hole you came from?"

"Aww." He cocks his head at me, stares at me from behind his dead eyes. "Now, is that a way to be? To your own dear daddy?"

I shake my head once, hard. It takes all the strength I have. I point the mouth of the bottle at him. "You're not my daddy. You were never my daddy."

He bows his head and shakes it slowly, then looks up sidewise at me. "You can keep on a-coming, boy, but this nut won't crack." He straightens his head. "You want I should go all soft and sugary on you? Is that it? Would that please you?" He sighs and a dry wind rattles the darkness. "Well, it's true I have lusted exceedingly in the wilderness and tempted God in the desert. I will agree with you on those particular points. My travels have transformed me into a shape monstrous and strange. You, too. *Damé mis papeles.*"

"No." The whole hillside is rocking slowly from side to side.

"*Damé!*"

No. I'm past fear, past pleading. He's right: there is no line. Or if there is, I don't care anymore. "You don't want the papers. What do you really want from me?"

He pauses, thinking. He scratches the side of his head. I can hear the crabwise scuttle of his mind at work. At last he speaks, slowly, hauling up each word one rock at a time. "I want what any daddy wants—relief. I want you off my back and out of my head."

My turn to laugh. "So there's a line after all. And I've crossed it."

"A line for me. Not for you."

"Tell me. Something. Anything."

A deep, hollow breath and he says, "All right. OK. Once while I served on Shore Patrol in the Casbah, I had to interview me a prostitute who'd just killed a man. We had no legal jurisdiction so I couldn't arrest her. All I could do was take down her story. She was so nervous as she told it that she ate her vinyl purse until there was nothing left but the brass buckle."

He gazes off.

"And once while I stood watch on the deck of a destroyer, a storm came up so fast and hard that it blew the man next to me right out of his boots. Gone. Adios. All she wrote. The ocean took him clean away."

I knew, even before I asked, that it was pointless expecting anything from him. "What do these things have to do with anything? Anything at all?"

"Only everything, sonny jim. Stop. Look. Listen. Just like the sign says. Tonight the desert is full of the dead. I seen them. I seen one fellow with his head buried in the sand. Six days of sun got to him and that was his only relief. He died that way. And oh, sonny, it's the saddest thing, but that man, he was you. I seen two corpses doing the dirty. *Both* of them were you. Once, a long time ago—do you remember?—I gave you a chance to come with me. It's not too late. *Venga, mi'ijo.*" Let's go, little man.

He leans forward. The open mouth stopped with frozen mist.

I scramble drunkenly to my feet and pull the knife from the back of my belt.

"You recognize this?" I hold the diver's knife toward him, blade first, the moldy, cracked leather grip tight in my hand. I found it today in the bags, wrapped in rags, one of my last finds. "Well? Do you? It's the knife you used to torture me."

"Torture," the shadow says. "Such a silly word."

"Yeah, torture. You cut me."

"I made you strong. Tried to. Guess it didn't take, did it. So now what? You want to cut me? Go ahead." He lifts his shadowy arms, his body making a crude cross against the darkness.

I down the last of the bottle, shift the knife in my hand, and charge him, stabbing at the darkness, slashing, cutting.

Only it's too late. He's gone, of course, or was never here. Nothing but a few square feet of pockmarked sand. A shadow among shadows. Nothing, nothing.

The man said, if they're on the river at night, kill them. But what if they're already dead?

The desert, a withheld breath while he was here, slowly comes back to life. The dark hillside is alive with different shadows, all shuffling down the hill toward the line in two's and three's. A low breeze noses around like a hungry dog. Behind me, the battered black shell of the ocean.

It was only a hallucination after all, a fever dream, an empty fantasy, a chemical reaction in the brain. My father is dead, laid to rest in Garland Brook Cemetery in North Vernon, Indiana. A team of soldiers was sent over from the armory to fire their guns over his grave. Someone played "Taps." A folded flag was pressed into my Uncle Carl's hands. Tears were shed. My brother and sister watched the mahogany box get lowered into the grave. Still, I can't help remembering the Mexican proverb: "A bad thing never dies."

I wish I had more *pox*. Or that Lunes, the *curandera*, were here. Cure this, I'd say. "Cure this!" I shout, a little alarmed at how drunk I must be. The desert goes silent again. I drop to the ground, blinking hard to keep away any hallucinations that might try to sneak up on me.

Every father is a mystery, a far country. I try to think of my father's world the way he might have. He was a Navy man through and through. It was his life, his bliss. He retired as a Commander and lived his last twelve years first in a camper and then on the sailboat that would eventually kill him. I can't help thinking that what he wanted was to hold onto the life he understood best, a sailor's life. I think the world was too wide open for him. He liked small spaces. He liked to be able to reach out and touch the bulkhead wherever he was. Throughout his life, the spaces he occupied got smaller and smaller, the way he wanted it. And now a coffin. Perfect.

It's late. I wish I had more *pox*. I said that. All around me shadows pass, lives moving through the dark. My father is not one of them. It's important for me to know this, to believe this. He died in the waters of Key West. He hung his boat on a jetty and was thrown into the sea, where he died of salt water drowning with asphyxia secondary to exposure to cold. About as dead as it gets. It was the *pox*. I drank too much. That's all.

The hill is alive with people now. They move in clusters, as silently as clouds, often with someone in the lead, a warning hand held out behind. *Cuidado! Danger!* They stop. Slowly they move ahead. Stop. Crossing from one world to another is hard. In the distance, I know, out of sight on the other side, the green vans of La Migra wait for them, for the undocumented, those without papers.

Documents. My father was the most documented person I will ever know. I've been traveling with a carload of garbage bags full of damp documents. And what have I found out about him? I have everything from his grade school report cards to his battle stars. I have nothing. What I have is less and less respect for the power of documents. And less and less respect for you, Dad. Your documents mean nothing, reveal almost nothing. In the end, you kept the wrong records, lived the wrong life.

Early today I found your datebook from the last year we lived together, the year of rage. Going through every page, I found almost nothing of importance. Pages and pages of homework due dates, social obligations, and shopping lists, one of them for Christmas presents. On it you list every living relative's name, including my brother and sister—even the names of your secret wife and daughter—but my name, the name of your first-born, does not appear. Perfect! I laugh out loud to think of it. I was never your son, was I? Not in any sense that matters. And there's the proof.

You spent your whole life building the box they finally put you in. First the study closet and then the camper and then the boat, special secret happy places, each one a well-appointed coffin. And it occurs to me that by poring through your papers I'm still the little kid sneaking into your secret space, crossing your border, trying to decode your private language, to see what the world looks like from inside your head, to understand the mystery of who you were and are. And of course I've failed. How not? And how strange. What a pitiful creature I am. But didn't you invite me here with your stories, your hints, even your silences?

Remember the story you told me once about a colleague involved in missile research for the Navy? "Here's a man," you said, "who spent a good big chunk of his life working on a single project. Day and night for years. That's dedication. Then one day the Navy goes and pulls the plug. Finito. No more project. That part of his life just out the window, wasted, gone with the wind. Would you blame this man for piling all his reports and test results into a wastepaper basket and setting them on fire? For dancing naked around the flames? Myself, I'd say that's the only *sane* response to something like that."

Even as you told me this story, I knew you were that man. Earlier that day the California State Police had called to ask if I knew where you were, warning me that you might cause harm to yourself or others, and that I should contact them if you showed up. How about that, Dad? And what was it like to see the work of years go up in flames, all those formulae collapsing into ash? All those families, those wives and children? Terrible. It must have been terrible. Why couldn't you just tell me? But I know why. It would be an admission of weakness, instability, loss of control.

I found phone numbers for more of your former colleagues today. Some of them are dead. But the few I was able to reach all said the same thing: "He was a good man." At first I thought that meant what it sounded like. But now I think maybe they meant, "He *was* a good man," a good man before you became a bad man, before you lost it. But that's probably just my bad animal talking. I never found out what the police wanted with you, and there's no piece of paper in the bags to explain it. You've covered your tracks well.

Still deep night. From this hilltop I can see the ocean, an immense blackness outlining the shore with a ragged strand of phosphorescent foam. I can feel the rise and fall of each wave, first the water building like a long intake of breath and then the shuddering collapse and sprawl, like broken breathing, a question unanswered, a thought falling back on itself, hope without help. And then again the long intake of breath leading, always, inevitably, to collapse. And then the darkness hiding behind the white light of tomorrow.

All these miles and all these pages, and all I have is this—a trip without a destination, a mystery without a solution, a book without an ending. Maybe that's the only kind of ending a book about fathers and sons can have, the relationship that never ends, that has no closure, that makes no ultimate sense. You were right, Dad. There is no line. You were—and are—an insoluble mystery standing outside the limits of time and space, alive and dead, here and everywhere, a dispenser of real vengeance for imaginary crimes. You taught me what all fathers teach their sons—fear, the word itself a sloppy anagram of "father," the only real legacy, the only real present you ever gave me.

I have come from nothing to nothing, and after hundreds of pieces of paper, I have learned nothing. I am, as you always told me, nothing.

A month from now, as the executor of your estate, I will open a storage locker in California in the renewed hope of finding a solution to the mystery of who you were. The long intake of breath, the wave rising. But the locker will turn out to be another dead-end, filled with nothing but old clothes and uniforms, ships' plaques, your medals, your dress saber, old letters of no consequence, and a few household objects. The wave collapsing back on itself, sucking back into the darkness.

A few weeks after that, I will learn that you had rented another locker, a bigger one, in Florida. The wave building again. I will call and call but get no answer from the owners. Finally, in desperation, I'll call the Marathon police department, asking for their help. They'll report back that the business is gone.

"Gone?" I'll ask. "You mean sold? But who are the new owners? And where's my father's stuff?"

"Gone. In that last big hurricane."

"But what's left?"

"Nothing. It was all swept out to sea, even the building. There's nothing there but an empty lot."

The wave collapsing, sliding back under deep water, sucked back into mystery.

The time to make peace with my father was while he was alive, of course. But he never gave me that chance. After death, a father becomes a legend. How can you make peace with a legend?

You were the stranger who stayed with us a while, who did this much harm, that much good. For some you were a walking blade; for others the shape of grace. I think of your brother Carl's words: "I don't excuse whatever bad he done, but I'm sure he had his reasons." It occurs to me that every garden-variety maniac has his "reasons" for what he does. What good is that?

You were married to two women at once and thought of violence as a valid form of child rearing. You tried to seduce—I'm afraid there's no other word for it—your own daughter. Maybe that's too harsh. Maybe you were only trying to let her into the secret circle of your life. Anything that intimate could easily be confused with sex. But it didn't work. She didn't go for it. There's only room for one in that box you built.

This whole trip has been a waste. It was meant to bring me to some kind of understanding, some kind of peace, and here I am more than two-thousand miles away from your body and worlds away from knowing anything more than I've ever known. Maybe I should have been there, at your funeral, but I was afraid I'd be overwhelmed by the myth, afraid those twenty-one guns would aim at me. And when I told my brother and sister I wouldn't be coming, no one was surprised. Mark was there, the son who never stopped loving you. Sheree, your daughter, big-hearted beyond reason. None of your wives went. But maybe I should have gone. I should have watched them put you into the ground, should have lowered you into the hole with my own hands, should have bowed my head over your grave. But I couldn't, you know? I just couldn't.

Instead, always the good English major, I turned your life and death into a library project, right down to an analysis of your autopsy. The word comes from the Greek for "to see for oneself." But what have I seen? And what do I know? All I'm doing is reconstructing bits and pieces of you, recreating you from the soggy evidence in garbage bags. Pathetic really.

Today—or I guess by now it was yesterday—the motel desk clerk narrowed his eyes at me as I dragged the last of the bags through his lobby to my room.

"*Mi padre en ésta*," I said. My father's in here. I patted the side of a bag.

"Don't let him drip on the carpeting," the clerk said.

For a time I thought you *were* there, in the bags, but you pulled a Houdini on me, leaving me with nothing but ink on paper. Before long, all the bags will be gone. I'll have dried out the last of the sheets and filed them carefully in boxes, each page crinkly as old parchment. I'll have files for "Receipts," "Correspondence," "Boat," "Photos," "Death," and every other category of your life. I'll have classified you. I'll have classified nothing. I'll have organized silence.

Until yesterday, I hadn't found a single photograph of any of your children or your wives. Not one. No pictures of any of us—only pictures of yourself as a child, you in the service, of bulkheads, sea spray, sailors, and ceremonies. But yesterday I found it, a photograph of you and me. I never knew the photograph existed. In fact, for years I thought my memory of that day might have been no more than a nightmare.

In the picture, a grainy black-and-white square with scalloped edges, I'm riding your shoulders into the surf at Norfolk. What was I—two, maybe three? You'd grabbed me by the wrists and hoisted me up from the sand and onto your shoulders in one powerful sweep. You walked down the crowded beach, straight into the water, and out through the breaking waves, even past them, with me holding on tight. I rode you like a greenbroke pony, feeling at last that I had complete control of you. I dug my heels into your sides the way I'd seen Roy Rogers dig into Trigger's flanks. I grabbed hold of your hair like a handful of reins. At last I could make you go, and not go, wherever I wanted.

Out there beyond the surf, the water was strangely calm but deeper with every step. Without a word, you kept walking. The water kept rising. Up to your chest, up to your chin, over your head. You walked out until you were completely under water, and then you just stood still, invisible, for what seemed like the longest time, leaving me above the surface as if I were clinging to nothing more than a submerged rock. It was a joke, I think, but to me, to a kid whose father had a habit of leaving, it was terrifying. It felt as if you had just disappeared and left me sitting on the surface alone and far from anything I knew, like it was only a matter of moments before I disappeared, too. But come on, how long could that moment have lasted, the gray-black water all around, my fists under water full of what might have been no more than seaweed? You must have stepped back into the shallows, must have come up for air, laughing and shaking me by the legs. But I don't remember that. What I remember is being lost on the vast gray plane of water, the shore no more than a faraway scribble of beige. It's a moment that has lasted forty-two years. And counting.

For a while I didn't know what to do with the blank sheets of paper in the bags, the ones where the ink had washed off. In the end, I put them in a file labeled "Blank," as if someday the words might come back, like birds, to the ground of their making. In the end, that may be the most meaningful file, the file that says the most about you and about our relationship. The chalkboard formula has been rubbed out—by you, by me, by the chemistry of the sea—and all I've done is guess at what's missing, trying to make sense of smudges, bound to get it wrong. What a fool I am. A two-thousand-mile fool. Soon I'll turn back to Nebraska, having wasted weeks, a ton of money, and most of my life.

The light comes up. Except for me, the hillside is empty. The long night is over. You're dead. I know that now, feel it. The water claimed you that night in Key West. You win, Dad. You'll be happy to know you died with most of your mysteries intact, your secrets locked behind your stony gaze. You've gone from one darkness to another. You've made your last border crossing. You've set sail for the open sea in the only boat you can't hole, escaping all my questions, all my analysis, all my blame, all my love.

LaVergne, TN USA
18 February 2011
217169LV00003B/5/P